W9-CEI-377

Dreamers of Dreams

DREAMERS
of DREAMS

Essays on Poets and Poetry

JOHN SIMON

Ivan R. Dee   Chicago   2001

DREAMERS OF DREAMS. Copyright © 2001 by John Simon. All rights re-
served, including the right to reproduce this book or portions thereof in any
form. For information, address: Ivan R. Dee, Publisher, 1332 North Halsted
Street, Chicago 60622. Manufactured in the United States of America and
printed on acid-free paper.

Library of Congress Cataloging-in-Publication Data:
  Simon, John Ivan.
  Dreamers of dreams : essays on poets and poetry / John Simon.
    p. cm.
  Includes index.
  Contents: On making the masterpiece — Laura Riding and her traveling
circus — Robed in images : the memoirs of James Merrill — Partying on Par-
nassus : the New York school poets — Wilde the poet — "When the ecstatic
body grips" — First-class mail : a wit and his world — Squaring the circle :
Stéphane Mallarmé — Rimbaud, the anarchic demiurge — A great, baggy
monster : Rilke's Duino elegies — Death fugues : the poems of Paul Celan —
Anna Akhmatova — Brodsky in retrospect — On translation — Traduttore,
traditore, or, The tradition of traducing — Victimized Verlaine.
  ISBN 1-56663-413-X (alk. paper)
  1. Poetry, Modern—20th century—History and criticism. 2. Poetry,
Modern—19th century—History and criticism. I. Title.

PN1271 .S55 2001
809.1'04—dc21

                                                                    2001032291

FOR PAT

who brings poetry into my life

We are the music-makers,
And we are the dreamers of dreams,
Wandering by lone sea-breakers,
And sitting by desolate streams;
World-losers and world-forsakers,
On whom the pale moon gleams:
Yet we are the movers and shakers
Of the world for ever, it seems.

Arthur O'Shaughnessy
(1844–1881)

Contents

Acknowledgments

THE ESSAYS THAT FOLLOW first appeared in the following publications:

Hudson Review: "When the Ecstatic Body Grips";

The New Leader: "On Making the Masterpiece," "Laura Riding and Her Traveling Circus," and "Brodsky in Retrospect";

The New Criterion: "Robed in Images: The Memoirs of James Merrill," "Partying on Parnassus: The New York School Poets," "Squaring the Circle: Stéphane Mallarmé," "Rimbaud, the Anarchic Demiurge," "A Great, Baggy Monster: Rilke's 'Duino Elegies,'" "Death Fugues: The Poems of Paul Celan," "Anna Akhmatova," and "Victimized Verlaine";

Poetry: "*Traduttore, Traditore*, or the Tradition of Traducing";

Washington Post: "First-class Mail: A Wit and His World."

I thank the editors and publishers of these publications for permission to reprint these essays here.

"Wilde the Poet" and "On Translation" in this revised form appear for the first time here.

J. S.

New York City
June 2001

Introduction

IN HIS BOOK *The Continental Pilgrimage: American Writers in Paris, 1944–1960,* Christopher Sawyer-Lauçanno remarks about the first year of *The Paris Review*: "The poetry department, perhaps because Hall [Donald Hall, the poetry editor] was at Oxford, tended to favor his British contemporaries—Geoffrey Hill, Thom Gunn, George Barker—and American formalists such as Richard Eberhardt, Richard Wilbur, Howard Moss, and John Simon (later better known as a critic)."

I am thrilled to have found my way, however ephemerally and undeservedly, into such august company. I am also tickled by Harvard's Widener Library catalog, which, after cards for my books, also has a card for an unpublished manuscript by one "John Simon, playwright," who, in fact, is the same John Simon, poet, now (I hope) "better known as a critic." And who, for all that, did not stop loving his first love, poetry.

If memory serves—and, as I grow older, it serves less and less— I learned to read and write at age four, and started writing sincere but unprodigy-worthy poetry at six. I wrote it in German, which for no other reason than that my parents wanted to start me out on a world-class language, was then the only one I had. Then came Hungarian, the language of my parents, and Serbian, my native tongue. By and by, I wrote verse in all my languages, including French and English, but only in the latter did I publish anything. I never had enough for a decent volume of poetry, even if I was printed in respectable magazines and a couple of anthologies, and earned commendations from some genuine poets.

Somewhere around the age of twenty-seven I stopped writing

poetry, except for occasional verse on such diverse occasions as the departure from *New York* magazine of some popular colleague, or the birthdays of my wife. I liked to romanticize my abandonment by the Muse as having been caused by the seismic effect of the suicide of a girlfriend. The sober truth lies elsewhere: I simply realized that I could be "better known as a critic."

But as I kept turning out my weekly, fortnightly, monthly, and quarterly reviews of drama, film, literature, occasionally art, and, latterly, also music, I tried never to forget my apprenticeship in poetry. I also cherished the friendship of some real poets: Yves Bonnefoy, Donald Davidson, Peter Davison, James Dickey, Hans Magnus Enzensberger, Donald Hall, Hans Egon Holthusen, Carolyn Kizer, Archibald MacLeish, Charles Simic, and Theodore Weiss. And I bought poetry volumes by both famous and lesser-known poets. From them, unconsciously, I learned to write better prose.

Some of the poets I fell in love with were celebrated, some obscure. I should like to reproduce here poems by some of the less obvious ones in very partial payment of what I owe them. One of my earliest enthusiasms was for Humbert Wolfe, a once very popular English poet, now completely forgotten. Though admittedly minor, Wolfe's poetry is charming, witty, graceful, and, above all, intoxicatingly musical. No one, I think, has rhymed better than Wolfe; no one could write, in very short lines and abundant rhyme, poems that penetrated the ear like earwigs, but, unlike them, could not be dislodged.

Here is the beginning of "A Little Music" from the volume *This Blind Rose:*

Since it is evening
    let us invent
love's undiscovered
    continent.

What shall we steer by,
    having no chart
but the deliberate
    fraud of the heart?

And, eight stanzas later, the final quatrains:

> Since it is evening
>> and sailing weather,
> Let us set out for
>> the dream together:

> set for the landfall
>> where love and verse
> enfranchise for ever
>> the travelers.

Yet just as Wolfe could be exquisitely lyrical, he could also be elegantly ironic, even satirical, with no loss in music. This, from *Kensington Gardens*, is "The Grey Squirrel":

> Like a small grey
> coffee-pot
> sits the squirrel.
> He is not

> all he should be,
> kills by dozens
> trees, and eats
> his red-brown cousins.

> The keeper, on the
> other hand,
> who shot him, is
> a Christian, and

> loves his enemies
> which shows
> the squirrel was not
> one of those.

Soon after that I came enthusiastically to E. E. Cummings, Yeats, and the early Pound. I also discovered my favorite modern English-language poet, Robert Graves. I got more pleasure from one of his lyrical or satirical poems than from forty-four quartets by Eliot or countless cantos by Pound. Next came Louis MacNeice, whom I preferred to Auden.

Among Americans I discovered John Crowe Ransom, whom I wouldn't trade for a king's ransom, and the unjustly overlooked Kenneth Patchen. "Do the Dead Know What Time It Is?" is as moving as a poem can get, but here is the no less fine but shorter "In Memory of Kathleen":

> How pitiful is her sleep.
> Now her clear breath is still.
> There is nothing falling tonight,
> Bird or man,
> As dear as she;
> Nowhere that she should go
> Without me. None but my calling.
> Nothing but the cold cry of snow.
>
> How lonely does she seem.
> I, who have no heaven,
> Defenseless, without lands,
> Must try a dream
> Of the seven
> Lost stars and how they put their hands
> Upon her eyes that she might ever know
> Nothing worse than the cold cry of the snow.

Like all young people, I had loved Edna Millay and even Sara Teasdale, but unlike many young or old people, I also happened upon the now sadly neglected Elinor Wylie. Here is the sestet of her "Little Sonnet":

> Remember how, asleep or waking,
> The shallow pillow of her breast
> Shook and shook to your heart's shaking,
> In pity whereof her heart was split;
> Love her now; forget the rest;
> She has herself forgotten it.

Later I was overjoyed to discover Stanley Kunitz and a number of Irish poets: the young and lyrical James Joyce, James Stephens, Donagh McDonagh, Patrick Kavanagh, and, eventually, Seamus Heaney.

It has always made me happy to come upon some worthy but truly obscure poet, which people have called my love of the second-rate. They may have been second-rate poets, but their best poems hit the mark. One of the beauties of poetry is that it springs up in unlikely places, and when you find it, it is like one of those blades of grass that push through cement—as lovely for its tenacity as for its verdure.

My life would have been poorer had I not stumbled across Harold Monro's "Midnight Lamentation," the first two of whose eight stanzas run:

When you and I go down
Breathless and cold,
Our faces both worn back
To earthly mould,
How lonely we shall be!
What shall we do,
You without me,
I without you?

I cannot bear the thought,
You first may die,
Nor of how you will weep,
Should I.
We are too much alone;
What can we do
To make our bodies one:
You, me; I, you?

Somehow I have tended to feel closer to British poets—Dylan Thomas, say, or Philip Larkin—than to American ones, perhaps because of my European origins, or perhaps my one year in a British public school had something to do with it. So, for example, I came to cherish John Pudney, the airman-poet, who delighted Auden by having stood for Parliament drunk. Take the second poem from what I would call "The Smith Trilogy," titled "Missing":

Less said the better,
The bill unpaid, the dead letter,

No roses at the end
Of Smith, my friend.

Last words don't matter,
And there are none to flatter.
Words will not fill the post
Of Smith, the ghost.

For Smith, our brother,
Only son of loving mother,
The ocean lifted, stirred,
Leaving no word.

It is too bad that rhyme has fallen into disrepute, no doubt be-
cause so many writers of doggerel capitalized on it. But what won-
derful finality rhyme can produce for those who can handle it
naturally, effortlessly—as, for instance, Monro and Pudney.

And now for a totally obscure British poet, A. S. J. Tessimond,
whose volume *Voices in a Giant City* I chanced upon as an under-
graduate while browsing in a long-gone bookstore near Harvard
Square. Of his many graceful or tongue-in-cheek poems, I adduce
"Talk in the Night":

"Why are you sighing?"
    "For all the voyages I did not make
    Because the boat was small, might leak, might take
    The wrong course, and the compass might be broken,
    And I might have awoken
    In some strange sea and heard
    Strange birds crying."

"Why are you weeping?"
    "For all the unknown friends or lovers passed
    Because I watched the ground or walked too fast
    Or simply did not see
    Or turned aside for tea
    For fear an old wound stirred
    From its sleeping."

This poem is simplicity itself, yet note how intricately far-flung its
rhymes are, and how unusual are its images made up from humble

building blocks, as in "Or turned aside for tea." A very English trope, that, yet how apt. What more natural way for an Englishman to evade the challenge of the new and different than to turn aside for his customary, dependably anodyne, hot cup of tea?

I could go on listing my enthusiasms for several Americans, such as James Dickey, James Wright, Galway Kinnell, W. D. Snodgrass, W. S. Merwin, James Merrill, and others, but let me cite one as unknown as it is possible to be, author of a slender, privately printed volume drolly entitled *Poems for Small Apartments*. His name is Edward N. Horn, and he was, I believe, a businessman whom I once met at the house of a high school friend whose relative he was. Here are two of his untitled miniatures.

In the tub we soak our skin
And drowse and meditate within.

The mirror clouds, the vapors rise,
We view our toes with sad surprise;

The toes that mother kissed and counted,
The since neglected and unwanted.

*   *   *

Pussycat sits on a chair
Implacably with acid stare.

Those who early loved in vain
Use the cat to try again

And test their bruised omnipotence
Against the cat's austere defense.

Now on to the American poet I feel closest to: Richard Wilbur. He was the assistant in a Harvard course on Victorian poets in which I got a well-deserved D for goofing off. When I nevertheless protested, Wilbur gave me a lengthy and kindly explanation that only a poet and a gentleman could find the time and heart for. What really did it, though, was an early poem of his, "Tywater," about a brutish redneck sergeant of his in the service. Here was a poem that could find beauty in, and forgiveness for, a menacing oaf.

I must at least name the foreign poets who mattered to me, skipping those, however, about whom essays follow. In France: Laforgue, Corbière, Valéry, Apollinaire, Queneau, and Prévert. In the German-speaking world: George, Hofmannsthal, Dauthendey, Spitteler, Morgenstern, Kästner, Benn, and, for one splendid poem ("An meinen ältesten Sohn") in particular, Wilhelm Lehmann. In Hungary: Ady, Babits, and József, and later Kosztolányi, Illyés, Pilinszky, and Radnóti. In Yugoslavia: Jovan Dučić and Vasko Popa.

It is frustrating to have to read poets in translation, but here are some who transcended that handicap: the Greeks Cavafy and Ritsos, the Spaniards Ramón Gómez de la Serna and Juan Ramón Jiménez, the Italians Umberto Saba and Eugenio Montale, the Turk Nazim Hikmet, the Pole Zbigniew Herbert, and Blok and Tsvetayeva among the Russians.

In particular, I want to stress how much I owe to poets. If anything distinguishes my prose style, it is things I might not have got from even the best prose. If it were up to me, no one would be allowed to write prose without having read—and preferably also tried writing—a certain amount of poetry. Beyond the pleasure it gives, it teaches you how to husband your words, how to make them say things more lapidarily and graphically, and, above all, how to make them sing.

It may sound presumptuous, or even preposterous, to assert that there can be music in the review of some humdrum movie or run-of-the-mill play. But if you choose your words lovingly, pay attention to rhythm and cadence, know how to use simile and metaphor—not to mention other tropes—you can enrich and enliven your prose. What you write may still be hogwash, but at least it will be attractive hogwash.

Along with other kinds, I have been writing poetry criticism over the years. If you wonder why the above-mentioned poets were not its subjects, it is because nobody commissioned anything about them. Once you are a professional critic, you rarely find the time or inclination to write pieces of a similar nature on spec. If your byline were irresistible, it might be otherwise; as is, the bottom drawer is not good enough for someone you love.

In fact there are not that many modern poets worth writing about at length. It is not that the rest are mere poetasters, but neither do they deserve the glorious title Poet. They are something in between, for which I just happen to have an appellation. Once, as a boy in Belgrade, I had a crush on one of those delightful young ladies who floated around what was considered Society, and were something in between debutantes and demimondaines. This particular one, since I was so much younger and known only as a toy-gun-toting kid, had no reason to pay me any heed—especially since I was still perfecting my French and beginning English, whereas she had already progressed to Italian.

Anyhow, one day I tried to impress her with my English and asked her in that language who was her favorite poetist. She burst out laughing, and if my handgun had not been a toy one, I would have probably blown my unworthy brains out. But now the term seems useful to designate those who, while really being physicians or insurance company executives, turn out respected poetry tomes. Robert Graves has fulminated against them with caustic mockery, even if he did include some who did not deserve it.

In any case, most of my subjects here are genuine poets, and may be an endangered species. We are witnesses to a disastrous divergence between a poetry that grows ever more esoteric and a public that grows ever more uneducated. At that rate, poetry may go from marginalized to extinct. This would not be a good thing. I don't know whether I would say about a nation, as Don Marquis, the charming bard of *archy and mehitabel* did, "They had no poet and they died." But I do think poets are needed by a society to keep language adventurous, to write pithy and pregnant things that people can carry about with them without benefit of briefcases or even pockets. And perhaps also to teach us prose writers how to write.

I hope that this book makes a contribution, however modest, to the interest in, and respect for, poetry. It is worth noting that Jean Vilar, the distinguished actor and director, but not poet, ended his 1953 book *De la Tradition théâtrale* with this marmoreal apothegm: "Le poète a toujours le dernier mot." The poet always has the last word.

Dreamers of Dreams

On Making
the Masterpiece

 FEW TWENTIETH-CENTURY POETS have elicited as much adoration as T. S. Eliot, and none, except for his friend Ezra Pound, has garnered so much hatred. Almost no one would deny that Eliot was one of the most influential "modern" poets in the English language—perhaps even more seminal than Yeats, and certainly more so than Hopkins, his two most conspicuous competitors. But whether that influence was entirely salubrious is still a matter for debate. To an older generation of scholar critics, men like E. M. W. Tillyard and H. W. Garrod, Eliot was a *bête noire*; yet a slightly younger academic like R. C. Churchill entitled the supplementary chapter he contributed to the *Concise Cambridge History of English Literature* "The Age of T. S. Eliot." Rare is the poet, to this day, who does not owe something to Eliot, if only through the mediation of Eliot's quasi-official heirs, Auden, MacNeice, Spender, and the rest.

To R. C. Churchill, "*The Waste Land* . . . is clearly the masterpiece of Eliot's first phase, as the *Four Quartets* are of the second." But here is Robert Graves: "Eliot's *Four Quartets*, taken in a lump, are lengthy enough and adult enough and religious enough and philosophical enough to pass as a masterpiece." And, twisting the knife, he adds, "I use the word 'masterpiece' without irony, in its original technical sense . . . a piece of work done by a journeyman which satisfies his guild-authorities that he is henceforth entitled to rank as a master, or full member of the Establishment. Here's a quotation dating from 1658: 'Taylors suffer none to set up his trade unless he have first made the masterpiece.'"

Among Eliot's admirers, too, there are those who prefer *The Waste Land* to *Four Quartets*. To quote Churchill again, "Some of us may miss the vigour and the irony of the younger Eliot and feel that the rhythmic movement of the *Quartets*, though distinguished, is a little slow and inclined at times to an almost pulpitarian solemnity." (I wonder, by the way, whether such solemnity is a function of rhythm or, rather, of diction and, indeed, content?) Those who dislike Eliot, like Rossell Hope Robbins, who wrote a whole book, *The T. S. Eliot Myth*, against him, put it more sourly: "The major difference in Eliot's borrowings in the early and later poetry is that in the latter his sources and analogues are from minor writers and non-imaginative authors. Even as a literary debtor he deteriorates." Graves, who concedes that Eliot "had once been, however briefly, a poet . . . [in] the haunting blank verse passages of *The Waste Land*," continues: "I wish that he had stopped at *The Hollow Men*, his honest and (indeed) heartbreaking declaration of poetic bankruptcy, to the approved Receiver of poetic bankruptcy, the Hippopotamus Church."

But to the true believers, the orthodox Eliot boosters, among whose number can be found many a major poet and critic of the Western, as well as the Eastern, world, the *magnum opus* is almost invariably *Four Quartets*. Had not Eliot himself virtually said as much when, with the publication of "Little Gidding" as a *plaquette* on December 1, 1942, he stopped writing serious poetry, although he was to live for another twenty-three years? Clearly, he felt that with *Four Quartets* he had said it all; there was no way of surpassing, or indeed equaling, this poetic testament.

There have been two or three book-length explications of *Four Quartets*, and innumerable shorter exegeses, but the publication of Dame Helen Gardner's *The Composition of "Four Quartets"* gives us at last the *Entstehungsgeschichte*, the full account of the writing of this work, some eight years in the making—taking into account the interruption of five years between the first quartet, "Burnt Norton" (1935), and the second, "East Coker." The heart of Dame Helen's book derives from a study and comparison of the numerous drafts, hand- or typewritten, that Eliot gave either to his close friend and, in some ways, mentor, John Hayward (who left them to King's College, Cambridge), or to Magdalene College, Cambridge; and from the perusal of the Eliot-Hayward correspondence during the writing of the three later *Quartets*. For Eliot was continually submitting manuscripts of the poem for annotation and commentary to Hayward and, to a lesser extent, other friends. Of these, Geoffrey Faber (of the publishing house in which Eliot, too, became a partner) headed a list that at times included such notables as Virginia Woolf and Herbert Read.

It was wartime, and communication by mail was often the only possibility; that and Eliot's eagerness for suggestions bordering on assistance resulted in one of the best documented records of composition by—what shall I call it? "Collaboration" is too strong a word, and often there was no "consensus," Eliot accepting, I would guess, only one or two out of every six or seven proposed emendations. Let me call it "creative midwifery," then, with Hayward as the obstetrician, and the others as interns and nurses, officiating at this difficult parturition. All the available stages are reproduced by Gardner in footnotes or as part of the text; for her extensive introductory sections and thoughtful running commentaries, she draws on far-flung materials providing literary, historical, biographical, bibliographical, and textual illumination. Though she modestly denies having prepared a critical edition of *Four Quartets*, she has done that and a good deal more.

There may be relatively little here that is absolutely new; some of it Dame Helen herself had set forth in her 1949 book, *The Art of T. S. Eliot*. But there is much useful information from out-of-the-way sources sedulously tracked down, abundantly quoted and shrewdly commented upon. But the rare new things are important ones: Gardner establishes the significance of Emily Hale, a friend from Eliot's Harvard undergraduate days, who may have accompanied the poet on a trip to New Hampshire in 1933, and whom he definitely saw during several subsequent summers in England. The meetings took place at the summer house of her relatives, the Perkinses, where Eliot, too, was asked to visit. It was during the summer of 1934 that Tom and Emily explored the gardens of Burnt Norton, and, although Dame Helen merely hints at this, Emily may

have been the muse whose unstated presence accounts for the sweet-
ness of some of the verses in "Burnt Norton."

Another major new contribution is Gardner's discovery of a
missing line from "Little Gidding"—a verse that, almost certainly,
dropped out of the finished poem by an oversight on everybody's
part. Surely "Where is the summer, the unimaginable / Summer be-
yond sense, the unapprehensible / Zero summer?" makes better
rhythmic, lyrical, and philosophic sense than the same passage with
the middle line omitted, as it now appears in all editions of the
poem. By showing that the verse was kept by Eliot in the first and
second proof, and merely left out of the "Final Recension" sent to
the printer, Gardner establishes an excellent case for its reinstate-
ment.

When Dame Helen proposes new literary sources, however, she
is on less firm ground than when she lists those put forward by other
commentators, which she has valiantly assembled through extensive
research. It is nice to be reminded again that among the sources for
this most cerebral of poems were *Alice in Wonderland* and bits of
filler material E. Martin Browne had asked for in *Murder in the
Cathedral* to give it livelier movement, then judged unnecessary.
Similarly, it is interesting to ponder that a bit of flaccid verse from
Mrs. Browning may have found itself echoed in "Burnt Norton" be-
cause it occurs in a story by Kipling, also a minor source.

But the attempt to trace Eliot's "ruined millionaire" to the Zeus
of Gide's *Le Prométhée mal enchaîné* is unconvincing; it seems to have
been dragged in to bolster up Gardner's earlier, and no more con-
vincing, identification of that figure (in *The Art of T. S. Eliot*) with an
aspect of Christ. All this in defiance of Hayward's, and apparently
even Eliot's, identification of this symbolic personage with Adam.
Significantly, though Gardner knew Eliot, she was too awed by him
to ask outright who the "millionaire" was; more significantly yet, she
notes that Eliot "would probably have evaded siding with either of
his readers."

On the other hand, how pleasant to find that Eliot's mind could
change. Gardner points out that the poet-critic repudiated his attack
on D. H. Lawrence (as, earlier, he had patched up his quarrel with
Milton), and was prepared to testify at the trial of *Lady Chatterley's
Lover* that "when he spoke of the author of that book as 'a very sick

man indeed,' he was very sick himself." (Too bad that Thomas Hardy, who had been bracketed with Lawrence in the attack, did not benefit from a like retraction.) Incidentally, it is instructive to note that psychiatry, contemptuously included in "The Dry Salvages" among such "pastimes and drugs" as astrology and palmistry, should have been rehabilitated in *The Cocktail Party*, where the Paraclete-like hero is a sort of psychiatrist.

It is absorbing to follow in this rigorously researched and exemplarily laid-out book (for $32.50, however, the publisher might have given us a photograph or two of the manuscripts) Eliot's relentless pursuit of the *mot juste*. Take, for instance, his agonizing over the verse in "Little Gidding" where the "dead Master" (Eliot's archpoet, a conflation of Yeats and several others) says that passage between death and life "now presents no hindrance." Hayward had queried the original word, "barrier," and suggested "hindrance" instead. Eliot replied, on October 2, 1942, "I changed 'barrier' to 'hindrance' but I am thinking of changing it back again, because it seems a little insolite [sic] to speak of a *hindrance between* two points, doesn't it? And the freedom of movement was not in one direction only, but to and fro." After nevertheless accepting Hayward's recommendation, Eliot, at the last minute, went back to "barrier" for the poem's publication in the *New English Weekly*. "But," he wrote Hayward on October 10, "I am not absolutely confident . . . are you still assured that it is proper to speak of a hindrance *between* two termini?" "Apparently Hayward was able to 'assure' him," Gardner concludes, for in *Four Quartets* we read "hindrance."

It is equally fascinating to learn that the lines in "Little Gidding" that troubled Eliot most, and elicited the lengthiest correspondence, were 89–91, where he describes, among other things, the time of meeting with the ghost as "the waning dusk." Originally Eliot had written "dawn"; then that became "first faint light." When Hayward proposed "faint half-light," Eliot replied that this was too close in sound to a terminal "night" a few lines earlier. We then observe him as he toys with "after lantern-end," "daybreak," "lantern-out," and "lantern-down," and starts fiddling (his word) with "the antelucan dusk" and other far-fetched possibilities.

Eliot complains: "It is surprisingly difficult to find words for the shades before morning; we seem to be richer in words and phrases for the end of day. . . . There is very likely some dialect word for this degree of dawn; but even if I could find it it probably wouldn't do." When, at last, he "fell back" on one of Hayward's versions, he remarked: "I perceive that these belong to that almost inevitable residue of items . . . for which the ideal is unattainable."

It is partly for this fanatical dedication to his art that Eliot elicited tributes like the one from Harold Nicolson, who doubted whether "any poet less selfless and saintly could have rescued our generation from apathy and cynicism." Still, as we gather from Gardner's book, this *poeta doctus* had considerable problems with spelling and syntax—sometimes even with the meanings of words. One would not expect the misspellings "rescension" and "moalars" from a Latinist, least of all a Latinist with as much dental trouble as Eliot had. He could also blithely write "asphalte" and "pig-stye," and "pentagon" for pentagram. Moreover, Geoffrey Faber was right (as Dame Helen implies) to question the loose and ambiguous syntax in, for example, verse 99 of "The Dry Salvages," where Faber wondered, "Who does not 'not forgetting'?" Yet, after her first meeting with Eliot, Virginia Woolf noted in her diary that "he believes . . . in writing with extreme care, in observing all syntax and grammar. . . ."

Grammar in particular bothered Eliot. Thus "Here and there does not matter" in "East Coker" remained uncorrected until the (posthumous) 1974 edition of the *Collected Poems*, despite Hermann Paschmann's pointing out the error to the poet, who commented, "How very odd," and added, "What I prefer is *Here or there does not matter*," magnanimously casting his preference on the side of grammar. There were times, too, when the great perfectionist remained at the mercy of the typesetter; Dame Helen shows how, through an accident in the printing, Eliot's intended (and eminently appropriate) line break after verse 128 of "East Coker" disappeared forever.

Even though *The Composition of "Four Quartets"* does not aspire to be an exegesis of the poem, it does supply interpreters of the work with invaluable data. Had it been available to Nancy Duvall Hargrove, her recent *Landscape as Symbol in the Poetry of T. S. Eliot* would not have insisted repeatedly that the church in "The Dry Salvages" is Our Lady of Good Voyage in Gloucester, Massachusetts. Dame Helen quotes the Reverend William T. Levy, who had it from Eliot himself, that it is Notre Dame de la Garde, overlooking Marseilles, regrettably misprinted here as "la Gard."

On the whole, the book is a marvel of typographical accuracy; when a couple of typos do occur in consecutive footnotes on page 202, they come as an astonishing exception rather than, as usual nowadays, the rule. But the good Dame Helen herself slips up on rare occasions: The book *Writers at Work* is named correctly once, and once as *Writers and their Work*; *Germelshausen* is by Gerstäcker, not Gerstärker; Gide called most of his fiction *soties* (not *sotties*, a possible alternative spelling); the plural of Perkins is "the Perkinses," and not, as she insists, "the Perkins." Her quotation from *Inferno* XV differs from my text in the Bodley Head Dante, but I am not qualified to determine which reading is better; the "sun" in Roger Fry's translation of a sonnet by Mallarmé should, of course, be "sin"—a misprint, but reprinting Fry's feeble translation is bad judgment.

One of the most useful services the book performs is making us reconsider our views of this important poem. In her earlier work on Eliot, Gardner had this provocative footnote: "An aversion to cats as strong as Mr. Eliot's confessed antipathy to Milton as a man, compels me to treat Old Possum, as Mr. Eliot treated Milton, as a musician, whose subject-matter is of no interest. . . ." She recognized merely "the brilliant dexterity of the verse." Since there is no eluding the fact, posited by Elizabeth Drew in words borrowed from Eliot, that *Four Quartets* is an "expression of 'the experience of believing a dogma,' " to which *I* have strong aversion—one person's cat is another's dogma—I too am at a disadvantage vis-à-vis *this* poem.

True, as Denis Donoghue has observed, "the poignancy of misgiving" makes the dogma less marmoreal and "keeps the poetry human," but there is also the circumstance Donoghue adduces, apparently without misgivings, that Eliot "writes of objects and experiences as if he had already left them—with whatever degree of reluctance—behind." Such excess of tranquillity in the recollection I find faintly dehumanizing.

And it is precisely in *The Dehumanization of Art* that Ortega y Gasset defined the role of the modernist poet, in this case Mallarmé, as disappearing, volatilizing as a man, in order to be "converted into a pure anonymous voice, which speaks disembodied words." Oddly enough, Eliot, who admired and emulated Mallarmé (Gardner duly points out the several quotations or paraphrases from him), nonetheless made some very un-Mallarméan efforts in *Four Quartets* toward personalizing his voice—fatal, I think, in a poet whose genius is for the suprapersonal. We get here those "it seems"-es, those "I have said before"-s, that Faber characterized as "lecture-stigmata"; plus such bathos as "you whose bodies / Will suffer the trial and judgement of the sea, / Or whatever event"; and such deliberate delyricization as in Section IV of "East Coker," where the mixing of tetrameter, pentameter and hexameter strangely undercuts the music.

In fact, George Williamson's assurance to the contrary, I doubt whether *Four Quartets* is more than intermittently "a lyric"; all too often it tries to be a kind of philosophical epic and hurtles, not infrequently, into prose—"closer sometimes," as Frank Kermode reminds us, "to commentary than to the thing itself." This strikes me as much nearer the mark than B. Rajan's assessment: "utter and relentless fidelity to the event."

An additional major problem for me is a certain schematic paradox-mongering, beginning right with the second Heraclitean epigraph to "Burnt Norton," and sometimes appearing as an adaptation of a mystical text, as in the following, derived from St. John of the Cross: "And what you do not know is the only thing you know / And what you own is what you do not own / And where you are is where you are not." Lawrence Durrell tries to defend this as a way of stating "something . . . beyond opposites in a language which is based upon opposites." He goes on: "Since statement qualifies, [Eliot] must at once correct it by introducing its opposite and measuring its claims against what he has already said." And again: "Under the terms of this metaphysic . . . any two opposites . . . are co-equals, sharers, partners. To let one have its head at the expense of the other would spoil the 'stillness' of the dance."

Well, my trouble is that whereas I can see the stillness, I tend to miss the dance. It is then a case of what Roy Campbell described (in another literary context) as using "the snaffle and the curb all right, / But where's the bloody horse?" Much of this looks to me like mere indecisiveness, tergiversation rather than equipoise. The poem has its undeniable beauties, but it seldom has that basis in sensuous reality that usually underlies even the most cerebral verse of a Mallarmé or Valéry.

Luckily, the work is not all metaphysic, as we are happily instructed by an epistolary exchange Gardner quotes with relish. "I do not get the significance of *autumn*," Hayward complains at one point, and Eliot responds: "'Autumn weather' only because it *was* autumn weather. . . ."

1979

Laura Riding and
Her Traveling Circus

❦ FOR ME, the arch poet of the modern English language has always been Robert Graves. E. E. Cummings, Louis MacNeice, Dylan Thomas, and John Crowe Ransom follow closely, but Graves is "it." He has lyricism and humor in equal measure, passion and satire, erudition and directness, immersion in myth and down-to-earth common sense. He himself said the poet has only two themes, love and death, an admirable precept that he felicitously kept forgetting. Other poets are greater (a vague concept)—Eliot and Auden, Pound and Stevens, perhaps—none is better.

Because of my love for Graves, I tried to read the poems of Laura Riding, the woman with whom he was deeply involved for fourteen years; all the more so because the one evening I spent with Robert Frost was taken up mostly with wittily mischievous stories he told me about Graves and Riding. Would that I had not forgotten them! But when I picked up Riding's *Collected Poems*, I was quickly bored, even repelled. The poems were clumsy, unclear, pretentious, and almost wholly lacking in sensuous appeal.

How could the splendid Graves have endured all those years living, loving, and working with Laura Riding? This awesome question is, if not exactly answered, exhaustively and exhilaratingly confronted by *Robert Graves: The Years with Laura, 1926–1940*, the second volume Richard Perceval Graves has devoted to the life and work of his uncle. It can be enjoyed on several levels, but it is nothing short of sublime as high farce, an amalgam of Feydeau, Coward, and Evelyn Waugh, plus a touch of Chekhov here and there. You read it with goosebumpy fascination between spells of roaring laughter and profound sadness.

In 1926, Robert Graves was thirty-one and a poet of some reputation who had been shell-shocked in the war and had not yet fully recovered. The son of pious Christians—Alfred Perceval Graves, a civil servant and minor religious poet, and Amalie ("Amy") von Ranke, Alfred's second wife and niece of the great German historian Leopold von Ranke—Robert was married, not especially happily, to Nancy Nicholson, daughter and niece of famous artists, and herself an artist and feminist. They had four children. The troubled *ménage* received much-needed financial support from both the elder Graveses and the Nicholsons.

This installment of the biography begins when Robert, who had studied at Oxford, accepted a professorship of English at the University of Cairo, a job friends and relatives living in Egypt had procured for him. He was already smitten by the poetry of a young American Jewish woman of Austrian origin, Laura Reichenthal. In 1920, at age nineteen, she had married Louis Gottschalk, a graduate student at Cornell, where she was a junior. Her poems soon made an impression on the group of Agrarian poets clustered around Vanderbilt University, led by John Crowe Ransom, Allen Tate, and Donald Davidson. They published her work in their magazine, *The Fugitive*, eventually even awarding her their big prize of $100.

These are the poems that Graves read. Laura, who changed her name to Riding, was someone he wanted to meet and collaborate with on a study of the "new" poetry, so he invited her to join him and Nancy and the children as they set out for Egypt. Having broken up her marriage and had a brief affair with Tate, she was eager for fresh adventure. She wrote the kind of verse that could truly be called "modernist," whereas he was still partially stuck in Georgian poetry—very English-countryside and steeped in poeticism. They had something to offer each other, and in those days poetry was a club whose members could extend such invitations to fellow members. Laura accepted.

She, Robert, and Nancy took to one another, especially she and

Robert. He was ruggedly handsome: tall, somewhat ungainly, with a shock of dark hair and a broken nose. Laura, though hardly beautiful, was a particular Semitic type that a good many WASPS perceive as exotic and sexy. When Tom Matthews, the writer and editor of *Time*, first saw her (and he, too, was for a stretch under her spell), he described her as "a small severe woman . . . as primly neat as Robert was gawky. She never had a hair out of place, and her clothes, which were old-fashioned, never seemed odd. When she was in full regalia her dignity matched and enhanced her costume [and no one thought it laughable] that she was crowned by [a gold band, fastened at the back with gold wire] that [in Greek lettering] spelled LAURA. She could indeed look royal—a Hittite queen."

Later, Matthews came to perceive her differently: "The texture of her skin was waxy to dead-dull, and her hands were surprisingly large and coarse for a woman's. It may have been partly her eerily brilliant brain . . . which seemed to me to render her asexual, sibylline." But the young classical scholar Eirlys Roberts, the mistress of J. Bronowski, a scientist collaborating with Laura, found her "beautiful" and "a pleasure to look at." Robert's brother John, on the other hand, was annoyed by Laura's frequent finger-wagging and pointing, her exaggerated consonants, her odd way of speaking (saying "blee-oo" for blue) and accenting "Robert" on the second syllable.

Harry Kemp, a young poet with whom Laura collaborated (she had a passion for working with men to whom she was attracted or vice versa), "found her physically unattractive" with "her undershot jaw, primly ascetic lips, rather prominent nose, curvaceous and tobacco-stained fingers, and wobbly eyes," not to mention her "too-theatrical costumes." To the sculptress Dorothy Simmons, Laura had power. "In a black cape, with something round her head, she could look truly sinister: She then became tight and ugly and horrible," said Simmons, and there was "something genuinely evil" about her.

Yet there was no denying her intellectual fascination that could somehow become sexual. As the biographer puts it (apropos Gertrude Stein's warming "to the ambivalent character of Laura's carnality"), "if people would only love her, Laura could respond just as easily to lesbians . . . she was almost always most attractive either to slightly masculine women or to slightly feminine men—like the young and still un-self-assured Graves."

The Robert-Laura-Nancy trio did not last long in Egypt. After a few months, to the dismay and detriment of those who had helped him, Graves breached his contract and returned to England, establishing domiciles both in the country and in London. For a while it was Robert and Laura in the city, working and playing, and Nancy in Islip with the children. In time, Nancy was sucked into what Laura called their "three-life." Graves' parents, brothers, and sisters, though initially drawn to Laura, soon felt that she had "vampirized Robert from the first," and thought the threesome "immoral."

Nevertheless, the *ménage à trois* chugged along, with Robert and Laura reading and commenting on each other's poetry and prose. She always played the genius-teacher, and he the disciple-slave. In fact, Graves was the real poet; Laura was published because of him, never widely recognized, and would shortly be forgotten. But they did produce at least two innovative, challenging, often highly pertinent critical-essayistic works, *A Survey of Modernist Poetry* and *Against Anthologies*. It is not far-fetched to argue that, either through the mediation of William Empson or directly, those works were a major influence on the New Criticism.

Once the "three-life" began to prove awkward, a young poet, Geoffrey Phibbs, was recruited to make it a "four-life." When he arrived with his wife, Norah, at the trio's Hammersmith apartment, Geoffrey was given a royal welcome; Norah was bundled off to a hotel and left to her own devices. The *ménage à quatre* commenced—a relationship the biographer calls "often baffling to [the four] themselves." Here I must quote at length:

> One of the problems was Laura's extreme jealousy of [Geoffrey's] continuing affection for Norah; and on one occasion she is said [by Norah] to have "locked herself in the lavatory for eight hours because Geoffrey said I was taller than she was (as I was). She only came out when Geoffrey lied for peace' sake and said I was much smaller."
>
> More serious was the fact that Laura had become more than a little unbalanced, and now revealed to Phibbs (as presumably she had already done to Graves) that she was more than human.

They could think of her as a goddess: She was certainly a figure of destiny . . . she embodied "Finality." So devoted was Robert to his spiritual guide that he unhesitatingly accepted Laura's estimate of her own significance. . . . Phibbs also began to believe that there was some truth in Laura's pronouncements, and even jotted down some notes about time and history being either "a projection from Laura," or "necessitated *by* Laura."

This comedy had a shifting locale, including two adjoining houseboats on the Thames that Graves had bought. But finally Geoffrey bolted to France to rejoin his wife. He was not happy with Norah either and wrote Laura, who, with Robert in tow, promptly set out in pursuit, intending to draw Norah into a "five-life." In a Rouen hotel Geoffrey and Norah declined the offer, and " 'God' in the Public Lounge threw herself on the floor, had hysterics, threw her legs in the air and screamed." She had to be removed by two waiters. Back in England, however, Geoffrey started falling more seriously for Nancy and before long had to go into hiding with David Garnett, the very man who had seduced Norah when she first left Geoffrey.

Now Graves showed up *chez* Garnett and threatened to "kill Geoffrey if he wouldn't return to Laura." The horrific climax was reached in Hammersmith, where the four-lifers argued furiously through most of the night. After a little sleep, the debate raged on. Geoffrey, emboldened by the prospect of exclusivity with Nancy, announced that he was leaving, whereupon Laura, aware that the poet Charlotte Mew had killed herself by drinking Lysol, imbibed some herself. Since this had no immediate effect, she said "Goodbye, chaps," and jumped from the fourth-floor window with a "doom-echoing shout." Graves started running downstairs after her, but on reaching the third floor, changed his mind and jumped in turn.

Robert got off without real injury. Laura broke four vertebrae, split her pelvis in three pieces, and bent her spinal cord severely. Robert's physician sister, Rosaleen, summoned by Nancy, administered morphine, got special consideration at her hospital for Laura, and later secured the services of Dr. Lake, the only up-to-date surgeon in England. Laura was to recover completely, but in the hospital, even when out of pain, she would scream for the fun of it, regardless of the discomfort to others. She showed no gratitude to Rosaleen, asking her fiercely, "How do you know that I didn't invent Mr. Lake?"

Rosaleen thought this was all out of "the most incredible Russian novel." And Martin Seymour-Smith, in his outstanding *Robert Graves: His Life and Work*, quotes Robert's friend T. E. Lawrence saying, "They are madhouse minds; no, not so much minds as appetites." Strapped as they were for money, Graves returned a generous check to his father because he didn't show enough sympathy for Laura. To Nancy, Robert wrote, "I love Laura beyond everything thinkable," while to Laura, Phibbs became "the Devil and also Judas and so on."

On and on the circus rolled, until Laura and Robert settled down in Deyá, Majorca, where life was rustic, pleasant and cheap. Geoffrey and Nancy remained together in England, in a relationship not destined to last. For seven years Riding and Graves lived it up in Majorca, chiefly off his two major hits, the autobiography *Good-bye to All That* and the novel *I, Claudius*, both enviously derided by Laura. Graves's journalism also made money, as did, miraculously, his poetry. Laura did not earn much more than Robert's servile adoration (Graves served her breakfast in bed and did all the household chores) as she frenziedly attempted one unrealizable project after another. Fiction collaborations between Laura and Robert misfired, too.

Other literary folks drifted to Deyá, many of them married or unmarried couples. Quite a few sat at Laura's feet and worked with the goddess on their or her projects, notably what she hoped would be her *magnum opus*, the ultimate Dictionary. According to Tom Matthews, that effort did not depend on "lexicographers to dig up the root definitions of key words . . . [rather, Laura] would supply the key definitions, making them not only exact but poetic."

Occasionally a four-life would reform, as with the young poet Norman Cameron and a tubercular German girl, Elfriede, impregnated by Robert. But Norman, who cared about Elfriede, recognized Laura's true nature and was filled with horror. Laura, no longer interested in going to bed with Robert, started starving him sexually and, at times, pushing him toward other women, only to reclaim him with insane possessiveness. To Matthews she suggested that he "work" with her and cede his beloved wife, Julie, to Robert. Amid this chaos, Robert was capable of writing his sympathetic sister Clarissa to accuse her of depravity and filthy-mindedness for failing to see that Laura was "absolute truth and goodness." It was not unlike the Shelley-and-Byron circle in Switzerland and Italy, except for involving a larger number of transient, and more maniacal, participants.

One who did not want to come, despite urging, was Matthews's friend Schuyler Jackson, poet and gentleman farmer in New Jersey. When first shown Laura's verse, he pronounced it philosophy, not poetry. Subsequently, in an article in *Time* on the state of poetry, commissioned by Matthews, he declared that the age had only two real poets, Rilke (already dead) and Laura Riding. For a long time before, Laura had nurtured, sight unseen, an *amour de tête* for Jackson, which she hoped someday to consummate. In the interim she was ordering oversized nightshirts for Robert as an anaphrodisiac. He was "in a constant swivet of anxiety" over Laura, Matthews reports, though she "treated him like a dog." Laura started fancying bullfights and "developed a morbid fascination [with] the beauty of cut flesh." She actually wrote an article about the joy of "seeing the interior of a man's leg . . . cut open in a motor-car accident." No matter. Graves believed she was a much finer poet than he, and Laura tacitly concurred.

Franco's takeover in Spain forced the abandonment of Majorca. The circus moved to England, where it suffered several setbacks: Alexander Korda's projected film of *I, Claudius* never materialized; other movie projects similarly evaporated; there were fairly serious problems with the eldest Graves daughter, Jenny; and Robert himself suffered from severe boils. Hospitalized, he was visited by a young disciple from the Deyá days, Alan Hodge, who brought along a friend, Beryl Pritchard. Laura continued to deny herself to Robert, and because his collaborator on a book about T. E. Lawrence, Basil Liddell-Hart, did not respond to her sexually, tried in various low ways to break up the collaboration.

Things became especially comic once the traveling circus moved to a villa in Lugano and then to a château near Rennes. Laura was now writing political tracts and gathering associates around her for "moral action by inside people" that could prevent war. Graves remained in the doghouse. Thus when she lost a topaz from one of her rings and he, "by rationalised search," found it for her, Laura merely sneered, "You ought to buy a grocery shop and sell jams and pickles and say 'I made them all myself.' That would be your madness." No; Laura was. There was even a time when Amy, Robert's mother, wished her son had died in the War rather than been driven insane by Riding. Yet in some ways Laura and Robert were well matched: When W. B. Yeats, whom they hated as they did almost every literary competitor, died, the two of them shared an "unholy satisfaction."

Early in 1939, Riding, Graves, and some of their retinue accepted an invitation to settle down in a renovated auxiliary building on Schuyler Jackson's large farm near Princeton. In preparation for the seduction of Schuyler, Laura gave up her chain-smoking and reduced her coffee intake from fifteen cups daily to one or two. Continuing to treat Robert abominably, she summoned him to her bedroom one night at 4 a.m. "simply to inform him of her sudden revelation that 'Love is a beautiful insincerity; and true.'" At the Jackson farm, Laura and her acolytes worked on the Dictionary and on further plans "to save the world from war." The Hodges (Alan had married the charming Beryl) lived with them, the Matthewses were down the road. Laura began to study Kit, Schuyler's wife and the mother of his children, for the best method of breaking up her marriage. She succeeded, driving Kit into a loony bin for a while. Laura "often seemed to those around her possessed of paranormal powers."

Schuyler and Laura became lovers, and flaunted the fact before the now often resentful yet still panting Robert. Then he and Beryl Hodge seemed to be falling in love; to remove that more serious threat, Laura pointed Robert toward Nancy, whom Geoffrey had left to marry another. Robert dutifully returned to England, where in spite of Nancy's hopes his passion was not rekindled.

To spoil Robert and Beryl's chances, Laura tried to get them to swallow a theory she had evolved. It held that women were primarily "two-in-hand," i.e., possessed of "intellectual grace combined with wisdom and self-control," and secondarily "one-in-the-bush," i.e., homemakers. Men were primarily "swingering swine," i.e., hard workers with control and determination, and secondarily "joulting pigs," i.e., possessed of an element of romantic wildness. Laura, as a pure two-in-hand, and Schuyler, as a pure swingerer, were perfect together. Robert and Beryl had some joulting pig and bush in them, respectively. This created a discrepancy in their characters that Laura named "Oscar" in Graves and "Lake Bottom" in Beryl. She warned Robert and Beryl that they were "in danger of letting the secondary nature rule [them] and getting mixed in a merely senti-mental Oscar-Lake Bottom way."

A series of fortunate incidents nonetheless did result in Robert and Beryl's marrying. Nancy was furious. Alan Hodge graciously yielded his wife to his master. Not only did he go on doing research for him, but the two even collaborated on a couple of books. Laura married Schuyler, who persuaded her to give up literature as incon-sequential. Following his death twenty-six years later, she started publishing again, mainly reprints of her poetry and screeds against literature. Reviewing a couple of her volumes, Donald Davie (see his *The Poet in the Imaginary Museum*) observed, "She has raised the stakes so high that she has to lose." But let's not forget that Auden, who learned much from Laura's work (to the point of being accused by Robert and Laura of plagiarism), called Riding "the only living philosophical poet." As far as I know, she is still alive in Wabasso, Florida.

Graves and Beryl resumed the old life in Majorca. She bore him another set of four children, and wisely allowed him affairs with much younger "Muses" whom he needed for inspiration. Unfortu-nately, all three relevant books, Seymour-Smith's, Matthews's *Under the Influence*, and this one, seem to have been written before Graves died in 1985, and so lack a sense of closure. But by 1955, reviewing the latest *Collected Poems*, Lionel Trilling could confidently assert, "We have to see Graves as a poet of the first rank. . . . He is in the tradition of the men who, by the terms upon which they accept their ordinary humanity, make it extraordinary."

Both Martin Seymour-Smith and Richard Perceval Graves end their books with tributes to Beryl Graves, and that seems wonder-fully fitting. Seymour-Smith estimates that Robert Graves "has made as long a journey—through nightmare—as most of us would wish to take, and one in which the baleful figure of Laura Riding stands out, a bleak and still enigmatic landmark." The nearest thing to an explanation of the Laura witchery (though unquoted by R. P. Graves) is to be found in Matthews's book. "To the question: Why did we put up with Laura? the answer is: Because people are in general vulnerable to bullying. . . . To someone with a good brain . . . and a bad conscience or even the normal amount of self-doubt, people with pretensions, who are *sure* they are superior beings, will always be dangerously attractive. . . . We are weakly and cowardly sane: they are strongly and indomitably crazy. So that when they demand our subjection, complete obedience, and instantly, our tendency is to hear and obey."

But Graves did at last, to use a word from one of his poems, disenthrall himself. He expunged Laura from the revised 1957 edition of *Good-bye to All That*, and, most likely, from his heart as well. She lives on, in sublimated form, as the White Goddess, as Livia in *I, Claudius*, and as the woman in a number of his love poems. She deserves no less. And certainly no more.

1990

Robed in Images: The Memoirs of James Merrill

FORGIVE ME if I start in a seemingly irrelevant way; there's a reason for it. As a sophomore at Harvard, in Robert Hillyer's advanced creative writing course, I wrote a play that I decided to produce myself (no one else wanted to) under the auspices of the United War Relief. It was 1943, in mid–world war, and the subject was appropriate. German officers were holding ten young Yugoslav girls as love slaves in a camp, until one of them managed to bump off a couple of the Nazi swine, whereupon all the girls lost their lives, but their honor was restored. Good for the war effort as the play was, my chief point in directing it and acting one of the two German soldiers was to cast ten of the prettiest Radcliffe girls I could find and then date as many of them as possible.

But the sponsoring United War Relief people were not all that forthcoming with the pittances required. To prod them, and to help with other production problems, I needed a production manager, and found one in Claude Fredericks. Claude was, like me, a bit of a loner; but, unlike me, he was not a Harvard student. Rather, he was a gifted autodidact who indirectly benefited from Harvard's cultural opportunities without indenturing himself to its curricula.

I liked Claude, and he seemed to like me, but I was too self-absorbed to find out much about him. I knew he came from Springfield, Missouri, had a fine grasp of the Classics, and was a charming conversationalist. Curly-haired, merry-eyed yet shy, he spoke with the softest of voices in a strange cooing accent that he had clearly invented for himself. He was gentle, wore bow ties, and was, unbeknown to me, a homosexual. Ignorant about such matters, I thought him a bit odd; but nothing about his behavior around me suggested a different sexual preference.

He was, however, a singularly inappropriate choice for a production manager because of his mild manner and general otherworldliness. Not the one to bully the United War Relief folks for a little more money, or exert pressure on the distinguished panel of academic sponsors to come through with other kinds of help. Only when I invented a *nom de guerre* for him, Dmitri Merezhkovskij (brazenly cribbing the name of the popular biographer, with a minimal change in the spelling), did his phone calls start getting results. Claude's self-effacing voice with the make-believe accent, which might just have been Slavic, now commanded respect.

After my play came and went, Claude went, too. I next heard of him as running a choice little printing press with a gentleman friend in the woods of Vermont, which struck me as a condign *modus vivendi* for a person of such rare and rarefied sensibility, and I was pleased for him. In 1949–1950 I spent a Fulbright year in Paris, and it was on my return to Harvard that I learned that Claude was living in Europe with a young poet whose first volume I owned and admired, and whose name was James Merrill. He was also the wealthy son of the millionaire head of Merrill, Lynch, and would surely help Claude develop into a literary figure, for which I thought him exquisitely suited.

I remember once running into Claude and James, perhaps even eating with them. I recall only that Merrill struck me as delicate and not very talkative, the latter seeming unusual for a poet. When I ran into Claude again, much later, he was no longer thick with Merrill. Having written a piece for *Vogue* about the best younger poets, which included Merrill, I was eager to pump Claude about him. Discreetly, he stuck to polite generalities. Then Claude became a popular teacher at Bennington College, and I lost sight of him for many years. One day in a Florida airport, I noticed someone reading a volume of Greek poetry in the original; he looked up, and was Claude. We sat together on the flight to New York, and he promised to stay in touch. But he vanished into Vermont, and was not heard from again.

Recently, I was amused to hear that a major character—albeit fictionalized to the point of caricature—in Donna Tartt's *The Secret History* was based on Claude, but the novel seemed too long-winded and short-breathed to bother with. And now Claude is back, co-starring in James Merrill's memoir, *A Different Person*, which I've been asked to review. I never got to know Merrill well. Once I was taken to the house in Stonington he shares with David Jackson; another time, to the one they own in Key West. In between, he and I were both guests at a dinner party of W. H. Auden's. He always seemed enormously civilized, distantly cordial, and (perhaps deceptively) frail. If Claude looked like a Murillo *putto* crossed with a Velázquez *picaro*, Merrill seemed a Renaissance princeling painted by an anonymous Italian whose name began in "Attributed to" or "School of."

But what made reading this book about James and Claude and divers others so strange for me was that I knew quite a few of the others as well. Take Tony Harwood (*né* Horowitz, as Merrill tactfully doesn't mention), James's second-best friend at Lawrenceville, and someone I stringently avoided at Harvard. Take the then married couple, the scholar Jonathan Bishop and the future novelist Alison Lurie, my neighbors and just about best friends during grad school. Or Irma Brandeis, who, as Merrill says, was *the* Italian Department at Bard College, where first he, and later I, briefly taught. Robert Isaacson, the third man of the memoir, I never met; but a common friend kept regaling me with stories about him. Does this sort of thing make reviewing a book easier or harder? We shall see.

A Different Person is distinguished by its style. It is written in a poet's prose, using the chisel, the burin, the goldsmith's scissors. The syntax scintillates, cadence is everywhere. Sometimes the tropes are too bejeweled, the preciosity becomes blinding. Consider this childhood reminiscence: "But the lesson of our Meissen plates and Sheraton chairs intimidated me. They kept their own counsel; our postures and hungers affected them hardly at all. The chair shrugged us off, each careful washing rinsed the dish of us, and the objects resumed, like heroines in Henry James, a gleaming, inviolable fineness their uncouth admirer could only fall short of." Or this mosaic at the Tomb of Galla Placidia in Ravenna: "Thousands upon thousands of glass-paste dice—each by itself dull and worthless as a drawn tooth—have been shrewdly cast to embed a texture now matte, now coruscant, with colors fifteen hundred years have failed to dim. Through narrow alabaster panels, their art-deco patterns lymph-washed and bloodless, like human tissue on a slide, comes a glow I try to resist. . . ." Even the shorter images sometimes hover on the verge of excess: "His manners were natural, even humble, like the hut of forest boughs that shelters a great wizard." Or: "Shaped by ideas like everybody else, I nevertheless avert my eyes from them as from the sight of a nude grandparent, not presentable, indeed taboo, until robed in images." There are reefs among the ripples of poetry, as in the recollection of an Amherst costume party: "It ended badly . . . but what was an ointment without flies? In memory the party shimmers and resounds like a *Fête* by Debussy. Freedom to be oneself is all very well; the greater freedom is not to be oneself." What kind of greater freedom ends in fisticuffs?

What is *A Different Person* about? It is principally an account of two years, 1950 to 1952, spent in Europe by the young poet between the ages of twenty-four and twenty-six. Reading his poetry at his alma mater, Amherst, he has an epiphany: "As I read, part of me listened to how I sounded, nasal, educated, world-weary as only those without experience of the world can be, and thought how much I would like this sound to change; or, failing that, what a relief it would be to live among French or Italians, who wouldn't automatically 'place' me each time I opened my mouth." He hopes to become a different person during these journeys and sojourns, or at least remove the trammels from his old self. "This is where a lover came in. For could I truly have contemplated stripping and plunging into the unknown without [Claude's] life-preserving arms about me?" After a long interval, he had just met Claude again at a party. They had hardly known each other then; now they were lovers embarking on a *vita nuova*.

The happy honeymoon cools as they trot from Austria to France, from Greece to Italy. In Rome, after fifteen months of this, they meet an old friend, Robert Isaacson. Claude hopes to start something with him, but it is James and Robert, who even look alike, that become lovers. Meanwhile Claude and James are both undergoing separate therapies with the same therapist, Dr. Detre, for about a year; then one after the other they return to the States, whither Isaacson has preceded them. Everyone remained friends with everyone, and nothing more.

This framework allows Merrill to write something between a long poetic meditation and a shortish autobiography. He travels even more freely in time than in space, and the narrative, as baggy as the latest Armani and Versace pants, can accommodate just about anything. The points of reference are chiefly lovers present, past, future, or imaginary; but also friends and family. Besides Claude and Robert, there is also the translator and anthologist Kimon Friar, James's teacher and lover at Amherst; David Jackson, Merrill's life companion, and, way in the future, Peter Hooten, a young actor. Also sundry Greek and Italian youths, picked up over the years.

Among the friends, we find Freddy Buechner, the novelist and best pal from Lawrenceville; Tony Harwood, aesthete, *poète manqué*, and school chum No. 2; Hubbell, an outré queen; Count Morra, a somewhat ambiguous war hero; and Hans, a (mostly) dying Dutch poet. A few women, too: Alice B. Toklas, Alison Lurie, Grace Stone. Also Mina, the older consort *cum* patroness of Kimon Friar; and Nina, the much older patroness and consort of Harwood. Both are very foreign, vaguely aristocratic, and good comic relief. Further, the art historian Marilyn Aronsberg ("Culture wasn't, in her case, the blind alley I sometimes feared it was in mine"), and Irma Brandeis, the Bard Italian hand, who turns out to have been Clizia, the lost love of Eugenio Montale.

But the most important woman is Mother, Hellen Ingalls Merrill, the book's heroine if it has one. James adores and dreads her, invokes and quotes her, conducts real and fantasy dialogues with her, reviews her two marriages, and romanticizes even her old age. The purplest passage of this supposedly risqué memoir is this love letter:

A tinted oval photograph shows her at eighteen with soulful eyes and Cupid's-bow lips, her forehead ringleted, the whole wrapped in a fichu of pink tulle against a studio backdrop of plantation oaks. It bears a clear likeness to my mother even now, while giving no clue to her uncanny, lifelong vitality. (One clue, no doubt, is the daily quarter grain of thyroid extract she has taken since my birth. This emerged when she broke a hip at eighty. Hospitalized without her medication, she lapsed before our eyes, like the beautiful girl at the close of *Lost Horizon*, into an old, old woman. Then she mended, and a tiny white pill again reversed the process.) Late in life, still glancing lovingly at the dance floor, all animation from her first drink, her dark hair barely frosted by the years, she has not lost the ability, or the desire, to draw her companion into that old complicity of vigorous nods and knowing smiles, her slender hand coming to rest on his arm for emphasis. At ninety, my mother has the smooth legs of a girl. Her breasts, glimpsed through a loose peignoir, are large and unwrinkled. The only physical sign of age is in the shoulders—giving out, as if they'd borne too much—and in the slow erosion of her once military spine to a fragile question mark.

Father also figures fairly prominently, but in a much more relaxed, easygoing way. After all, James has already settled his score with him in *The Seraglio*, a *roman à clef* published, revised, and republished. Other family members likewise put in pleasantly anodyne appearances. Back and forth weaves the memoir until, at last, some sort of web or structure emerges, not entirely cohesive and purposeful, but artfully deployed to suggest a transcendent, albeit opaque, order.

Yet there is something queasy about this book, described by the blurb as "perhaps the most lucid and inward account we have had of a homosexual life in a world of intellect and art." The problem is not the homosexuality (that has long since turned from onus to bonus) or even the somewhat wearisome promiscuity, whether indulged in or merely fantasized. It is rather the question of tact, discretion, accountability, and also of truthfulness. One wonders how seemly it is to tell a tale this intimate about real people with their real names. I am told, too, that Claude Fredericks thinks that he hasn't been accurately portrayed, and some of the others may also feel compromised.

There is always something problematic about a memoir that

quotes long-past conversations in great, seemingly authoritative detail. Did Merrill keep a diary? And even then, does one record conversations at such length, in such detail? Or does he perhaps have total recall? Or is he just re-creating the feel of those conversations? Both Fredericks and Isaacson are evoked with affection and respect, but even if (I don't know for sure) they agreed to such publication, might they not feel that too much is revealed, or that there is a slant or distortion here and there? True, though sex is omnipresent, there are no detailed descriptions; even so, there is a scene in the book where Claude objects to the mere use of "Portugal" in the title of one of James's poems, Portugal having meant something special to the two of them; well, much more than Portugal is given away here.

Merrill himself is as possessed by art as he is obsessed with sex throughout the book, from his days as lustful ephebe, through his maturity as poet and *bon vivant*, into his incipient old age, surrounded by his *Lebensgefährte* and some younger lovers. I am reminded of these lines from his early poem "Salome": "Whosoever faithfully / Desires desire more than its object shall / Find his right heaven, be he saint or brute." Could Merrill be speaking for himself here? Does he believe this? He certainly wants to, for it would justify his libidinal lingerings. Consider, further, these verses from a later poem, "From the Cupola":

> . . . This is me, James,
>   Writing lest he think
>   Of the reasons why he writes—
> Boredom, fear, mixed vanities and shames;
>   Also love.

I see all the above motives represented in *A Different Person*, except the last: there is not much genuine love to be found here, despite some elegant, rather operatic, posturing. And truth, you will have noted, is not mentioned in Merrill's etiology.

What I trust least in the book is the figure of the psychotherapist, Dr. Detre. There is a medical doctor as well, Dr. Simeons, who, in his amiably bumbling way, is quite believable. Not so Detre. He is supposed to be Hungarian, but his name, whatever it may be, is not Hungarian. And he is too perfect, even for a Hungarian: not only omniscient, but also able to couch his couchside omniscience in epigrammatic, lapidary utterances a Gautier might envy, such as "Sex between men is by its character frustrating. . . . The anus is full of shit; the mouth is a well of flattery and untruth. The honest penis is left with no reliable place to go." This sounds very much like the analysand writing the analyst's lines, as do other passages. Why, then, not stick your honest pen into fiction?

And while I am complaining, there is one particularly murky passage between pages 189 and 192. It begins: "It was a truth universally acknowledged in those innocent decades from 1950 to 1980 that a stable homosexual couple would safely welcome the occasional extramarital fling." The implication is that this was a mistaken belief of those "innocent decades." Yet on the next pages we get a glowing account of what fun it was for David Jackson and James to seek out threesomes and foursomes in Italy, Greece, and New York bathhouses. "For me those hours were the adolescence I'd been too shy or repressed to put into action at the time. Their polymorphous abundance spilling over into our lives kept us primed and sexually alert towards each other." Well then, those innocent decades must have been more wise than naïve, especially since no one seems to have incurred AIDS. Greek youths are particularly recommended because they all have a fiancée stashed away somewhere but need to have innocent fun until they can afford to marry. This "seemed to ensure our never going overboard in Greece. David and I could follow with no harm to him the faun incarnate in this or that young man, and without losing ourselves or each other." This sounds contented, even smug. Yet why, then, the tone of rebuke in the next sentence, "We were very optimistic to think so"? And why the numerous hints throughout that the optimism continues? The author wants to have it both ways, extolling the polymorphous decades, yet wagging his finger at them; endorsing the sober ways of the post-AIDS Nineties while flouting them.

Which is not to say that the book doesn't have its beauties. It sovereignly evokes a picture of rich, highly cultivated young American homosexuals living near-idyllic lives (there is a bit too much ego in Arcadia) in an as yet unspoiled Europe, where the very flies enhance the ointment. There are heady portrayals of opera-going in some of Europe's best and worst opera houses. There are enthusiastic descriptions of the wonders of painting, sculpture, architecture lined up in espaliers for the cognoscenti. There are impassioned accounts of privileged landscapes and cityscapes. There are stimulating conversations and sportive confrontations, glimpses of an America better comprehended from afar, and a Europe better enjoyed from inside its nooks and crannies. Merrill catches bits of jaunty dialogue, such as the Roman matron's comment to her fellow diner about Maria Montez dead in her bathtub: "At least she died clean."

There are witty aperçus, as when Merrill observes two of his male friends together: "Pangs reserved exclusively for the gay shot through me—I was jealous of both parties at once." Or this encapsulation of differences between lovers: "Where I was content to 'find myself' in a Fauré song or a Degas interior, Claude identified manfully with a Zen scroll or the *St. John Passion*." Or take this charming vignette *chez* Toklas: "The big white poodle Basket, the original Basket's replacement but still the most famous animal I've ever met, lay at her feet. His manners were plain, even perfunctory, like an old countrified nobleman's; as man of the house, he clearly had his share of nonsense to put up with." There is a delightful account of what words mean to our poet, of how one's art matures through the words one favors:

> What were my recurrent words? No longer, as at sixteen, "pale" or "dim," or even the irresistible names of colors—"violet" or "rose," scented respectively by turbulence and upward movement. The words I never wearied of were rather those adverbs like "still" or "even," or adverbial phrases like "by then" or "as yet" or "no longer," which, sharpening a reader's sense of time, suggested a reality forever in the process of change. . . . "Still," with its triadic resonance of immobility, endurance, and intensification ("Eleanor grew still more animated"), was perhaps the hardest to resist. Deep in the pinewoods of my vocabulary, it yielded an intoxicating moonshine I would keep resorting to in small, furtive sips.

Say what you will against this Merrillian world, it has something to recommend it. It has culture down to its fingertips, erudition down to its most frivolous allusions, style suffusing its most trivial pursuits. No matter how well or badly you use it, so much recondite knowledge, concentrated into a sestina or prodigally scattered in small talk, commands wonder. We shall not see the like of it when Merrill and his likes are gone, and we shall be the poorer for it.

Perhaps the most engaging passage in *A Different Person* is this one, which truly conveys "a reality forever in the process of change":

> The house I return to most regularly in America is Claude's. Its rooms remain of a gleaming, exemplary bareness, the books high-minded and intently read. The sad truth is that I shall never live up to him—he who has no more than one lover at a time; who seldom travels farther than thirty miles from home, and then only to meet his students at Bennington; who, exchanging his recorder for a *shakuhachi*, came back from Kyoto a Buddhist. By now he looks like one, rotund and roseate, eyes alert under heavy lids, a loose, much mended kimono sashed round him: Zenmaster Time's favorite pupil. Visiting him is restorative.

Could it be that Claude found what James was looking for? He certainly sounds like a different person, which Merrill, surrounded by David, Peter, and Jerl, and the silly Ouija Board that has ruined so much of his fine poetry, does not. But there is time as yet even for him. Still.

1993

Partying on Parnassus: The New York School Poets

DAVID LEHMAN'S *The Last Avant-Garde: The Making of the New York School of Poets* examines the lives, work, and influence of John Ashbery, Frank O'Hara, Kenneth Koch, and James Schuyler in what seems to be order of importance. To put my cards on the table, as Lehman would have a critic do, I declare that none of these poets has written what I would call a single poem of any importance, although some of them have written plausible light verse.

Lehman states the problem succinctly:

> Though he is America's best-known poet, with a strong readership in Britain and a larger international following than any of his contemporaries, Ashbery remains an issue and for some a litmus test. A respected editor declared that one cannot like both Ashbery and Philip Larkin, and though I feel that one can, I understand the logic of her position. Ashbery's poetic assumptions are the opposite of Larkin's. Larkin set store by his sincerity and his control; Ashbery by his fancy and his abandon. If your sense of literary tradition extends from Keats and the Romantics to Emerson and Whitman and from there to Wallace Stevens, Ashbery's your man; if, on the other hand, you derive your sense

of tradition from Thomas Hardy and William Butler Yeats, Ashbery will seem a renegade.

Except that I would not abandon Keats and the Romantics to the other camp, and would not limit my tradition to Hardy and Yeats, I agree with this assessment, and especially with the "respected editor." To like what I consider anti-poetry as much as poetry bespeaks not catholicity but wishy-washiness, which, to be sure, has been enshrined as a virtue in our time. Does my attitude, then, entitle me to review Lehman's book?

It would be a sorry state of affairs in which, say, books on religion could be reviewed only by true believers. There are at least two sides to every question, and a critical dialogue should be just that— a dialogue. Surely Lehman would not be content with preaching only to the converted and gathering their encomia in his collection plate.

So, by way of further laying down of cards, let me state my idea of poetry. It comprises music, painting (imagery), insight, and pregnancy or memorableness of utterance, the first two, of course, in a special sense. Ambiguity, too, may be a legitimate device, but it should not be confused with the mainstay of much New York School (henceforth NYS) stuff: openness to infinite, arbitrary, private readings—*quot homines, tot sententiae*. That way lies formlessness, dissolution, anarchy, and, yes, madness, when free association, becoming too free, hurtles into dementia.

By accepting such scot-free association, anything the NYS poets tossed off or elucubrated could be proclaimed poetry. That these poets were closely associated with some painters (mostly of the NYS of painting) and some composers explains one of their major fallacies: the bland assumption that the procedures of the other arts could be readily appropriated by poetry, so that, for instance, the techniques of Jackson Pollock and John Cage could be applied to writing poems.

Lehman's book divides into three main parts, although he acknowledges only two. He begins with an introductory section acquainting us with the early days of his four poets at Harvard and elsewhere, and the New York literary and art scene in the Forties and Fifties—an avant-garde at odds with contemporary modes in art and life. Next come individual sections on each of the four poets, in which, however, a lot about other poets and artists figures as well. In the third part, "The Ordeal of the Avant-Garde"—although the ordeal seems to me that of the readers—we get affiliations, influences, cross-fertilizations, the work of some of the painters as both painters and poets, also the roles of some art critics, and the most recent developments involving both the heirs of the NYS and rival movements.

Lehman has been a journalist, poet, and teacher, and displays some of the virtues of each profession. He is well-read and readable, knows most of the poets and some of the painters personally, and tells good anecdotes. We also get a sense of the hangouts some of these figures frequented, and probably just enough about their personal relations as well.

John Ashbery (born 1927), Frank O'Hara (1926–1966), Kenneth Koch (born 1925), and James Schuyler (1923–1991): three out of four of them went to Harvard, three out of four wrote professional art criticism, and three were, or are, homosexual. But even in these respects there was no real odd man out. We read, "The painter Alex Katz delighted Schuyler by refusing to believe him when he said that he attended [without graduating] Bethany College in West Virginia. 'Nah, you're Harvard,' Katz said." Koch, who has not written art criticism, "wrote plays partly for the pleasure of collaborating with painters who did the sets." And though he was the one heterosexual in the group, his friend and collaborator Larry Rivers recalled that he "talked and acted as gay as the rest."

Lehman is at his best documenting the numerous collaborations on poems, plays, and even fiction among these poets, usually in pairs, thus conveying the sense of a school. But he fails to note that, with very few exceptions (and even those not usually in the top bracket), such collaborations have proved artistically negligible.

In further pursuit of honesty, let me mention that I graded Ashbery's papers in Harry Levin's "Proust, Mann & Joyce" course at Harvard, as I did those of his classmates Donald Hall and Robert Bly. All three poets got straight As. I got to know Ashbery—slightly—only later, when we were fellow critics at *New York* magazine. I also run into him at parties. I find him reserved, civilized, and witty, dangerous only when he picks up a pen—or, actually, type-

writer—to write a poem. I once reviewed his *Tennis Court Oath* un-
favorably, but I did not, as Lehman claims in another book, and
Richard Howard alludes to in *Alone with America*, call it garbage. I
merely quoted from the autobiographical poem "Europe" the line
"He had mistaken his book for garbage," adding that "I do not think
it is up to us to know better than the poet."

I knew Koch at Harvard equally slightly. He did me the kindness
of getting a couple of my poems into the *Harvard Advocate*, on
whose board he was. Frank O'Hara I would glimpse around Har-
vard, and probably spoke to at the Poets' Theatre, where he was
very active and I acted in two plays. I never laid eyes on James
Schuyler.

I must also state that the review of Ashbery's play *The Compro-
mise* in the Cambridge broadsheet *Audience* was not, as Lehman
speculates, by me; everything I published there was signed, as the
byline was one's only recompense. I learn from Lehman that this re-
view, though mostly favorable, elicited an "Ode," jointly written by
O'Hara and Schuyler, that starts out lampooning me and then pro-
ceeds to one of the "harmonious workings of two 'quite singular'
sensibilities." The best lines, as quoted by Lehman, begin: "if I did
go out on the fire escape and piss on myself in the rain / which is, I
suppose, the male equivalent of a good cry / I might not ever want
to come in again / I would be emptying myself forever like a mast-
head for love." Who, I wonder, in this harmonious outpouring, is
the pisser on the fire escape, O'Hara or Schuyler? For all their kin-
dred sensibilities, they were not, after all, Siamese twins.

To be sure, some of the NYS poets had, as I learn from the book,
uncanny resemblances: "On different occasions both Ashbery's
mother and O'Hara's companion were fooled [on the phone] into
thinking that one was the other." Even in the flesh, with her back
turned, Mrs. Ashbery once mistook Frank for her son. And sure
enough, many a NYS poem could have been written by another
member of the group.

Which is not to say that there are no salient differences. French,
of which they were fond, has apt terms for all four of our poets—
what I would call the 4F categories. For Ashbery, *fumiste*; for
O'Hara, *flâneur*; for Koch, *farceur*; and for Schuyler, "who was prone
to psychotic fits [and] spent most of his life in and out of psychiatric

institutions," *fou*. Let me investigate them, and Lehman's treatment of them, one by one. If what follows is more a polemic than a review, let me point out that Lehman's book is more a panegyric than a serious work of criticism.

For Ashbery—whom the poet-critic Thomas M. Disch refers to as "the poet-laureate of spaciness," whom James Dickey called "a very difficult and perhaps impossible poet," and about whom William Arrowsmith wrote, "I have no idea most of the time what Mr. Ashbery is talking about or being . . . his characteristic gesture is an effete and cerebral whimsy"—Lehman has nothing but praise. In *Beyond Amazement*, a collection of essays about Ashbery that he edited and contributed to, Lehman declared, "Ashbery's poetry [is] far from inaccessible; on the contrary, it could be said to open up a path of entry to whole areas of consciousness that could not otherwise be reached."

In *The Last Avant-Garde*, Lehman holds up many poems and passages from Ashbery for our admiration. Here, from what is described as one of his "most admired" poems, is the beginning:

> They dream only of America
> To be lost among the thirteen million
>   pillars of grass
> "This honey is delicious
> *Though it burns the throat*"
>
> And hiding from darkness in barns
> They can be grownups now
> And the murderer's ashtray is more easily—
> The lake a lilac cube
>
> He holds a key in his right hand
> "Please," he asks willingly,
> He is thirty years old. . . .

It seems that "it is possible to read this haunting poem as an allegory about the poet's relationship to Pierre Martory." Martory was Ashbery's lover for some of the ten years the poet lived in Paris. How such a relationship lends itself to allegory—and just what here is allegorical as opposed to, say, aleatoric—is not explained. But to give you a sense of Lehman the exegete, take "the strangeness of the adverb in the line ' "Please," he asks willingly,' is not easily explained, and that is one of its virtues." What its other virtues are, we are not told.

Now here is something from a later piece, "A Love Poem," one of "the great works of [Ashbery's] maturity":

The dripping is in the walls, within sleep
Itself. I mean there is no escape
From me, from it. The night is itself asleep
And what goes on in it, the naming of
the wind. Our notes to each other, always
    repeated, always the same.

Such marvels came from Ashbery "for more than thirty years, as long a stretch of sustained creative productivity as any American poet has enjoyed." And why not, if one considers Ashbery's method, as described in an earlier Lehman book, *The Line Forms Here*: "Ashbery approaches his typewriter once a week or so to write poetry, confident that he will tap his unconscious in the very act of tapping the keys." And "should the phone ring during the hour or so . . . he'll welcome the interruption—and allow it to modify the poem in progress."

Lehman's hero-worship of the NYS's *chef d'école* is often ludicrous bordering on the pitiful. When Ashbery goes to France on a Fulbright, he is "like the hero in a medieval romance embarking on a test, a quest, and an adventure." When W. H. Auden, not caring much for either O'Hara's or Ashbery's submission to the Yale Younger Poets Series in 1956, nevertheless had to choose between them, he "was as though thrust into the position of God choosing between the gifts of Cain and Abel." And Lehman adds, "The competition for Auden's nod stands somewhere behind the epistolary quarrel between O'Hara and Ashbery on the question of which of the two was more like the James Dean figure in Elia Kazan's *East of Eden* (1956)." Lehman devotes the next three pages to the running argument between two silly queens (my term) about who looked more like James Dean.

Gush like "brilliant," "seminal," and "diabolically clever" proliferates. "Ashbery's poems," we read,

defeat the analytical methods. . . . Like mysterious equations in
which the terms take on multiple values, they cannot be easily

reduced to syllogisms. The effort to make conventional sense of the poems would be wasted; rather, the reader should approach them without preconception, or with the willingness to allow expectations to be dashed. ["Please," we should say willingly.] For Ashbery . . . the poem is the performance of experience rather than the commentary on the experience. [By that token, the performance of a sexual act, say, is a poem. Does it even have to be written down?] So radical a departure from the norm is this that critics today are still catching up with poems Ashbery composed nearly half a century ago.

Personally, I have given up trying to catch up with them; I prefer to keep a safe distance.

The reader can conclude from what I have quoted, or from any poem of Ashbery's he might open by way of *sortes Vergilianae,* that all this is sheer camping, sheer nonsense, or, as the French would call it, *fumisterie.* A *fumiste* is, literally, an oven repairman or chimney sweep. The fin-de-siècle wits, with regard to all the smoke and obfuscation, turned the word into argot for a fake artist or pretentious poetaster, or, as the Larousse has it, a *mystificateur, mauvais plaisant.* Or an Ashbery. We read, "Poems are 'going on all the time in my head and I occasionally spin off a length,' Ashbery has said." That's the old sausage machine method: you let the meat be ground a while, then you arbitrarily cut it off, wrap it in casing, and presto, a sausage—I mean, a poem.

But Ashbery's greatness is not confined to his poetry. His "incidental literary criticism adds more to our literary knowledge than any score of scholarly dissertations." That may indeed be true when you consider Lehman's idea of a scholarly dissertation. After quoting from a poem of O'Hara's in which "the most ordinary of activities seems endowed with a nobility"—to wit, "the Manhattan Storage Warehouse, / Which they'll soon tear down. I / used to think they had the Armory / Show there"—Lehman comments, "A thesis could be written on O'Hara's error." I dare say twenty such might begin to equal one piece of Ashbery's incidental criticism.

What, however, about Lehman's criticism? In *The Last Avant-Garde,* he speculates a good deal about a relationship between Ash-

bery's titles, with which the poet begins, and their texts, with the text
of a poem having apparently nothing to do with its title. He must
have forgotten his interview with Ashbery, in which the poet pro-
nounced,

> Very often my poems diverge from the areas or concerns the
> title has announced, and I think it's profitable in this way to add
> a further dimension to poetry. I mean, one can write a poem "To
> a Waterfowl" [as Ashbery has done, stooping to despoil poor
> Bryant] that has nothing to do with waterfowls, and the reader
> is obliged to consider the poem as somehow related to the sub-
> ject indicated only in the title.

If this is not *fumisterie*, I don't know what is: not only writing the
poem to a cheaply prankish title, but also erecting a whole *ars poe-
tica* on this campy procedure. To be sure, Lehman opines, "camp,
like any other style, can furnish the technical means to ends that are
serious and complex." Accordingly, he reports seriously that "Ash-
bery persuaded Koch that 'shapely as an amoeba' was a better sim-
ile than "shapeless as an amoeba.'" This is what Lehman calls "the
poets [getting] a contact high from one another." With equal seri-
ousness, he quotes Ashbery: "As I have gotten older, it seems to me
that time is what I have been writing about during all these years
when I thought I wasn't writing about anything." Proof, I think, that
one should always trust one's first impressions.

About Frank O'Hara, Lehman has scarcely less reverential
things to say, although none as poignant as this sentence: "O'Hara's
father died while he was at Harvard, and his journals of the period
show him in a soul-searching mood." (Given Lehman's faulty syn-
tax, one wonders how this poetical father, dying at Harvard as a
mere youth, found time for marriage, procreation, and soul-search-
ing.) Son Frank, however, was an un-soul-searching *flâneur*. Most of
his poems are street poems (derived from Apollinaire's *poème pro-
menade*) in which O'Hara records his *flâneries*, or else "list poems" in
which he enumerates whatever comes to his mind with perfect
Whitmania. "Personal Poem," for example, begins with a walk at
lunchtime, then describes meeting up with LeRoi Jones. They walk
and eat together as the poem continues:

> we get some fish and some ale it's
> cool but crowded we don't like Lionel Trilling
> we decide. We like Don Allen we don't like
> Henry James so much as we like Herman
>   Melville. . . .

and ends:

> I wonder if one person out of the
>   8,000,000 is
> thinking of me as I shake hands with LeRoi
> and buy a strap for my wristwatch and go
> back to work happy at the thought possibly so

Note the absurd use, or lack, of punctuation and the inane enjamb-
ment that, as the NYS fantasizes, turns prose into poetry. But
Lehman evaluates, "So casual and spontaneous is this poem, so com-
mitted to the rhythms of actual speech, that the reader may not even
hear the closing rhyme. And that is as it should be: the music is at
the heart of the noise, the poetry something subtle in the midst of
all that seems wildly antipoetic." The poem is thirty-four wildly an-
tipoetic lines long, but ends with two lines rhyming, albeit so dis-
creetly we may not even notice it, and indeed shouldn't. Yet the
rhyme is "the music at the heart of the noise," the hidden poetry for
whose sake we must put up with thirty-two lines of noise. What
Lehman fails to mention is that all thirty-four lines, rhyming or not,
are equally banal.

There is no end to the grandiose claims Lehman makes for the
Four Horsemen of the NYS. Thus a verse about a bank teller, "Miss
Stillwagon (first name Linda I once heard)," "has an interest beyond
the sass in the speaker's voice, it helps evoke a once commonplace
situation remote from us today, used as we have been to automatic
teller machines and the universal American first-name basis." The
source of the line is "The Day Lady Died," a putative elegy for Bil-
lie Holiday. It is not until the concluding five lines of the poem that
O'Hara remembers Lady Day, which Lehman justifies as putting
"the poem into the company of other great elegies, notably Milton's
'Lycidas.'" So, too, we learn that "O'Hara's poetic preoccupation
with Miles Davis . . . and with Billie Holiday . . . is evidence less of

white-negroism than of peerless aesthetic taste." The grand conclusion is "it could be said that if all that survived of 1959 was 'The Day Lady Died,' then historians a century hence could piece together the New York of that moment." Note the poor grammar and syntax, and poorer judgment.

Gilding by association, as in O'Hara-Milton, is one of Lehman's favorite ploys. Kenneth Koch's "poems are unthinkable without a meat-and-potatoes diet of Ovid, Ariosto, Lorca, Pasternak, Mayakovsky, and a dozen French poets," though Lehman doesn't make clear for whom this diet is prescribed: the poet, the reader, or both. He situates Koch in the tradition of satire's "greatest practitioners," Pope and Byron, as he elsewhere brackets Schuyler with Montaigne. Koch's poetry "demands to be read in the context of . . . Rabelais, Lord Byron, Lewis Carroll, and Oscar Wilde," even as Ashbery is "in the visionary company" of Wordsworth, Emerson, and Stevens. O'Hara and Schuyler "revised the lyric model" of Whitman, Crane, and Williams, and "Ashbery resembles Kierkegaard in the quality of his irony."

Such gilt by association climaxes in the comparison of Koch's two circus poems, "Circus" and the much later "Circus II," which Lehman uses both in class and in public lectures. To choose between them, it seems, is to choose, as Lehman asks his hearers to do, "between art and life. In terms derived from William Blake," one stands for innocence, the other for experience. "In Schiller's terms, the first 'Circus' is naïve, the second sentimental. . . . In Wallace Stevens's terms, the first represents the principle of the imagination, the second that of reality." Indeed, "the second is like Koch's version of Coleridge's 'Dejection Ode.'" All this show apropos of two poems by our *farceur* from which I quote:

"What is death in the circus? That depends on if it's spring.
Then, if elephants are there, *mon père*, we are not completely
    lost.
Oh the sweet strong odor of beasts which laughs at decay!
Decay! Decay! we are like the elements in a kaleidoscope
But such passions we feel! bigger than the beaches and
Rustier than harpoons." After this speech the circus practitioner
    sat down.

And the second:

> I never mentioned my friends in my poems at the time I wrote
>   The Circus
> Although they meant almost more than anything to me
> Of this now for some time I've felt an attenuation
> So I'm mentioning them maybe this will bring them back to me
> Not them perhaps but what I felt about them
> John Ashbery Jane Freilicher Larry Rivers Frank O'Hara
> their names alone bring tears to my eyes. . . .

As to which of the poems is greater, Lehman avers, "I know the answer, but my lips are sealed," surely an aporia worthy of Jesting Pilate.

It should not surprise us that Lehman, as he says, decided to become a poet when taking his only writing course ever as a Columbia sophomore from Koch, and also by reading Donald Allen's notorious anthology *The New American Poetry*—and especially O'Hara's "Why I Am Not a Painter" contained in it. This "made poetry seem as natural as breathing, as casual as the American idiom, and so imbued with metropolitan irony and bohemian glamour as to be irresistible." He does not, however, tell us what made him also espouse literary criticism, samples of which follow.

"Koch, our funniest poet, has had the misfortune to be a protean genius at a moment when the lyric poem is the be-all and end-all of verse and is mistakenly held to be incompatible with the spirit of comedy." It is elementary knowledge that comic verse has never fallen out of esteem, but is held, now as before, to be light verse rather than poetry, with the exception of Pope and Byron, Chaucer and some epigrams by Rochester and Belloc. Koch, whose entire output traffics in sometimes funny, sometimes unfunny burlesque verse, has not been critically shortchanged.

Now here is Lehman on James Schuyler, whose "Freely Espousing" is "a brief statement of his poetics." For Schuyler, "who is sparing with figurative language, the literal description suffices more often than not, making similes seem supererogatory." So Lehman quotes admiringly from the above-mentioned poem: "The sinuous beauty of words like allergy / the tonic resonance of / pill when used as in / 'she is a pill' / on the other hand I am not going to espouse any short stories in which lawn mowers clack." After quoting from another Schuyler poem, "there is a dull book with me, / an apple core, cigarettes, / an ashtray," Lehman comments, "the unembellished 'apple core' is sufficient to suggest the mythic dimensions of another lost garden paradise."

This kind of associative diarrhea is frequent. Koch told a student that "The Lost Golf Ball" would be a good title for an abstract painting because, though people looking for the ball would not find it, "they'll look more closely at the painting." From this, Lehman leaps to these lines of Schuyler's: "Kenneth Koch / could teach a golf ball / how to write pantoums," as if this juxtaposition shed critical light on either poet. Similarly, from among questions "as compelling today as when Koch first asked them," Lehman cites "Is there no one who feels like a pair of pants?"; Lehman then finds a "shared aesthetic" in the following from "Personism," O'Hara's poetic manifesto: "that's just common sense: if you're going to buy a pair of pants you want them to be tight enough so everyone will want to go to bed with you." A manifesto all right, but not exactly a poetic one.

Again, the ending of Schuyler's "Korean Mums" is "a notable example of an allegory emerging from literal truth": "what / is there I have not forgot? / or one day will forget; / this garden, the breeze / in stillness, even / the words, Korean mums." But does not all allegory take off from a literal meaning, and just what is allegorized here? Lehman perceives "a case of exact identity between 'the words' and what they mean." Is *that* the allegory then? Lehman probably knows, but once again prefers to keep mum. Or mums.

Here is a further example from Ashbery, who "does to conventional syntax what Robespierre did to the monarchy." "When the poet remarks . . . that we . . . 'have been given no help whatever / In decoding our own man-size quotient and must rely / On secondhand knowledge' the *hand* in that phrase vibrates with meaning, like the sound of one hand clapping." Has exegesis ever been more elucidating? So, too, when O'Hara writes "to be more revolutionary than a nun / is our desire, to be secular and intimate / as, when sighting a redcoat, you smile / and pull the trigger," Lehman helpfully explicates that it "is conceivable that the 'redcoat' O'Hara envisions was a coat of red paint," though I am more inclined to see it as a coat to be worn over skintight pants making everyone want to go to bed with you.

But then Lehman lauds crazy Schuyler for seeing "the poetic possibilities of the laundry list," as in this "quintessential" passage, "unglib, fresh, and free of fake language," from the poem "Things to Do": "Walk three miles / a day beginning tomorrow. / Alphabetize. / Purchase nose-hair shears. / Answer letters. / Elicit others. / Write Maxine. / Move to Maine. / Give up NoCal. / See more movies. / Practice long distance dialing." How odd that Lehman doesn't see NoCal as a tribute to a fellow *fou*, Robert Lowell. But Lehman's sharpest moment comes when, in Gertrude Stein's *Stanzas of Meditation*, much admired by Ashbery, he notes that "in one poem . . . Stein places periods in the middle of sentences—an experimental move that still seems fresh today." Fresh? I'd say downright impudent.

There are, moreover, errors of every stripe. *Cadavre exquis* is not a "one-line poem"; Baudelaire is not the inventor of the prose poem, which harks back to Bertrand and Guérin, if not indeed to Evariste Parny. You cannot write "neither true or false" in good English, any more than *bête noir* in either English or French. We read that the NYS poets' pleasure would have been diminished if any of them "felt that the others' approbation were automatic." Lehman makes the common error of using *paraphrasing* to mean twisting someone else's phrase around for effect; he often misuses *supernal* for something like sublime, and he subliterately employs *critique* as a verb.

Again, a steady refrain does not *orchestrate* a poem. In a sentence about Pierre Reverdy, the singular *poetry* makes a poor antecedent for the plural "their enchantment." *Astrological* is misused for astronomical. "O'Hara's 'exoticism' of blacks" is extremely clumsy. Baudelaire's *mauvais vitrier* is a *bad* glazier, not an *evil* one, and the prose poem wherein the glazier occurs does not end with cries of "Life is beautiful!"—*Vivre en beauté* means "live in high style." But then Lehman's French allows for *jeu du* [sic] *paume* and *Bibliotheque de l'Arsénale* [accent missing, *arsénal* feminized], his Italian Hispanicizes Francesco Parmigianino into *Francisco*; his German takes *Schadenfreude* to mean envy.

But Lehman is at his least appealing in his continual aggrandizing, as when Ashbery becomes a "hero in a fantastic tale," because a bookstore he bought something from supposedly vanished without a trace when he next looked for it. So Koch is a "poet of the highest originality" because he "has revived the epic and the drama as viable vehicles for verse [surely that statement has been stood on its head] and revealed an uncanny knack for marrying unusual forms to unconventional matter." It takes only a cursory glance at Koch's verse drama or verse epic (and isn't epic ipso facto verse?) to ascertain the hopelessness of each. As for pantoums and sestinas, they can no more be helped by unconventional matter than that matter can be ennobled by marriage to them.

David Lehman studied with Kenneth Koch, who "convert[ed] a generation of Columbia students into sorcerer's apprentices." He was the colleague of John Ashbery both on the faculty of Brooklyn College and at *Newsweek*, where he reviewed books and Ashbery art. With *The Last Avant-Garde*, he proffers a collegial and sorcerer's apprentice tribute to them and their NYS fellows. Whether he has rendered a similar service to his readers remains open to doubt.

In *The Line Forms Here*, Lehman wrote, "For many of us, any key or code to the poems—however ingeniously put forth—might well work to diminish rather than enhance our delight." Ashbery's poetry "induces [a] state of mystified alertness that only the most intense esthetic experiences can afford." One of Ashbery's most cited and debated nonsense phrases, "Murk plectrum," may have finally acquired its critical counterpart in Lehman's murk spectrum.

1998

Wilde the Poet

OSCAR WILDE'S great literary achievement was the full exploitation of the paradox. Obviously he was not the first to make use of this fascinating trope, known in its most concentrated form as oxymoron. The Greek meaning of paradox is (I am quoting J. A. Cuddon's excellent *Dictionary of Literary Terms*) "beside, or beyond, belief," but it gradually acquired its modern meaning: "an apparently self-contradictory (even absurd) statement which, on closer inspection, is found to contain a truth reconciling the conflicting opposites." Interestingly, a basic tenet of Christianity is the oxymoron *felix culpa*, or fortunate fall, referring to Adam's sin, which paradoxically enabled humankind to earn salvation. Though why this should be considered fortunate compared to the initial state of paradisaic bliss is one of those religious mysteries beyond my comprehension.

But back to Wilde. In 1895, the week after Wilde's sentencing, the distinguished music critic Ernest Newman published in *The Free Review* a defense of Wilde the artist—and, by implication, the man—a brave thing on the part of both author and publisher. Newman placed particular emphasis on Wilde's paradoxes. He wrote:

> A paradox is simply the truth of the minority, just as a commonplace is the truth of the majority. The function of the paradox is to illuminate light places, to explain just those things that

everyone understands. For example, everyone knows what Art is, and everyone knows what it is to be immoral; but if a thinker says "Art is immoral," the new synthesis puzzles people, and they either call it a paradox, or say the writer is immoral. In reality, he is doing just what they cannot do; he can see round corners and the other side of things. Nay, he can do more than this. . . . We ordinary beings can see objects in three dimensions only; a great paradox is a view in the fourth dimension.

Newman then goes on to point out that Wilde's paradoxes are "to the Philistine an insult and to Mrs. Grundy shameful. Yet there is not a single one of these paradoxes of Mr. Wilde's that does not contain—I will not say a half-truth . . . but a good truth and a half at least." And, once more, "a paradox is a truth seen round a corner."

The simpler and more prosaic way of putting it is that a paradox is a contradiction capable of reconciliation. Even folk wisdom propounds the equal truth of opposites, hence such antithetical adages as "Absence makes the heart grow fonder" and "Out of sight, out of mind." It takes someone as philistine as Robert Benchley to parody Wilde with (I quote from memory) "I love red roses—they are so yellow." That is not a paradox: "I love red roses" is not a commonly held truth, and "they are so yellow" is not its opposite.

Now look at Wilde. In "Phrases and Philosophies for the Use of the Young," he writes: "There is a fatality about all good resolutions. They are invariably made too soon." This *is* a paradox. But a couple of phrases on, Wilde writes: "To be premature is to be perfect." The young user of these phrases may find that the second paradox contradicts the first. The great paradoxer would explicate that the first means that we are all too weak to live up to our good resolutions; the second refers to someone whose ideas are ahead of their time and thus better than accepted but outworn opinions. Both phrases, of course, apply to Wilde himself.

However, even if Wilde contradicted himself, as he sometimes did, he might well have said with another homosexual poet, Walt Whitman, "Do I contradict myself? / Very well then I contradict myself, / (I am large, I contain multitudes.)" Or he might have said: A contradiction is merely an unfinished paradox—one that has yet to be fully enunciated. There is another major homosexual writer, one who in his youth seems to have been Wilde's lover and greatly influenced by him: André Gide. In his novel *The Counterfeiters*, Gide makes contradiction a hallmark of homosexuality; the homosexual boy Boris undercuts his every yes with a no.

There seems to exist an important nexus between homosexuality and the perfected form of contradiction which is paradox. Until recently, an accepted synonym for homosexuality was inversion. I think the only reason it became offensive is that it was thought to be a reference to intercourse from the rear, whereas it referred merely to a reversal of sexual partners from the opposite to the same sex, an inversion of prevalent practice. Similarly, the paradox is an inversion of accepted wisdom, which yields a new truth that, when embraced, may yield a new *modus vivendi.*

This is essentially the thesis of Robert Merle, who published in 1948 his *Oscar Wilde: Appréciation d'une oeuvre et d'une destinée*, revised in 1984 and published as *Oscar Wilde*. Merle sees Wilde as progressing from a *perversion refoulée* to a *perversion satisfaite* and resulting in a two-way movement between "une tendance à l'aveu" and "une volonté de secret." As Norbert Kohl (about whom more anon) summarizes Merle's thesis, the "nihilistic attitude towards the established social and moral order, together with the anti-realism of Wilde's aesthetics, makes it very easy to understand why the paradox—as a means of undermining the validity of conventional beliefs—was one of Wilde's favorite literary devices."

What both Merle and I, and not a few others, are saying is that Wilde was a genius not despite of, or alongside of, his homosexuality but, in large measure, because of it. The great Austrian poet-playwright-librettist-essayist Hugo von Hofmannsthal published a beautiful tribute to Wilde as early as 1905. He defended Wilde against squeamish moralizers who tried to salvage the work by cutting it off from the life: "One must not trivialize life by tearing asunder the creature and his destiny by setting apart the unhappiness and the happiness. One must not separate everything. Everything is everywhere. There is something tragic in superficial things and something foolish in tragical ones. There is something chokingly uncanny in what we call pleasure. There is something poetic in the frippery of tarts, and petty bourgeois in the sentiments of lyric poets. It's all inside the human being."

Oddly enough, the otherwise so perceptive Ernest Newman goes on to say in the same article, "One would have thought that with his genius for delicate humor Wilde would have done some work at least of this kind in verse. The curious thing is that he keeps all his humor and paradox for his prose writings, and is serious—even terribly serious—in his poetry." Newman may be partly excused by Wilde's later poetry not yet having been available to him, but some paradox and a little humor can be found even in the early, mostly conventional verse.

The tension that leads to contradiction and thence to paradox is almost omnipresent even in the earliest poems. There is a deep-seated schism in the poems' oscillation between Christianity, indeed Catholicism, and paganism; between Christ and Mary on the one hand, and Greece and its mythology on the other. As Norbert Kohl puts it in the German title of his seminal *Oscar Wilde: Das literarische Werk zwischen Provokation und Anpassung* (the literary work between provocation and compromise)—which David Henry Wilson's excellent translation renders as an oxymoron, *Oscar Wilde: The Works of a Conformist Rebel*—the paradox in the early poems is in the would-be Catholic's yearning for Arcadia, and the contrary longing of the would-be pagan to embrace Mother Church or, failing that, Queen Victoria.

This already comes through in the Oxford undergraduate's Newdigate Prize–winning poem "Ravenna," in which Oscar describes himself as one who "watched the sun by Corinth's hills go down, / And marked the 'myriad laughter' of the sea / From starlit hills of flower-starred Arcady; / Yet back to thee [i.e., Christian Ravenna] returns my perfect love. / As to its forest-nest the evening dove."

That, too, is what Karl Beckson and Bobby Fong perceive in their important essay "Wilde as Poet" in *The Cambridge Companion to Oscar Wilde*. They call it "the tension between Wilde's avowed aestheticism and his Victorian sensibility." It is expressed clearly in the great near-concluding sentence of Wilde's essay "The Truth of Masks" (from *Intentions*, 1891): "A truth in art is that whose contradictory is also true." But as Kohl reminds us, "the *Poems* (1881) do not yet offer a clear picture of the basic tension between provocation and conformity that was such a vital element of Wilde's work and character."

Wilde felt himself to be the poetic heir of Keats and Shelley, and, more immediately, Rossetti, Morris, and Swinburne. He admired the great Catholic poet Dante, but no less the Greek bucolic poets, thus replicating his moral or, if you prefer, sexual dilemma. At this stage, though the inclination must have been there, he did not think of himself as a homosexual, even if his beloved mentor Walter Pater was a closeted one and, as Wilde later claimed, made passionate advances to him. This was never substantiated, and most likely constituted a neo-Greek myth.

To begin the examination of Wilde's poetry, let's take the sonnet "Hélas," affixed as headpiece to the first collection, *Poems* (1881). It may be that the very title is a hidden pun: on the one hand the repentant sigh, *hélas*—but why in decadent French? On the other, with just one added l, Hellas—a tribute to Greek hedonism.

The sonnet starts in medias res with "To drift with every passion till my soul / Is a stringed lute on which all winds can play." But this is not Shelley's image of the poet as Aeolian harp for inspiration to play on; these winds are the winds of passion, all passions. Yet regret immediately sets in with an attempt at retraction: "Is it for this that I have given away / Mine ancient wisdom, and austere control?" Wilde's harp becomes a palimpsest: "Methinks my life is a twice-written scroll / Scrawled over on some boyish holiday / With idle songs for pipe and virelay." We note that the poet's youth is scrawled over in a boyish prank, not entirely innocent, what with virelay, a French poem form, hence probably decadent, and the pipes presumably pertaining to the god Pan.

"Surely there was a time I might have trod / The sunlit heights. . . ." Originally Wilde had written "august heights," i.e., nearer Heaven. So he would "from life's dissonance / Have struck one chord to reach the ears of God." Lost, then, was some great religious achievement. As Beckson and Fong see it, the yearned-for life of sensations derives from a letter of Keats's; the drift with every passion, from Pater's *Renaissance*, "in which Pater urges readers 'to be for ever curiously testing new opinions and courting new impressions!" Richard Ellmann, in his magisterial *Oscar Wilde*, adduces Pater's "drift of momentary acts of sight and passion and thought."

But ambivalence is ripe here, and forthwith we are back to the

Bible, but to a passage Pater also quoted in his essay on the homo-sexual scholar Winckelmann: Jonathan's appeal to Saul, "I did but taste a little honey with the end of the rod that was in my hand, and lo! I must die." It doesn't take a Freudian to explicate that rod in hand that yields honey, but Wilde makes it even more explicit: "Is that time dead? lo! with a little rod / I did but touch the honey of romance," which is more sexual and, as in the case of Saul and Jonathan, homosexual.

And the consequences? "Losing a soul's inheritance," i.e., damnation. The duality is clear, even if garbed in that archaizing, putatively poetic diction Wilde could not as yet shake off: "mine an-cient," "methinks," "do but mar," "did but touch," and "lo!"

The poems go from long-winded narrative or descriptive pieces, seemingly determined to prove Poe right about there being no such things as long poems, to short lyrics, sometimes religious or politi-cal. And sometimes both: "Sonnet on the Massacre of the Christians in Bulgaria" ends, "Come down, O Son of Man! and show thy might, / Lest Mahomet be crowned instead of thee." It is a bit sur-prising to find a poem to Louis Napolen ending with the triumphal news "that the great wave of Democracy / Breaks on the shores where Kings lay crouched at ease." Leaving aside the infelicitous image of royalty lolling in beach chairs, do we not wonder at Wilde's being on the side of those opposed to superiors couched, if not crouched, at ease? Wilde states his position in another poem where, as often elsewhere, he bemoans England's materialism and concludes, "in dreams of Art / And loftiest culture I would stand apart, / Neither for God, nor for his enemies."

Let us now turn to "Theocritus: A Villanelle." This Renaissance Italian and Provençal pastoral form derives its name from *villano* or *vilain*, meaning peasant, and was originally a type of bucolic poem, becoming more sophisticated with the passage of time. Wilde ap-propriately returns it to its pastoral origins and beyond, to Theocri-tus, the third-century B.C. poet of the *Idylls* and father of pastoral poetry.

> O singer of Persephone!
>   In the dim meadows desolate
> Dost thou remember Sicily?

Still through the ivy flits the bee
   Where Amaryllis lies in state;
O singer of Persephone!

Simaetha calls on Hecate
   And hears the wild dogs at the gate:
Dost thou remember Sicily?

Still by the light and laughing sea
   Poor Polypheme bemoans his fate;
O Singer of Persephone!

And still in boyish rivalry
   Young Daphnis challenges his mate;
Dost thou remember Sicily?

Slim Lacon keeps a goat for thee,
   For thee the jocund shepherds wait;
O Singer of Persephone!
Dost thou remember Sicily?

The curious thing here is the interrogation of Theocritus about characters and situations from his own poems. Surely it is the questioner, Wilde, who laments the lost pastoral paradise, Sicily or Arcadia. But, paradoxically, this idyll in which human and superhuman beings blithely mix is still there waiting: slim Lacon still awaits him who dare seize, not a bull perhaps, but a goat by its horns.

Wilde, who was not the most easeful of rhymers, cheats a bit: to rhyme polysyllables ending in an unaccented *-ly* and *-ne*, as in *Sicily* and *Persephone*, makes for facile, uneuphonious rhyme. The distinction of the prosody here lies in the alliterations and in the bright assonance of "Still through the ivy flits the bee."

Consider now a much finer poem and anthology piece, "Requiescat." It is a sad comment on Wilde's poetic reputation that there exists a disc with little-known art songs of Samuel Barber that includes a setting of this poem. In parentheses, where the name of the poet is placed, we read "Barber?" This is doubly wrong: Barber never wrote poems, and "Requiescat" is, or should be, well enough known for easy identification.

Tread lightly, she is near,
    Under the snow,
Speak gently, she can hear
    The daisies grow.

All her bright golden hair
    Tarnished with rust,
She that was young and fair
    Fallen to dust.

Lily-like, white as snow,
    She hardly knew
She was a woman, so
    Sweetly she grew.

Coffin-board, heavy stone,
    Lie on her breast,
I vex my heart alone,
    She is at rest.

Peace, Peace, she cannot hear
    Lyre or sonnet,
All my life's buried here,
    Heap earth upon it.

Anyone reading this would assume it to be an elegy for a dead lover, but it is for Wilde's sister, Isola, who died when she was nine and Oscar twelve; the poem was written twelve years later. There is something odd about that "young and fair" and "She hardly knew / She was a woman," implying someone rather older than nine, unless she was one of those Peruvian Indians, among whom girls have been said to give birth at an even younger age. Melissa Knox, in her *Oscar Wilde: A Long and Lovely Suicide*, may be right in alleging "a sexual current flowing between" the siblings. But when Knox, based on Wilde's adopting the meter of Thomas Hood's "The Bridge of Sighs," about a beautiful drowned prostitute, argues that Oscar thought of Isola as an erotic prostitute, I part company.

There is a quaint inconsistency here, perhaps even a paradox. The dead girl can hear the daisies grow, so graveside visitors should

speak in hushed tones. Yet she cannot even hear music or singing—
"lyre or sonnet"—coming from aboveground. Perhaps she has be-
come part of the soil and can hear earth sounds, the daisies growing,
but not human voices. In that case, why that "Speak gently" of
stanza one?

The poem comprises only two images. First, "golden hair tar-
nished with rust," striking enough because gold, unlike silver, does
not tarnish. Second, the hyperbole, "All my life's buried here," made
more concrete and palpable by "Heap earth upon it." Again, though,
what truly distinguishes the poem is its exquisite music: the alterna-
tion of trimeter and dimeter lines with alternating abab rhymes (to
my ear, the most satisfying of rhyme schemes), the self-contained
quatrains, each with a strongly clinching last line. The rhymes are
apt, what with the a-rhymes usually high-pitched, as in *near-hear*;
the b-rhymes low, as in *snow-grow*; or else it is the reverse, but always
well contrasted. There is even a canny echo effect from the *near-hear*
rhyme to the *hair-fair* one, and in the *snow-grow* picked up later by
snow-so, and by the concluding stanza's *hear-here* recalling the open-
ing one's *near-here*.

English prosody, however, does not condone identities, as in
hear-here, even if the homonyms have very different meanings. Yet
attention from this lapse is skillfully deflected by that same last
stanza's b-rhymes, *sonnet-upon it*, the first feminine rhyme in an oth-
erwise masculine-rhymed poem. That richer disyllabic rhyme, with
its ampler sonority, adds headier music and perhaps also greater fi-
nality to the conclusion. Ellmann notes that Oscar paid regular vis-
its to Isola's grave and that "the melancholy which he always
afterwards insisted underlay his jaunty behavior may have been
awakened by this early death."

As important as the rhyming is the artful rhythm. It would be
easy for a poem with such short lines to turn into singsong, which
Wilde avoids through slight but shrewd irregularity. Making the
first foot of an iambic line trochaic is, of course, a time-tested de-
vice, which he, however, varies further by introductory spondees:
Tread light-, *Speak gent-*, *She that*, *I vex*, *Peace-Peace* (the spondaic
beat underlined by the emphatic capital P on the second *Peace*), and
Heap earth, the weightiest and most apposite spondee of all.

Finally, the indisputable appearance of paradox: the dead girl is alive enough to hear the daisies grow, whereas the living poet's heart is buried in her grave; but this is still a very mild paradox compared to what was to come.

In several short, pictorial poems, Wilde is emulating the paintings of his friendly enemy, or inimical friend, James McNeill Whistler, with perhaps the added influence of a poem such as Théophile Gautier's "Symphonie en blanc majeur." Here is "Impression du Matin":

> The Thames nocturne of blue and gold
> 　　Changed to a Harmony in grey:
> 　　A barge with ochre-colored hay
> Dropt from the wharf: and chill and cold
>
> The yellow fog came creeping down
> 　　The bridges, till the houses' walls
> 　　Seemed changed to shadows and St. Paul's
> Loomed like a bubble o'er the town.
>
> Then suddenly arose the clang
> 　　Of waking life; the streets were stirred
> 　　With country wagons; and a bird
> Flew to the glistening roofs and sang.
>
> But one pale woman all alone,
> 　　The daylight kissing her wan hair,
> 　　Loitered beneath the gas lamps' flare,
> With lips of flame and heart of stone.

Beckson and Fong suggest that the poem recalls Monet's innovative painting "Impression: Sunrise"; more to the point is Norbert Kohl's derivation of it from Whistler's "Nocturne in Blue and Gold: Old Battersea Bridge," as the first line clearly proclaims. But Beckson and Fong rightly stress the use of "such musical terms as *nocturne* and *harmony* from Whistler's titles to focus on the artifice of art and its color harmonies rather than on 'message.'" Also involved, I would add, is synesthesia, a favorite device of Impressionists and Symbolists.

So far the critics approve, but then "a prostitute appears, loiter-
ing beneath a street lamp. The attitude expressed in the final line is
precisely what a conventional Victorian reader would expect—in-
deed, demand—a fallen woman devoid of the capacity for love." But
wait a minute: Wilde was perfectly capable of sticking to pure
painterly impressions, as in "Symphony in Yellow"; the streetwalker
may be more than a sop to the goody-goody Victorians. The poem
begins with cool blue and warm gold; it ends with "lips of flame," a
hot color, and "heart of stone," i.e., grey, and, like that of the "pale
woman," a cold color. The palette has come full circle.

But that is not all. This is a cityscape in which objects—a barge
with hay, bridges, walls—come to a ghostly halflife: the shadows in
yellow fog, the bubble of St. Paul's dome. These waken to full life at
the clutter of wagons and song of the bird. But the living woman,
paradoxically, fades with the dying lamps, turns to stone like her
heart. Against all this capitalized Harmony of line two, the dehu-
manized woman is the one discordant note, her falsely glowing lips
a wound at the core of things.

From here it is but one step to one of Wilde's finest poems, "The
Harlot's House," which Donald Davidson has aptly summarized in
the introduction to his anthology *British Poetry of the Eighteen-
Nineties.* He calls it "for all its artificiality . . . as perfect a statement
as can be found of that Vision of Evil, seen by Wilde as in a Beards-
ley picture, in which love by deliberate choice passes into the house
of lust which is also the house of death." True, although that "delib-
erate choice" may be more like hypnotized sleepwalking.

> We caught the tread of dancing feet,
> We loitered down the moonlit street,
> And stopped beneath the harlot's house.
>
> Inside, above the din and fray,
> We heard the loud musicians play
> The "Treues Liebes Herz" of Strauss.
>
> Like strange mechanical grotesques,
> Making fantastic arabesques,
> The shadows raced across the blind.

We watched the ghostly dancers spin
To sound of horn and violin,
Like black leaves wheeling in the wind.

Like wire-pulled automatons,
Slim silhouetted skeletons
Went sidling through the slow quadrille.

They took each other by the hand,
And danced a stately saraband;
Their laughter echoed thin and shrill.

Sometimes a clockwork puppet pressed
A phantom lover to her breast,
Sometimes they seemed to try to sing.

Sometimes a horrible marionette
Came out, and smoked its cigarette
Upon the steps like a live thing.

Then, turning to my love, I said,
"The dead are dancing with the dead,
The dust is whirling with the dust."

But she—she heard the violin,
And left my side and entered in:
Love passed into the house of lust.

Then suddenly the tune went false,
The dancers wearied of the waltz,
The shadows ceased to wheel and whirl.

And down the long and silent street,
The dawn, with silver-sandalled feet,
Crept like a frightened girl.

Here our Freudian scholar, Melissa Knox, really hits her stride. The poem, she avers, "echoes the hidden meaning of 'Requiescat,' by describing prostitutes as 'strange mechanical grotesques,' 'skeletons,' and 'phantoms.' I think that the seductive little sister comes alive in these phrases." Skeletons seem an odd way of coming alive, but, I guess, the fun-loving dead have a limited number of options. After reminding us, as others have before her, that Wilde may have got the title "Requiescat" from Matthew Arnold's poem of the same name, which includes the lines "In quiet she reposes; / Ah, would that I did, too," Knox again goes off the deep end: "through imitating the meter of Hood's poem ["The Bridge of Sighs"], borrowing Arnold's title, and producing a number of erotically charged poems concerning young girls and, often, their deaths . . . Wilde expresses obsessive erotic fantasies about his sister." So much for scholarship.

"The Harlot's House" is in tercets, but not exactly, as one might expect from an admirer of Dante, in terza rima. The rhyme scheme is aab, ccb, dde, ffe, and so on through a dozen iambic tetrameter stanzas. It begins with feet, "the tread of dancing feet" as heard by the poet and his beloved, and it will end with other feet. The lovers arrive at the brothel from which issue the sounds of dancing to Strauss's "Treues Liebes Herz," though there seems to exist no such Straussian waltz, and the title does not translate, as Beckson and Fong would have it, as "Heart of True Love" but as "Dear True Heart." Either way, though, this is ironic in a setting where there is no love or faithfulness.

The style, as Beckson and Fong note, is derived from Baudelaire and Gautier, but there are also strong suggestions of Dante Gabriel Rossetti and Thomas Lovell Beddoes. The dancing skeletons are medieval Dance of Death–derived. The horn and violin may be erotic and seductive, but everything else is funereal, starting with the black leaves and progressing through automatons and skeletons to horrible marionettes. The rhyme *automatons-skeletons* is uneuphonious and jarring, but in this context, why not?

The dance changes from a fast waltz to a "slow quadrille"—and note the chilling way *sidling* suggests creepy, crablike movement. Then it slows down even more to a "stately saraband"; if this were a movie, slow motion would have set in. The "thin and shrill" laughter is mirthless; the failed attempt at singing further emphasizes the stifling joylessness.

Particularly powerful is the "horrible marionette" smoking its cigarette "like a live thing," that *its* especially ghostly. Whereupon the inconceivable happens: the living beloved enters "the house of lust," where "the dead are dancing with the dead." At first it would seem that it is only for the bereft lover that "the tune went false." But no, the dancers themselves have stopped. Why? And what does the last tercet mean? Beckson and Fong speak of "a questionable simile" and conclude, "The obvious morality of the poem again reveals Wilde's difficulty in adhering to *l'art pour l'art.*"

I am not sure this carping is deserved. The shadows stop dancing because night and death are superseded by dawn. But this personified dawn is frightened by her awareness of the realm of night and death into which she, too, will eventually sink. Traditionally she is, as Homer described her, rosy-fingered; here, however, she is distinguished by her silver-sandaled feet, a vision of purity that recoils at the horrible sight before her, but nevertheless slowly, hesitantly faces up to it.

There is, however, more to this poem. It has been observed that Wilde, even in fiction, always writes about himself; that, for instance, all the main characters in *The Picture of Dorian Gray* are really Oscar Wilde. So, too, in "The Harlot's House," one gets the feeling that the beloved who enters the fateful brothel is one part of Wilde, that the lover watching in dismay is another part of him, and that the dawn, aghast at this split world and hesitant about confronting it, is yet a further aspect of himself.

Norbert Kohl observes, "The link between eroticism and death that is made by the dance of death taking place in the harlot's house—a link that typifies the literature of *décadence*—was already to be found in 'Charmides.' It is a theme that Wilde was to vary once more in *Salome*, and to take up again in *The Ballad of Reading Gaol.*" Well, "Charmides" is one of the more interesting of Wilde's early long poems which, however, I do not propose to discuss. Despite incidental felicities, they do not come off as wholes, and are primarily of autobiographical interest, expressing more or less covertly Wilde's sexual fantasies. They also show off his recondite knowledge of mythology, zoology, and botany, a veritable Sears, Roebuck catalogue of fauna and flora. Kohl remarks pertinently, "One cannot escape the impression that the poet regarded his lists of flowers as an essential prerequisite for 'intensive' nature poetry. The fact that he occasionally makes mistakes in botany strengthens the suspicion that his knowledge came from sources other than observation of nature." It is a matter, Kohl goes on, of "conforming to the conventional clichés of nature poetry, as well as striving to create a decorative effect."

Furthermore, these long poems show how eclectic and derivative much of this poetry is. So it was that the young and erudite Oliver Elton (later a distinguished Oxford don) to whom Wilde had expectantly sent his poems, caustically remarked that they were "for the most part not by their putative father, but by a number of better-known and more deservedly reputed authors. They are in fact by William Shakespeare, by Philip Sidney, by John Donne, by Lord Byron, by William Morris, by Algernon Swinburne, and by sixty more." More recently, Harold Bloom has—unjustly, I think—lumped *The Ballad of Reading Gaol* with them, calling it "an embarrassment to read, directly one recognizes that every luster it exhibits is reflected from *The Rime of the Ancient Mariner*; and Wilde's lyrics anthologize the whole of English High Romanticism."

There is some truth to this, but not the whole truth. Before Reading gaol, Wilde may have been the captive of his reading, but with his best poems, and notably the *Ballad*, he managed to escape. Of the earlier stuff, Kohl could write with some justification that it "often seems that the poet has no direct contact with reality—as if it has never made its mark on him through experience." But two years at hard labor put an end to such laborious elucubrations. When the *Ballad* was published in 1898, Arthur Symons observed in his notice in the *Saturday Review* that the poem is not innovative in form and diction, which is still "poetic," and that it evidences a struggle "between personal and dramatic feeling, between genuine human emotion and a style formed on other lines." But, as Symons concluded, "We see a great spectacular intellect, to which, at last, pity and terror have come in their own person, and no longer as puppets in a play."

What might be added is that here Wilde fully realized the applicability of his trademark paradox to poetry. Symons sensed this but called the poem—rather too cautiously, I think—"half, but no more than half, paradox." It is, in my view, paradox of one kind or another from first stanza to last, the only ones I can deal with here.

The poem concerns one Charles Thomas Wooldridge, a trooper in the Royal Horse Guards, who, out of jealousy, slit the throat of his young wife, Laura Ellen. He spent a relatively short time in Reading prison, where he was observed by Wilde, and was there hanged to Wilde's lasting horror. He died bravely. Wilde changed a few facts: Charles killed Laura in the road near her house, and not in bed; and he was not drunk on wine or anything else. Here is the opening sestet:

> He did not wear his scarlet coat,
>   For blood and wine are red,
> And blood and wine were on his hands
>   When they found him with the dead,
> The poor dead woman whom he loved,
>   And murdered in her bed.

Note the initial paradox: Wooldridge did not wear his scarlet uniform when he killed; it sufficed that there was red in his wine and in the blood on his hands when he was apprehended. This has deeper meaning. It implies that in uniform it would have been correct and commendable for him to kill some innocent enemy soldier. But as a civilian, he had no right to kill his putatively cheating wife. The further implication is that passionate, foiled love is not considered even a mitigating factor in killing, whereas, paradoxically, cold-blooded military killing is sanctioned, indeed demanded. The last stanza runs:

> And all men kill the thing they love,
>   By all let this be heard,
> Some do it with a bitter look,
>   Some with a flattering word,
> The coward does it with a kiss,
>   The brave man with a sword!

People kill love in one way or another. By the bitter look of satiation, boredom, and revulsion; by calculating, feelingless flattery; or by the Judas kiss, the supreme, craven betrayal. The brave man—who, like Wooldridge, was fully prepared to pay the price—does it with a sword. Actually, the trooper did it with a razor borrowed for the purpose from a friend. But what might do in Georg Büchner's naturalistic drama *Woyzeck* would not do in a poem that, while in part shatteringly realistic, still observes certain nineteenth-century poetic proprieties. It is thus more proper to kill your wife in her presumedly adulterous bed with a heroic weapon than to slit her throat with a borrowed razor in the roadway. When the lover who helped cause Wilde's downfall, Lord Alfred Douglas, later on asked Oscar what he meant by that last line, Wilde answered, "*You* ought to know."

The closing stanza is a consummate paradox. For one thing, we all kill the one we love—even Laura, the victim, killed her murderer with lying kisses; for another, to kill swiftly with a sword, however heinous, is less culpable than slowly starving someone with lack of love and perhaps even humiliating him with adulterous deception.

We come now to the *Poems in Prose*, which first appeared in the July 1894 issue of the *Fortnightly Review*. Here the very genre, poem in prose—or, as it is more often called, prose poem—is a paradox in itself. If it is a poem, why in prose? If it is prose, why call it poem? Well, the prose poem, with its long, illustrious, and international history (about which, incidentally, I wrote my doctoral dissertation), has, like the heart, its reasons. It is an endeavor to combine the freedom from rhyme, meter, and having to indent every line (as is granted prose) with an emphasis on imagery and intensity, cadence and concentration (as in lyric poetry). It is too short to call itself "story," even when its aims include storytelling (which it usually avoids), and so it calls itself prose poem or poem in prose.

Some of the greatest poets the world over have written prose poems, but Wilde's, truth to tell, are not the greatest. He was probably introduced to the genre by his friend Pierre Louÿs, author of the novel *Aphrodite* (a favorite of masturbating schoolboys) and the prose-poem sequence *Les Chansons de Bilitis* (a favorite of lesbians, some of whom call themselves Daughters of Bilitis). Many of Louÿs's prose poems do indeed have anecdotal form, though the anecdote, being essentially prosy, is least congenial to prose poetry. Still, Rilke managed it with his sequence *Die Weise von Liebe und Tod des Cornets Christoph Rilke*, which may be the most famous prose poetry ever written.

Baudelaire, too, wrote some anecdotal prose poems, but the best prose poetry, notably Rimbaud's *Illuminations* and Mallarmé's *Divagations*, is not anecdotal. Wilde's prose poems, however, for the most part are. They originated in witticisms, usually clever paradoxes he uttered in conversation. Then, with the raconteur's art, a *boutade* would be stretched out into a miniature tale. The painter Charles Ricketts recalls that "sometimes a prose poem would be retold without change." At other times Wilde would elaborate and polish. One *bon mot* in particular would have made a jolly prose poem. At a party given by the poet Heredia, Wilde asked André Gide, "Do you know why Jesus hated his mother?" Gide didn't know. "Because she was a virgin."

But this one, of course, would then have been unpublishable. So, too, another one reported by Ricketts, about a goddess worshiped by Sicilian fishermen as the Lady of Sorrows. On midsummer eve she would strip naked and revel with the fauns, nymphs, and centaurs, but always depart early. When her son Eros "besought her not to leave him," she explained that she had to return whence she came, "for know I have another son who suffered greatly."

That son, of course, was Jesus, with whom Wilde liked to identify himself. That may be one reason that the language of his poems in prose is biblical; another is that the prose of the King James Bible is justly admired for approaching poetry. Some of Wilde's prose poems, however, are better in the shorter versions in which he first talked them. Such is the case of "The Master," as reported by Adela Schuster.

On the night when Jesus died, Joseph of Arimathea went down from Mount Calvary and came upon a young man weeping bitterly. And Joseph spoke to him: "I know how great thy grief must be, for surely He was a just Man." And the young man made answer: "I am not weeping for Him but for myself. For I too have wrought miracles; I have turned water into wine, healed the sick, given sight to the blind, fed the multitude, cast out devils, caused the barren fig tree to wither, and raised the dead. All that this Man did, I have done. And yet they have not crucified me."

In the printed version of "The Master," Wilde poeticizes fiercely. Take this added *verset*: "And kneeling on the flint stones of the Valley of Desolation he saw a young man who was naked and weeping. His hair was the color of honey, and his body was as a white flower; but he had wounded his body with thorns, and on his hair he had set ashes as a crown." Such additions do little but dilute the impact, though they do add a decorative and homoerotic flavor. Was Wilde that young man weeping for not having been accorded the supreme tribute, crucifixion? Publicity is what he ardently sought; for it, even crucifixion was not too high a price. And did he not seek something of that sort when, ignoring his friends' urgings to flee to France, he seemed to want to be arrested, courting a horrible sentence that was to destroy his life almost as surely as crucifixion? Paradoxically, he may have been right; infamy brought him his greatest fame: the posthumous one of a martyr.

Significantly, the other of Wilde's two best prose poems, "The Disciple," forms a diptych with "The Master." In this instance I adduce not the shorter version, as given by Hesketh Pearson in his *Oscar Wilde: His Life and Wit*, but the published one.

When Narcissus died, the pool of his pleasure changed from a cup of sweet waters into a cup of salt tears, and the Oreads came weeping through the woodland that they might sing to the pool and give it comfort.

And when they saw that the pool had changed from a cup of sweet waters into a cup of salt tears, they loosened the green tresses of their hair, and cried to the pool, and said, "We do not wonder that you should mourn in this manner for Narcissus, so beautiful was he."

"But was Narcissus beautiful?" said the pool.

"Who should know better than you?" answered the Oreads. "Us did he ever pass by, but you he sought for, and would lie on your banks and look down at you, and in the mirror of your waters he would mirror his own beauty."

And the pool answered: "But I love Narcissus because, as he lay on my banks and looked down at me, in the mirror of his eyes I saw my own beauty mirrored."

A pretty little paradoxical parable, prettily told. Both it and "The Master" proclaim self-love as the only real love: the weeping youth in that poem weeps not for Christ but for himself; the pool in this one weeps not for Narcissus but for—which is it: herself or himself? In his recent book on the prose poem, *Invisible Fences*, Steven Monte argues for the masculinity of the pool and thus a homoerotic element: "The pool is male, to judge by what it believes to be its reflection." This is not convincing: just because Narcissus's eyes are male, what they reflect need not be male as well. Yet the important thing is not the gender of the pool; the crux of the matter is that any lover loves himself or herself in the eyes of the beloved, regardless of what sex. In a sense, "The Disciple" is the poetic version of Wilde's famous prose epigram about the perfect marriage being based on a mutual misunderstanding.

Wilde's third-best prose poem, "The Artist," is a portrait of the artist as a dedicated hedonist. In all his poems, in verse or prose, Wilde gives himself away, which adds to their interest. If, however, the intrinsic merit of this handful of prose poems is modest, their influence on Anglo-American poetry was not inconsiderable. It is felt most clearly perhaps in the too-little-known prose poems of Stephen Crane.

Yet along with the boost Wilde gave to the genre came also a kick in its groin. When Sir Edward Clarke, Wilde's lawyer, tried to defend Oscar's most notorious love letter to "Bosie" Douglas, the one containing "those rose-leaf lips of yours should have been made no less for the music of song as for the madness of kisses. Your slim gilt soul walks between passion and poetry" etc., etc., he called it, as he said Wilde had called it, "a prose sonnet." And indeed, in his testimony, Wilde repeatedly referred to that letter as a prose poem. As I wrote in my doctoral thesis, "If anything beyond the name of Oscar Wilde was besmirched . . . it was, I suspect, the name of the prose poem." And so in her book, *A Tradition of Subversion*, Margueritte Murphy contends, "the stigma of effeminacy, of a lack of strength and virility, remained with the form."

Oscar Wilde's poetry, like his life, was a mixed bag; but the good and the bad in it are interconnected, part of Wilde's glittering yet vulnerable, ostentatiously amoral yet also childlike and sentimental persona. The formerly so reprehended but now so vindicated figure that gazes at us from T-shirts and shopping bags, that can even in so flatfooted a docudrama as Moïses Kaufman's *Gross Indecency* delight unsophisticated theatergoers, is today as famous as any nineteenth-century writer, English or other. It would be a shame if Wilde's poems and prose poems, a significant if secondary aspect of his output, were overlooked to his and our diminishment.

The poems, after all, were an important training ground for the incomparable comedies, just as an early grounding in poetry has benefited numerous other prose writers. Consider only this exchange between Cecily and her governess, Miss Prism, in Act Two of *The Importance of Being Earnest*. Miss Prism has just confessed that in her youth she wrote a three-volume novel. Exclaims Cecily: "I hope it didn't end happily? I don't like novels that end happily. They depress me so much." To which Miss Prism replies: "The good ended happily, and the bad unhappily. That is what fiction means." Let me write this out as verse:

> Thĕ goód éndĕd háppĭlў,
> Ańd thĕ bád únhăppĭlў.
> Thát ĭs whăt fíctiŏn meáns.

What you have here is three lines of iambic trimeter, with subtle variations. In line one, the second foot is inverted into a trochee, and the third into a dactyl. The second line begins with an anapest, a relative of the iamb, and proceeds to a trochee and iamb. The third, by way of a customary inversion, begins with a trochee, followed by two perfect iambs. Consciously or not, this speech cunningly scans.

Equally important is that Wilde made good use of the paradox in his poetry. In "Charmides," for example, life is called "A fiery pulse of sin, a splendid shame." A mere oxymoron. But what about this from *The Ballad of Reading Gaol*, where fellow prisoners are watching the man condemned to death: "As molten lead were the tears we shed / For the blood we had not spilt"? You expect "had spilt" but, paradoxically, get "not spilt." Why? Because weeping out of compassion is even sadder, truer than weeping out of self-pity. These fellow inmates know that "had each got his due. / They should have died instead: / He had but killed a thing that lived, / Whilst they had killed the dead."

What does that paradox mean? Wilde goes on to explain:

For he who kills a second time
    Wakes a dead soul to pain,
And draws it from its spotted shroud,
    And makes it bleed again,
And makes it bleed great gouts of blood,
    And makes it bleed in vain!

This is the most mysteriously paradoxical stanza in the whole poem. It says that killing a living person once, with a sword, is less evil than what the other prisoners—other people—have done and keep doing: killing the same person over and over again with flattery or treachery, dissimulation and humiliation. Thus are their victims, already hurt and humbled and deadened, made to suffer repeatedly and continually, which, in their weakened condition, is even uglier torture, bloodier murder.

By the time he wrote this piece of gallows humor, Wilde had discovered how funny—balefully or bracingly funny—the paradox could be, and thus the great achievement of his comedies. Before that, the paradox could startle, shock, and by provoking us into thinking, instruct. Wilde taught it how to laugh.

2001

"When the Ecstatic
Body Grips"

🌿 IT WOULD BE PRESUMPTUOUS, indeed foolish, to try to pick the greatest love poem in the English language. But I will stick my neck out and name my candidate for the finest overlooked love poem in modern English, one deserving a place in every anthology and every poetry lover's consciousness. It is a poem to be savored, reflected upon, indeed learned from, even though didacticism is the farthest thing from its mind. I discovered "When the Ecstatic Body Grips" by Eric Robertson Dodds in *The Viking Book of Poetry of the English-Speaking World*, compiled by the poet Richard Aldington, and published in 1941. I have not come across the lyric in any other anthology.

The poem affected me more than any other in that worthy collection, which, alas, gave its author's name as Dobbs rather than Dodds: it was not till much later that I gathered that "Dobbs" was in fact E. R. Dodds, the distinguished Regius Professor of Greek at Oxford, best known for his *The Greeks and the Irrational*, a classic in its own right. In his youth, he had published a slim volume of poetry containing this remarkable poem. I got the volume out of Harvard's Widener Library in the hope of more such gems, but found nothing in it of comparable stature. Still, not a few poets have made it on one immortal lyric, the most famous being, I suppose, Félix Arvers with his celebrated sonnet.

There was in one of my Harvard Humanities sections a Radcliffe undergraduate from Rumania, as it was then known, whose name, like those of my other students, I have long since forgotten. But she was considered one of the sexiest Cliffies of her era, a student in one of Albert Guerard's creative writing classes, and held to be very talented by her teacher. To me, one day, she handed in an assignment consisting of an original poem, in which I promptly recognized "When the Ecstatic Body Grips." Only the canny creature had substituted a synonym for one word in every one of the poem's twenty-eight lines—seven quatrains in iambic tetrameter rhymed abab—assuming to be thus cleared from possible charges of plagiarism.

When I confronted her with her misdeed, she denied any knowledge of Dodds's poem, and brazenly ascribed the similarity to coincidence. I forget how I handled the case (mildly, I imagine, given the girl's allure), but one thing sticks in my memory. Not ungifted though she was, her every change was for the worse. This proved to me the poem's supremacy: twenty-eight times out of twenty-eight, Dodds had unerringly chosen the *mot juste*.

Let us go through the poem stanza by stanza. Readers would do themselves a service by not skipping ahead to read the entire poem in advance. Later, they should read it over as a whole; for now, it is better to follow and consider the twists and turns as each stanza zigzags ahead.

> When the ecstatic body grips
> Its heaven, with little sobbing cries,
> And lips are crushed on hot blind lips,
> I read strange pity in your eyes.

The poet-narrator is recollecting—whether in tranquillity or not remains moot—the carnal act with his beloved. The approach of consummation is graphically evoked by word after precisely descriptive word. "Grips its heaven" is particularly apt in its conjoining of the transcendent *heaven* with the animalistic *grips*. Even the punctuation—or its absence—in "hot blind lips" conveys a frenzy unchecked by commas. But then, surprisingly, the "strange pity" in the woman's eyes. All is not so simple as might be expected in the sexual act.

For that in you which is not mine,
And that in you which I love best,
And that, which my day-thoughts divine
Masterless still, still unpossessed,

That ambiguous *For* creates suspense: is the pity *for* something
or *because* of something? It emerges that the best-loved thing about
the mistress is that unattained, perhaps unattainable, innermost self.
Human nature, being what it is, craves most what it doesn't, and
possibly cannot, have. That something is the cynosure of the lover's
fantasies, nicely referred to as *day-thoughts*, for by nightfall the
woman is there in the flesh. *Divine*, too, is apt: though meaning *guess
at*, it has overtones of divinity—the godhead of the new, the un-
known, the yet-to-be-conquered, like the summit of an even less ac-
cessible Mount Everest. "Masterless still, still unpossessed" further
clarifies the psychological situation: the man is after complete pos-
session, total mastery over his mistress. Note how the chiasmus jux-
taposing "still, still" emphasizes the yearning and frustration.

Sits in the blue eyes' frightened stare,
A naked lonely-dwelling thing,
A frail thing from its body-lair
Drawn at my body's summoning;

The very first word strikes the right note. The lovers in bed are
horizontal, but this something *sits*: it is semi-upright, at least partly
evading the posture of fusion. The eyes almost have to be blue, the
color of virginal purity. This is a naked, hence vulnerable thing; it is
lonely-dwelling, a timorous animal in its den, as confirmed by *fright-
ened* and *body-lair*. It hides in the body, but is not a part of it, as the
animal is not part of the sheltering lair. Could it be the soul? It is
drawn by the man's sexual *summoning*, with the ambiguous *drawn*
equally suggestive of compulsion as of fascinated eagerness.

Whispering low, "O unknown man,
Whose hunger on my hunger wrought,
Body shall give what body can,
Shall give you all—save what you sought."

Here the tragedy of the situation unveils itself. The shy thing "whispers low" and reveals that the man is as *unknown* to the woman as she is to him. What unites them is mutual *hunger*: the repetition of the word stressing that the sexual act is compulsive, instinctual, urgent, and primitive—that it bypasses intellect and freedom of the will. The reiterated *shall* (rather than *will*) makes the coercion more palpable; the repeated *body* underlines the physical, animalistic, primordial at work. And then the devastating "save what you sought," with that sibilant alliteration hissing out the woman's negation of total surrender. Again, perhaps, the soul, clinging to its independence.

> Whispering, "O secret one, forgive,
> Forgive and be content though still
> Beyond the blood's surrender live
> The darkness of the separate will.

Again, the man, too, remains *secret*, but is supplicated (two *forgives*, prominently placed at the end and start of consecutive verses) to forbear and moderate his demands. And, once more, that *still*, which here reverberates with its other meaning of silence, impenetrable otherness. Now it is not just body, but also *blood* that joins in the copulation—everything, in short, save "the darkness of the separate will," where *darkness*, tersely and powerfully, conveys the *terra incognita* into which there is no access. The *will*, the essence, remains *separate*, whether tragically or triumphantly remains unresolved, although *darkness* suggests bleakness.

> "Enough if in the veins we know
> Body's delirium, body's peace—
> Ask not that ghost to ghost shall go,
> Essence in essence merge and cease."

Body, blood, veins: the locus of orgasmic frenzy and subsequent repose. Left out is *ghost*—this time clearly revealed as the spirit or soul (as in "ghostly father," for a priest ministering to the soul), or *essence*, again with spiritual and philosophical implications. This is the quiddity that remains above the fray, as it were, seeking and maintaining its separateness (no *merge*) and its life (no *cease*, as in some kind of death). This sounds proud and noble: even if sad on one level, surely grand and heroic.

> But swiftly, as in sudden sleep,
> That You in you is veiled or dead;
> And the world's shrunken to a heap
> Of hot flesh straining on a bed.

Here, at last, the unambiguous dénouement in the orgasm—the, so to speak, anti-climactic climax. That capitalized *You* is plainly the higher self, the soul, subjugated or slain. And the "world's"—note the urgency and effectiveness of that colloquial *'s* rather than the formal *is*—"shrunken to a heap." How pitiful that diminishment; how pathetic, a mere *heap*! And what a heap: *hot*, which returns us to the "hot blind lips," and *flesh*, which patently eliminates the soul. And that heaving heap is "straining on a bed," with *straining* implying the desperateness of it all (like that initial *grips*), and *bed* locating it in the mundane, the real and mortal—the place where not only the upper-case self (*You*), but also the rest (*you*) dies. What now of the soul? Gone? For good?

If we now glance back at the whole poem, what do we get? An extraordinarily sensitive, penetrating, and evocative depiction and analysis of the sexual act in both its physical and psychic aspects, and the raising of the deepest, insoluble problems of identity, sharing, fusion, confrontation of the One with the Other—in short, the lineaments and limits of love. Great art almost never hands out answers as do lesser works: it merely raises, as precisely and profoundly as possible, the great questions, and leaves the rest to us.

Here the question of human sexuality—and, ultimately, identity—is viewed in lyrical form, but whether tragically or with thickly black humor is up to us to decide; in any case, the poem is not a piece of snide sarcasm or a facile diatribe. The Regius Professor of Greek at Oxford was a good man, as you could learn most recently from a charming anecdote in Roger Rosenblatt's memoir *Coming Apart*, and his younger self was clearly no less humane. What informs the poem is pity for the human condition, that "strange pity" the poet *reads* in his beloved's eyes in stanza 1. That pity radiates outward, and, in stanza 7, encompasses the lovers' whole world shrunken to a pitiful and pitiable heap.

Even the choice of meter attests to Dodds's astuteness. Had he used pentameter, there would be something statelier, more formal about the poem: iambic pentameter, after all, is the stuff of English heroic and dramatic verse, although, to be sure, of love sonnets as well. Still, by choosing tetrameter, a more tripping measure, Dodds achieves a fragility as well as narrative speed suited to the urgency and breathlessness with which the poem hurtles to its shocking conclusion. For shocking it is: in stanza 6, after the woman's soul has pleaded, seemingly unsuccessfully, for her essence not to merge with her lover's and so yield up its autonomy, that is precisely what happens in stanza 7, as hot flesh strains in a heap on sheets foreshadowing winding sheets.

Or is it? Might that merging be only temporary body's delirium, transcended into body's peace and resumption of the soul's selfhood? Or is the delirium of flesh a permanent abdication of innermost independence? Something tragic does seem to take over when that capitalized *You* becomes veiled or dead. But the final answer—if such there be—is up to the individual reader. Only let him or her be warned by a splendid thought from Professor Dodds's *The Greeks and the Irrational*: "We must resist the temptation to simplify what is not simple." *Caveat lector*, and beware all of us when the mighty Cyprian goddess grips our ecstatic bodies.

1999

First-class Mail:
A Wit and
His World

✿ WHAT A GUY, this Philip Larkin! At twenty-something he feels old age creeping in; at thirty-something he starts fearing death. At forty he thinks life has passed him by; at fifty he is sure he has achieved next to nothing, and wants to start all over. Yet he is one of Britain's most honored and beloved poets. A cherubic child, a gangly youth, he becomes a homely man, especially after most of his hair departs, his waist overreaches, his lenses thicken, and hearing aids take over both ears. After a homosexual flirtation, he becomes ravenously heterosexual, and has considerable success with the ladies, though none of them is much of a looker. He wants more from sex and becomes an avid purchaser of porn.

His career could not be more staid. After graduation from Oxford, he becomes a librarian (poor eyesight keeps him out of the war) and works in university libraries in Leicester, Belfast, and finally Hull, where he spends the three decades leading up to his death from cancer at age sixty-three in 1985. He never marries, though he has, among other women, one steady girlfriend to the finish. He takes good, perhaps excessive, care of his widowed mother, who lives to be ninety-one. He drinks like a fish—or two. In underheated England, he inhabits mediocre lodgings, where he squats close to the heater, always wrapped in blankets or overcoats, reading, writing, and freezing. He has quite a few male and female friends scattered across the country with whom he keeps up a lively correspondence. Wanting at first to be a novelist (with two novels to his credit), he finally settles into poetry. His poetry gets more and more successful, earning him numerous prizes, awards, honorary degrees, and other honors. But his poetic vein dries up, and for the last six years of his life he writes only prose, mostly reviews.

His *Collected Poems* runs to two hundred rather loose pages—mostly short poems—plus some eighty pages of unremarkable juvenilia. He despises most of the famous and not so famous poets and novelists of his time. Later, when editing *The Oxford Book of Twentieth-Century Verse*, he has to read and include many of them. His early favorites are Hardy and Auden, and the fiction of D. H. Lawrence. He detests modern art but loves jazz, about which he writes a newspaper column for a while. He thinks Louis Armstrong has done more for our age than Picasso. His politics are ultraconservative, and his jibes about the working class, unions, minorities, liberals are withering. He is witty about everything, including himself, whom he never tires of lampooning. A curmudgeon, then, but an oddly likable one.

With his publishers, Larkin drives hard bargains. He is a loyal friend, most helpful to the writers he admires, even knocking himself out for Barbara Pym. Kingsley Amis is a chum from school days, and remains so; other literary friendships include John Wain, John Betjeman, Robert Conquest, to whom many of these letters are addressed. Griping about the world, deriding others, depreciating himself, or just telling about daily doings and dawdlings, he is never deserted by humor.

All his life, Larkin remained a provincial Englishman, full of xenophobia ("Filthy abroad!"), love of cricket (he exchanges cricket cards with Harold Pinter), cantankerous toiling in his garden ("anything that looks bright and positive I take to be a weed"). He hardly ever ventures onto the continent, is terrified of America, has no languages save a smattering of French, and is often shaky about English spelling. But he understands the possibilities of English cadence, rhythm, and rhyme better, perhaps, than any of his British or American contemporaries, His spare, crabbed, wrenching, gallows-humor-laden verse, sometimes crisscrossed by flashes of rueful lyricism, has inched its way to the absolute forefront. Why? It has the smell of lived life, the odor of humanity—as do these letters.

In recent years we have had an authoritative edition of the poems by Anthony Thwaite, a useful biography by Andrew Motion (both men are also poets, friends of Larkin, and his literary executors), and now Thwaite has edited these *Selected Letters*, covering the years 1940–1985. They make a thick tome, not quite a door-stopper but much more than a stocking-stuffer, even if two major sets of letters were not made available to the editor. Still, these cheerful, despairing, frolicsome, often foul-mouthed, grouchy, self-assertive, and self-depreciating missives should not be missed by anyone who appreciates Larkin's verse, has the slightest interest in British literary life, values authentic eccentricity, or enjoys the company of a crotchety, uproarious, perennially schoolboyish yet amazingly canny human being.

Some letters, as we know, are written with an eye to print and posterity; others care only about intimacy, conviviality, and getting things off one's heaving chest into a heedful ear. Larkin's are of the latter kind, and often feel as if they were addressed to you. Larkin's concerns have a way of becoming your concerns; his tribulations, your tribulations; his friendships, enmities, loves, and rivalries yours as well. Obviously you don't read all this in one sitting, but you pick it up every time with an anticipation scarcely distinguishable from opening your mailbox. You feel about the epistolarist as about a favorite character in Dickens, Trollope, or Jane Austen, whom you know better than your own friends. (It has to be a typical nineteenth-century character, whose idiosyncracies are epic, rather than a contemporary one, whose very grandeur is apt to be mundane.) Even the frequent cuts in the text, duly noted by tantalizing ellipses, finally stop bothering you: Larkin is so much of an endearing muchness that more might be surfeit.

At age twenty-three, he writes a friend, "I am a long way off being capable of any emotion as simple as what is called love." Four years later, "The days are like a beer tap left turned on—jolly fine stuff all running to waste." The one time he proposes to a woman is recorded in a letter to someone else, "I cannot think what maggot was in my brain to produce such a monstrous egg. Or rather I can think . . . the maggot of loneliness, the maggot of romantic illusion, the maggot of sexual desire." To a mistress leaving him (we're now in 1953), he writes: "You are the sort of person one can't help feeling . . . ought to come one's way once in one's life—without really expecting she will—and since you did, I feel I mustn't raise a howl when circumstances withdrew you—it would be ungrateful to fortune. . . . But oh dear, oh dear! You were so wonderful!"

"I think a poem is a sort of verbal device to preserve a feeling you have had, so that anyone who inserts the penny of his attention will receive that emotion neatly wrapped," he reflects. "Beware . . . of trying to transport the best of the old life into the new," he advises. "Giving things up means giving up the nice as well as the nasty." "Sorry about your wives and families," he writes Robert Conquest. "I feel I ought to offer to take one set off you." He allows how "publishing a book is like farting at a party—you have to wait before people stop looking at you before you can behave normally again." By 1958, a book jacket makes him look "like some crazed balding unfrocked cleric who goes about stealing candlesticks from churches." To Barbara Pym, he writes, "I think autumn & winter are better than spring & summer in that they are not supposed to be enjoyable."

Asked on the radio whether William Golding is any good, he answers, "I prefer to bypass that aspect of his work," and clucks to Barbara Pym, "Rather nice, don't you think?" "Marriage," he tells a woman friend, "is a marvelous thing for other people, like going to the stake." A distinguished Australian, coming to lecture at Hull, "tells me he's never seen a kangaroo. A pity: I was hoping for some informed criticism." Trollope's novels, he pronounces, "are so grown up . . . beside Dickens' three-ring circuses." At age forty-eight: "I suppose if one lives to be old one's entire waking life will be turning on the spit of recollection over the fires of mingled shame, pain or remorse." To a fellow poet, he complains, "It's terribly unfair that one never gets any better at writing . . . not like making a window frame or seducing women." And about himself: "I don't think I write well—just better than anyone else."

About a celebrated colleague: "At Ilkley literature festival a woman shrieked and vomited during a Ted Hughes reading. I must say I've never felt like shrieking." He declares to Amis, "I'm more or less all right, except that I never put pen to paper or penis to—to— Ah, my memory is going." There's consolation in one's job: "One wakes up wanting to cut one's throat; one goes to work, & in 15 minutes one wants to cut someone else's—complete cure!" When Ted Hughes is reading at Hull, "for £4.50 you can go to a reception and 'meet Ted Hughes.' . . . Feel like walking up & down with a placard reading 'Meet P. L. for £3.95.' "

Yet always the fear of aging and death: "I think," he writes in 1982, "it's a bit hard to call someone sixty just because they've been fifty-nine for a year." About his acclaimed collection of criticism, *Required Writing*: "My trouble is that I have only two ideas or so to rub together, and when they are rubbed together remorselessly for 150 pp. the reader gets restive." About his good friend Amis: "The only reason I hope I predecease him is that I'd find it next to impossible to say anything nice about him at his memorial service." A lifelong distrust of the young is summed up: "In a student paper . . . I was said to have 'judged it prudent / Never to speak to any student,' which abashed me rather, though not enough to make me speak to one." He marks his next-to-last birthday "by discarding one of my weighing machines. It is just too erratic at high figures. The other is marked in kilograms I can't understand . . . and pounds so small I can't see . . . I have only one pair of trousers that will meet at the front."

He bewails his "sagging face, an egg sculpted in lard, with goggles on," but is still capable of youthful enthusiasm about authors he likes: Julian Barnes, Jonathan Price. He bemoans the piles of fallen leaves he has to rake: "Perhaps they'll dry and blow away. . . . Perhaps I'll dry and blow away myself." To an inquiring broadcaster, he replies, "Sometimes I think the writer is the last person to know what he is doing." On receiving a fan letter from "a whole form of Welsh schoolgirls, seemingly inviting mass coition," he sighs, "Where were they when I wanted them?" Asked by his doctors to cut down on his conspicuous imbibing, he remonstrates, "The trouble is . . . most people drink nothing at all except at Christmas and weddings and this drags the national average down."

A few months before his death, he writes his favorite poet, Gavin Ewart, about his doctors promising complete recovery, "an opinion

I embrace when drunk but doubt when sober." An electric type-writer (rejected) makes him feel "put at the controls of Concorde after five minutes' tuition." He reiterates on his last birthday the outcry he made at most previous ones: "What have I done to be sixty-three? It isn't fair." In what may have been his last critical judgment, he reads Dylan Thomas's letters "with almost supernatural boredom." Some years earlier, after "castigating" Evelyn Waugh's letters in *The Guardian*, he wondered "how my own would rank for 'charity'—not very highly, I should imagine, and a good deal duller."

I would hate to have to adjudicate a charity contest between Waugh and Larkin, but I can affirm that there is not a trace of dullness in either. Read these enthralling letters, beautifully edited by Anthony Thwaite. Like Mozart about his music, Thwaite can claim about his editing, not a note too many, or too few.

1993

Squaring the Circle:
Stéphane Mallarmé

IF STÉPHANE MALLARMÉ was not the greatest poet of modern times—although an impressive case for that, too, could be mounted—he was certainly the most poetic. And poetic not only in his work, but also in his life. No one else has lived poetry quite so single-mindedly as he did.

The tendency persists to think of the "poetic" poet as Byron, Baudelaire, or Rilke. But Byron's womanizing, incest, covert homosexuality, swimming the Hellespont, and early death for the Greek cause (in a sickbed, to be sure) are poetic only by narrowly romantic standards. Baudelaire's bohemian existence as a *poète maudit*, with drink, drugs, a mulatto mistress, venereal disease, and premature demise, is poetic only within a similarly narrow, *décadent* frame of reference. Rilke, a great poet, carried sensitivity to new, indeed sickly, heights; wrote reams of verse and even more letters (many to women he bedded, others to rich, aristocratic ladies who extended him limitless hospitality amid gracious surroundings), was "poetic" chiefly in the current academic sense: good for graduate theses, what with enough poetry, alternative versions, and fragments to stuff dozens of doctoral dissertations.

Mallarmé lived the poet's life—the poetic vocation—much more truly. He made his toilsome living as a schoolmaster, for a long time in the provinces, and was a good husband and father, save for one brief and ultimately harmless affair with the glamorous Méry Laurent. He traveled little, worked hard at the tasks he hated and labored lovingly on the poetry he adored, had a number of literary friendships and even his own modest but prestigious literary salon. He dedicated his inner life to the *Livre* or *Grand'Oeuvre*—a kind of poetic masterwork that would alchemically transform the world— which he kept writing in his head and in fragmentary notes he urged his wife and daughter to destroy after his death. What he did finish and publish was some of the world's finest lyrical poetry (small in quantity compared to his voluminous occasional verse and syntactically opaque prose), but so intricately and dazzlingly crafted as to attain the nearest human equivalent to perfection, and to almost completely defy translation. This difficult, untranslatable poetry is what keeps Mallarmé far less known than he deserves to be. Typically, *Bartlett's Familiar Quotations* dismissed him summarily until recent editions; finally included, he is represented by a measly quintet of entries, one of them a misquotation. To add insult to injury, all of them (including the misquotation) are clearly transcribed from Norbert Guterman's *A Book of French Quotations* rather than from the original texts.

So the appearance of a fresh Mallarmé biography and new translation of all of Mallarmé's major poetry in verse and prose *cum* much-needed commentary is to be saluted, even if the result—at least in the case of the translation—is less than a blessing. I refer to *A Throw of the Dice: The Life of Stéphane Mallarmé*, by Gordon Millan, and *Stéphane Mallarmé: Collected Poems*, comprising translations and commentaries by Henry Weinfield. Let me proceed, in an order Mallarmé would have frowned at, by putting the life ahead of the work.

Gordon Millan is a professor of French at Strathclyde University in Glasgow, and a co-editor of a three-volume critical edition of Mallarmé's works (three volumes of correspondence are to follow) for the venerable French publisher Flammarion. His book, in large, readable print, runs to just under four hundred pages, forty-four of them notes—about as concise as a serious biography gets these prolix days; no wonder it was written by a Scot. It is true that Mallarmé's life was uneventful, but since this is a critical biography of the world's hardest modern poet, the book's terseness is to be applauded.

Mallarmé was born in 1842 into a family of bureaucrats on both sides. His father, Numa, was to end up as a mid-level civil servant who, for reasons of health, retired early. Stéphane lost his mother when he was five, his beloved sister Maria ten years later. Brought up largely by his strict maternal grandparents, especially the formidable grandmother, Fanny Desmolins, he was sent to a fancy boarding school and then to a Jesuit *collège* in Passy, where he alternated between winning prizes and doing poorly. He was especially hostile to Religious Study, and was resented for being a loner. Some of the time, though, he lived with his father and young stepmother, Anne, who proved a most understanding protectress to the boy at crucial turning points.

Numa Mallarmé became *conservateur des hypothèques* in the cathedral town of Sens, seventy-five miles southeast of Paris. Accordingly, Stéphane transferred to the Lycée Impérial of Sens, his holidays to be divided between the grandparents at Passy and the parents at Sens. At age eighteen, very much against his wishes, he started working at the Registry Office in Sens, with a dull bureaucratic career in the offing. But he was to get support for his rebellion from a young schoolmaster and published poet, Emmanuel des Essarts, who befriended the budding poet-registrar, for Stéphane was already scribbling verse imitative of his idols, Hugo and Baudelaire.

Anne Mallarmé, the intelligent stepmother, listened to Des Essarts, and helped get permission for Stéphane to change careers, for which, as a minor, he needed the permission of his stern Catholic grandfather and guardian, André Desmolins. The idea, only reluctantly agreed to by André, was for Stéphane to become a teacher of languages, specifically English, wherefore he was to undertake an extended stay in England after some private English lessons. But he was loath to lock himself up, as André wished, in a Catholic boarding school in England. The deadlock was broken by Anne, and Stéphane was soon taking his morning lessons, then reading the newer poets: Leconte de Lisle, Banville, and Gautier. Also Shakespeare and, discovered through Baudelaire's translations, the poet he was himself to translate and love all his life, Edgar Allan Poe.

Thanks to Des Essarts, Stéphane met a young Parisian law clerk, Henri Cazalis, who was to become his best friend, correspondent, and confidant. A crucial incident for the young poet was an outing in the forest of Fontainebleau with Cazalis and his gang, which included the painter Henri Regnault and the future *salonnière* Anne-Marie Gaillard, later known as Nina de Villars. (Renaming oneself was quite the fashion: Mallarmé himself was baptized Etienne, which he ennobled into the Hellenic Stéphane, from *stephanos*, a garland or crown.) Also present were the daughters of the English journalist Edward Yapp, the elder to be Cazalis's Dulcinea. In the romantic Franchard Gorge of the forest, Mallarmé was later to propose to his future wife, and it was in this forest that, much later still, he would spend some of his happiest hours.

Stéphane rhapsodized about the charms of the English girls: "Those perfect Greek waists, not a pretentious wasp waist but the waist of an angel who would unfold her wings from beneath her corsage." He at first mistook Marie Gerhard, the rather plain, uneducated German governess, seven years his senior, for one of those "adorable creatures" from Albion, which probably accounts for his courting and, eventually, marrying her. By this time the pair were living, somewhat strainedly, in London, where, after a break-up or two, the wedding took place in 1863, with Stéphane, at the time, a sexually very inexperienced twenty-one-year-old. Having acquired a not quite ironclad expertise in English, Mallarmé was sent to teach, not as he hoped in or near Paris, but in the provincial town of Tournon on the Rhône, 350 miles from the capital, and, to the disappointed young man, a place of Ovidian exile. "The inhabitants of this dismal village," he wrote at first (he was to soften a bit later on), "live in too great an intimacy with their pigs for me to find them anything other than disgusting."

Just before heading south, though, Mallarmé met the poet, man of letters, and womanizer Catulle Mendès, who was to become one of his closest friends along with Edouard Manet and the novelist and dramatist Villiers de l'Isle-Adam (best remembered for his influential *Axël*), who might be described as a *prosateur maudit*. This eccentric, impoverished Breton nobleman symbolized for Mallarmé "the absolute figure of the Poet," as Alan Raitt has said in his life of Villiers. Tournon was a bitter pill after such scintillating company, yet, strangely, London came to Mallarmé's rescue: its memories were from then on to haunt his imagination. But Tournon, that "dismal

hole," also brought about with its foul weather the recurrence of the
rheumatic condition that was to plague Mallarmé much of his life.

Still, it is here that some of his very good earlier poems began to
take shape, and work commenced on the poetic drama *Hérodiade*,
with which Stéphane wrestled all his life, and which survives only in
fragmented form. In an 1864 letter to Cazalis, Mallarmé formulates
his lifelong poetics, "Paint not the thing itself, but the effect that it
produces." Writing in 1865 to another important friend, Eugène
Lefébure, Mallarmé sounds one of his most constant refrains: "The
artist *becomes himself* in front of the blank sheet of paper." And he
conceived of the passionate struggle with poetic creation as inimical
to domestic happiness, though he "would always remain," in Mil-
lan's words, "a loving father and a loyal and devoted husband."

In the same year, Mallarmé complains to Cazalis: "Imagine
being a washed up old man at the age of twenty-three when all
the others whom we love live amid sunlight and are ready to write
their masterpieces." But he cheers up when, with the first version of
L'Après-midi d'un faune, he imagines having invented a new form of
dramatic verse "insofar as the line breaks are quite slavishly calcu-
lated to follow the gestures of the actor without abandoning poetry
aimed at mass effects." Poor Mallarmé, mass effects were not part of
his repertoire, then or ever. The work was rejected by the Comédie
Française for not having a story line strong enough to sustain audi-
ence interest.

Although the Mallarmés lived rather comfortably—not on a
teacher's salary, but on a trust fund from Stéphane's mother—the
poet was spending too much on ever fancier apartments and fur-
nishings. But he now had a fine view of the Rhône, and soon sun-
rises and sunsets began to figure prominently in his verse. There
were, however, problems with his job: then and throughout, Mal-
larmé the teacher was getting low ratings from students, headmas-
ters, and inspectors. On the other hand, on visits to Paris, he was
starting to frequent important fellow poets such as Leconte de Lisle,
Heredia, and Coppée. In the south, notably in Avignon, he was be-
friending Théodore Aubanel and other members of the *félibrige*, the
circle of poets writing in Provençal.

As significant as that long-ago excursion to Fontainebleau was a
trip to the Riviera with Eugène Lefébure. They explored Cannes,

Nice, and environs, and had a wonderful time discussing poetry. It lasted only one week, but it echoed strongly in Mallarmé's work, and eventually gave rise to the major poem "Prose (pour des Esseintes)." These talks with Lefébure also resulted in two capital insights. One concerned the difficulty of writing, of the rarity of that precise harmony, or correlation, between sound and sense Mallarmé strove for in verse. The other involved the precariousness of life itself, brought home to him by his recent illnesses. Language was no more than a collection of meaningless conventional signs, and life could absurdly end at any moment. He became aware, in Millan's words, "of the extremely fine line separating absence and presence, being and nothingness, life and death, which later . . . he could place at the very centre of his work and make the cornerstone of his personal philosophy and his mature poetics." And he launched on a pursuit of what he first called "Beauty," and subsequently "the quintessential but totally elusive quality of life itself." Art now loomed as a substitute for religious belief, to which, after his discovery of the void—*le néant*—underlying the world, he could no longer subscribe. Contemplating a volume of poetry to be called something like *The Glory of Lying*, he declared, "I shall sing as a man without Hope."

In letters to Cazalis, he announced, "Having discovered the void, I have discovered Beauty" (1866), and, the following year, "I have descended deep enough into the Void to be able to speak with certainty. There is only Beauty, and it has only one perfect means of expression, Poetry." Such obsessiveness merely made his teacherly activities suffer the more. His publishing of poems in the "avant-garde" *Parnasse Contemporain*, moreover, was considered outrageous in Tournon; some parents even contemplated removing their children from his tutelage. The principal of his *lycée* pronounced on his English teacher: "Talks a lot about poetry and the ideal, but professes only modest esteem for his fellow men."

Mallarmé's next teaching job was at Besançon, where he did not do much better and wasn't any happier. He kept living beyond his means, and expecting his grandmother to bail him out. He rejected Christianity completely, which took courage considering that it put him at odds with his wife and entire family. In the bitterly cold winter of Besançon, he kept looking at the stars and became obsessed with the Great Bear. Somehow the Great Work he was planning was to mirror the structure of that constellation: there was to be an "ultimate correlation between Poetry and the Universe." The *Grand'Oeuvre* was to be the equal of the Venus de Milo and the Mona Lisa, "absolute and unconscious Beauty." Meanwhile the agony of an ailing body, in that unprecedentedly cold winter, found expression in the famous sonnet "Le vierge, le vivace et le bel aujourd'hui," whose magnificent swan has become trapped in winter's ice.

By now the father of a growing girl, Geneviève, Mallarmé came to realize that excessive intellectual activity to the exclusion of everything else was extremely harmful. "To be truly human," he wrote Lefébure in 1867, "you have to think with your entire body." Yet it is at this point that, transferred to Avignon with its pleasant climate, he writes one of his most rigorously cerebral poems, the notorious "-ix sonnet," beginning "Ses purs ongles très haut dédiant leur onyx." It is based on the decision to have one set of its rhymes in -ix, no easy feat in French. Millan does scant justice to this sonnet; he does not even quote the important passage from the annunciatory letter to Lefébure: "I may write a sonnet, and as I have only three rhymes in -ix, do your best to send me the true meaning of the word ptyx, for I'm told it doesn't exist in any language—something I'd much prefer, for that would give me the joy of creating it through the magic of rhyme." But the word does occur in Greek, where it means a fold or a shell, of the kind that pressed to the ear suggests the sound of the sea. Millan reproduces this sonnet without explicating *ptyx*, which I find remiss.

Mallarmé's own comment on this poem in a letter to Cazalis, to whom it is dedicated, is significant: "Its meaning if it has one (but I would be quite consoled if this were not the case, thanks to the large dose of poetry that to me it seems to contain) is conveyed through a hidden mirage suggested by the words themselves." The bantering tone, Millan observes, is misleading; Mallarmé very seriously tried "to encapsulate . . . his absurdist vision of the world as a glorious and tantalizing mirage. Its theme is the absence/presence paradox which lies at the very centre of his poetic universe."

Foolish expenditure on redecorating the Avignon flat plunged Stéphane into hysteria and forced him to take to his bed for a few days. His attempts to raise money, as his salary underwent various cuts, were pitiful. But the death of his grandmother jolted him back into writing again, the result being the curious Poesque tale "Igitur." He grasped at a variety of desperate projects to make more money, especially as Marie was about to give birth to their second child, Anatole. Luckily the pull he had through friends at the Ministry of Education finally paid off, and he obtained a job at the Lycée Condorcet in Paris. He was almost thirty years old.

He settled in the inexpensive district near the Gare St. Lazare on rue de Moscou, whence he could walk to school and to the boulevards with the theaters he loved. Further pull got him promoted to senior-class teacher and better pay. Life improved. There were the literary and artistic friendships old and new, Manet becoming especially dear to the poet. Through him, Mallarmé got involved in the art world and its controversies, and turned into a passionate champion of Manet and the Impressionists. He became editor of the fashion magazine *La Mode Dernière*, and, under various pseudonyms, often its sole contributor. He discovered the village of Valvins on the Seine at the edge of the forest of Fontainebleau. This was to become his steady summer home. He published a deluxe edition of his translation of Poe's "The Raven," illustrated by Manet; then went to London on an invitation that resulted in his contributing a regular column to *The Athenaeum* on the literary and artistic life of Paris. The final version of *L'Après-midi d'un faune* appeared in a limited edition likewise illustrated by Manet.

Immersed in the literary life, in art-world infighting, in often vain attempts to get his poetry published, Mallarmé neglected his teaching even more. On a commission from England's *Art Monthly*, he wrote an article in defense of Manet that, as Millan puts it, "can now be seen [as] one of the earliest and most enlightened attempts to define and explain the history of modern painting." But, reprimanded by the school authorities upon publishing his famous sonnet to Poe's memory, Mallarmé stopped bringing out any more verse for a goodly number of years, and rather than jeopardize his family's future, tried to concentrate on his teaching. He did, however, publish a philological treatise, *Les Mots anglais*, and a free adaptation of an English book on mythology, *Les Dieux antiques*. He also worked on his Poe translations. But in many ways he remained a very parochial Frenchman, refusing even to set foot in Germany, his wife's country, because of the Franco-Prussian War, in which his painter friend Henri Regnault was killed.

Another project was to be a major play "to be performed at a fixed period of the year." "I am not concerned with a single genre," he elaborated, "but with all those I consider to belong to theatrical performance: magical, popular and lyrical drama." But soon a heavy blow was to dampen Mallarmé's spirits: eight-year-old Anatole died of a rheumatic condition that affected his heart. "That charming, exquisite child had captivated me to the point where I still include him in all my future projects and my dearest dreams." Stéphane had even hoped that Anatole would someday finish the *Grand'Oeuvre* that he himself would only begin, and that he kept ceaselessly revolving in his head.

At this point Méry Laurent becomes stellar in Mallarmé's life. The daughter of a laundress, she was born Anne-Rose Louviot, had been an unsuccessful actress, and was now a successful *mondaine*. Millan writes, "Renowned for her stately good looks, her statuesque and buxom features [can features be either of those?], luxuriant blonde hair and a perfect complexion, she had become the mistress of a rich American" dentist, and had her winter apartment off the rue de Rome, on which the Mallarmés lived now too. She had been a model and close friend of Manet, perhaps also his mistress, and Stéphane thus got to know her; but it was not until Manet's death that she became important to the poet, partly as a reminder of his lost friend. He would visit her almost daily in winter, a few doors down the rue de Rome; and often, too, at her summer villa on the Boulevard Lannes. They also corresponded extensively. It is fairly certain that, ill-matched as they were, they had a brief affair, but their letters confirming it won't be made available till the year 2000.

In any case, it is to Méry that Mallarmé wrote his finest love poems; one need only compare such a dignified but cool poem as "Don du poëme," written to his wife, with the sonnet to Méry, "O si chère de loin et proche et blanche," to appreciate the difference. In fact, a French girl from the bourgeoisie whom I knew on my Fulbright year in Paris and tried to sell on Mallarmé, wrote me in America that she would have had little use for the poet were it not for that poem, the only one she could truly warm to. It is indeed a great love poem. Mallarmé's fellow poet and friend, the aristocratic and straitlaced Henri de Régnier, found Méry rather common, but

Stéphane thought her the ideal person to relax with from the chores of teaching and the exertions of the literary life. "The charming and frivolous quatrains with which he embellished her fans and other possessions" are among the jewels of Mallarmé's copious occasional verse.

By this time, he was beginning to be recognized as the leader of the Symbolists, and the Tuesday evenings on the rue de Rome were the place to be for artists both French and foreign. Mallarmé would be holding forth almost uninterruptedly, and Marie, assisted by Geneviève, would tend to the modest amenities. Two men, at this time, greatly contributed to Mallarmé's unsolicited and not especially welcome celebrity. J.-K. Huysmans had sought his help with the writing of *A rebours*, the paradigmatic novel about an art-for-art's-sake dilettante, and Mallarmé's old friend Paul Verlaine published a three-part study of him in *Lutèce*, as part of a project on the *Poètes maudits*. It was accompanied by Manet's beautiful portrait of the poet, which also graces the jacket of Millan's biography. The articles then came out in book form (1884) almost simultaneously with *A rebours*, which named "Mallarmé, along with Rimbaud, as one of the most exquisite poets of the age."

Mallarmé was indeed an aesthete in the admirable yet somewhat troublesome sense of *japonaiserie*, Wagnerism, calligraphy, *lavallières*, the hieratic role of the artist (particularly the poet), and all the rest. But Romanticism having become *embourgeoisé* on the one hand and decadent on the other, the time was ripe for a poet who took his mission seriously, even mystically, especially if, like Mallarmé (unlike many of his disciples), he also had a smiling, playful side to him. The sense of mission is reflected in further words of the letter to Cazalis, part of which I quoted earlier. Other than poetry, "everything else is a lie—except in the case of those who live the life of the body, for love, and for that love of the mind, friendship." Thus does a touch of hedonism enter the hierophantic; the latter gets its apotheosis in a missive to Léo d'Orfer (1884): "Poetry is the expression, through human language reduced to its essential rhythm, of the mysterious meaning of the various aspects of existence. In this way it authenticates our sojourn on this planet and constitutes our sole intellectual challenge."

Yet there remained, behind everything Mallarmé was writing, the Great Work, sometimes referred to as The Book, of which "there is only one, which has been attempted, whether they knew it or not, by all who have ever written, including men of genius." In the conversations of the famous Tuesdays, with the many distinguished *mardistes*, and in those fragments that have posthumously come to light, the pursuit of that Book was paramount. Wretched Mallarmé; as he wrote John Payne in 1886, "I never sleep any more and that is how I imagine the state of eternal damnation." Millan is averse to including the anecdotal in his biography; otherwise he might have mentioned Mallarmé's telling someone that he had not slept in twenty years, and upon that person's rejoinder, "You mean *hardly* slept?" exclaiming, "No, not at all!"

Tough going as Mallarmé's poetry is, his prose is even more difficult. The first drama review he wrote for his disciple Edouard Dujardin (the official inventor of the *monologue intérieur* and editor of the *Revue Indépendente*) seemed to the latter much too obscure in places. To every respectful objection, Mallarmé replied, "But this is perfectly clear!" That, for him, was the truth and no affectation. Yet, as another anecdote has it (and, as such, likewise excluded by Millan), Verlaine's funeral procession was already under way when Mallarmé was still sitting at a café table, fiddling with his eulogy. Asked what he was doing, he answered he was adding a few last-minute obscurities.

Be that as it may, his arcane style certainly was a failure on the lecture circuit. A telegram from Brussels to his wife and daughter runs, "FIRST LECTURE LASTS 2 1/2 HOURS. STUPEFACTION. MALLARME." Cut down to an hour, it still didn't go over, with even the friend Edgar Degas bored and fidgeting. The Banquet Years were at hand, but Mallarmé, at first an enthusiastic participant in these gastronomic literary tributes, was soon remarking, "The world of literature is becoming very strange, and there is something indecent in appearing to be connected with it in any way whatsoever." But his sense of humor did not forsake him. Thus when he received a telegram from Whistler (whom he considered "the very personification of the artist") that the "magpie" Oscar Wilde was coming to a *mardi*, "WARN DISCIPLES PRECAUTION FAMILIARITY FATAL KEEP TIGHT GRIP ON PEARLS OF WISDOM," Mallarmé replied, "The evening was as dull as you would have wished."

Occasionally Gordon Millan's acuity is dulled too. Throughout the book, he prints Mallarmé's poems with unassumingly serviceable translations. But in rendering "Salut," the prefatory piece to the *Collected Poems*, Millan errs badly. This banquet poem begins

> Rien, cette écume, vierge vers
> A ne désigner que la coupe;
> Telle loin se noie une troupe
> De sirènes mainte à l'envers.

Millan translates this as "Nothing, mere froth, virgin verse / If I am referring to the cup; / Just as in the distance a troop / Of many sirens drowns upside-down." Surely, Millan should have given the second verse as "To characterize only the cup," and the fourth, with its deliberate poeticism *mainte*, as something like "Many a one upside down." It is words like *mainte, aucun,* and *telle* that become most telling in Mallarmé. On the other hand, we can't blame Millan for not being able to reproduce in English the wordplay to which Charles Chassé has called attention,[1] the puns on *vers* (verse) and *verre* (drinking glass) and *coupe* (cup or caesura).

Mallarmé's often serious humor manifested itself to a journalist seeking his take on an anarchist bomb exploded in the Chamber of Deputies: "The only bomb of which I am aware is a book." To some of his *mardistes*, as Henri de Régnier reports, he was even sharper: "There is only one person who has the right to be an anarchist, and that is I, the poet. Because I alone supply the product for which society has no use, and in exchange for which it does not provide me with enough to live on." By this time, to be sure, he was able to give up his detested teaching, even if only six years were left him in which to enjoy his blessed liberation. Now there was more time for everything, including his beloved concert-going, and working undisturbed on The Book. Yet there was also his gregariousness, which elicited Geneviève's comment, "You are not really a solitary monk, no, not at all."

He was now a regular at the dinners of Berthe Morisot and Méry Laurent, and became a steady contributor to Natanson and Fénéon's *Revue Blanche*. He became a favorite subject of *enquêtes* (celebrity in-

---

1. *Lueurs sur Mallarmé* by Charles Chassé (Paris, Editions de la Nouvelle Revue Critique, 1947).

terviews or questionnaires), so popular at the time, the frenetic pace at which he pursued his alleged "doing nothing" actually impairing his health. There were recurrent bouts of flu and rheumatism, aggravated by heavy smoking and near-permanent insomnia. His election as "prince of poets" upon Verlaine's death, with its attendant publicity, gave him little pleasure. Somewhat reluctantly, he published his prose poems and other prose under the dismissive title *Divagations*. In some of these he "created a new hybrid," as Millan states, "somewhere between the traditional prose poem and the review article," which he called "poème critique."

Then, too, he undertook his longest, most daringly innovative, and most hermetic poem, "Un Coup de dés" ("A Throw of the Dice"), which, though a culmination of sorts, was not meant to be the Great Work.[2] It was to have been published in a luxury edition illustrated by Redon which never materialized. To Elémir Bourges, he wrote, "Each day I descend a rung on the ladder into emptiness and disgust." Even a banquet in his honor, organized by the greatest of his disciples, Paul Valéry, misfired because of rivalries between the older and younger literati. With Valéry at Valvins, Mallarmé had grand times boating, walking, and chatting, and enjoying simple, hearty meals. I would give anything for a transcript of the incident Valéry reports in a letter to Gide, another admirer of Mallarmé's: "In the evening, after some boating and some drinks (always too many), we had a rather interesting and serious but rather dirty conversation." Serious dirt from Mallarmé and Valéry ought to be worth its weight in gold.

Work on the verse play *Hérodiade* proceeded fitfully but stubbornly, the great actress Marguerite Moréno hoping to play the heroine. When Zola was on trial for having defended Dreyfus, Mallarmé dispatched an admiringly supportive telegram. He also commiserated with Rodin, whose statue of Balzac was rejected by the people who had commissioned it: "After all," he wrote to his sculptor friend, "you have the glory of knowing you are right." When literary work got too taxing, there was puttering in the Valvins garden,

2. "The last work . . . which, with its diverse fonts and word-islands in an amorphous sea of broad white surfaces, comes across at first as a graphic foretaste of Cubist painting." *Mallarmé: Dichtung, Weisheit, Haltung,* by Kurt Wais (Munich, C. H. Becksche Verlagsbuchhandlung, 1952).

or playing with the cat Lilith. At this time, a sore throat turned into tonsillitis. On September 8, 1898, the doctor came; the poet joked that, from coughing, he was as red in the face as an exotic rooster. "In the middle of his sentence, a coughing fit overcame him. He looked quickly at his daughter, then made a grab for the doctor and collapsed on top of him, asphyxiated by a sudden contraction of the glottis. He was fifty-six years old." In photographs of that period, he looks a good deal older.

Many peasants of Valvins attended the funeral of "Mossieu Mallarmé," whom they considered a genial neighbor. Paul Valéry, scheduled to speak, was too choked up. In a farewell note, Mallarmé advised his wife and daughter to burn all his papers, but he left the note unfinished, giving rise to speculations about whether he might have changed his mind. It is significant that James Joyce possessed an edition of "Un Coup de dés" as he worked on *Finnegans Wake;* both works are terminal, unreadable masterpieces. Gauguin, learning in Tahiti of the poet's death, remarked, "The best part of his work was his life." Three weeks before his death, Mallarmé answered a query with, "I have been sufficiently faithful to myself for my humble life to have retained some meaning." As in his final poem, so in all his work, Mallarmé's achievement was, to quote Millan, "a heroic and defiant throw of the dice."

It seems to me that Mallarmé foundered on a grandiose self-contradiction, though such a defeat may surpass most victories. His poetic aim was a pure contradiction (remember Rilke's epitaph for himself, with its *reiner Widerspruch?*): to have poetry not say, but suggest; yet to create with words something as solid, shapely, and unalterable as a constellation. On the one hand, the cultivation of the misty aura; on the other, the obsession with the indelible contour.

The other great problem, of course, is the obscurity. Though he never saw it that way, Mallarmé was the most mandarin, most abstruse of poets. Not because of any recondite references, but because of the complex imagery, complicated syntax, and expressly cultivated ambiguity. And also because of his compression. Writing poetry for him was like translating the baroque into telegraphese. Yet at the same time—and this makes an enormous difference—there was the verbal music, equaled perhaps by a few, but never surpassed. For Mallarmé—and this was a first—sound could become tantamount to meaning. As he told Degas, who showed him one of his poems (another anecdote excluded by Millan) and defended the ideas in it, "Poems are made with words, not ideas." Mallarmé's poetry is in the sound of those words, their etymologies, their unstable equilibrium and polyvalent interaction.

Still, the hermetic aspect can be exaggerated. Mallarmé's earlier poems are also remarkable, yet totally perspicuous. Many of his verses have that musical magic that on one exposure etches itself into the memory. Who can forget "La chair est triste, hélas! et j'ai lu tous les livres"? Or "Le vierge, la vivace et le bel aujourd'hui"? Or take the famous verses about Poe, who undertook to "Donner un sens plus pur aux mots de la tribu," but came into his own only in death, "Tel qu'en Lui-même enfin l'éternité le change." (This one inspires wits. I shall never forget coming across a headshot of Henri Troyat in a *bouquiniste*'s window, with the author's superscription, "Tel qu'en lui-même enfin le photographe le change.") Or, about a prostitute, "Toi qui sur le néant en sais plus que les morts." And the eponymous key line that winds its way through the entire final poem: "Un coup de dés jamais n'abolira le hasard." It is misquoted both by Norbert Guterman's *A Book of French Quotations* and by the copycat *Bartlett's* as "Un coup de dés n'abolira jamais le hasard," which kills the rhythm and illustrates the difference between Mallarmé's verbal music and the prose of the tribe, anthologists included.

There are many more great lines. One could go on, though not quite forever, for Mallarmé's poetry, not counting the occasional verse and poems in prose, constitutes almost less than a tome— something rather like a *plaquette*. In this, too, he is a father of such moderns as T. S. Eliot, John Crowe Ransom, and that fine poet better known as a publisher, Francis Meynell.

But to return to the verbal music. Mallarmé, as we have seen in connection with the sonnet in -ix, was not averse to letting the music do more than mirror, actually *become* the meaning. Even so, unlike the later Surrealists and Dadaists, he did not really favor divesting himself of content. Hence his comment on Victor Hugo: "What a poet he would have been if he had had something to say." Millan cites in a note that, in 1886, *Le Gaulois* printed an attack by Tolstoy on Mallarmé's incomprehensibility. He does not mention that this became part of *What Is Art?*, a book-length polemic, in which the Russian master contemptuously quotes Mallarmé's famous dictum, "To name an object is to take away three-quarters of the enjoyment of the poem, which consists of the happiness of guessing bit by bit: to suggest it, that is the dream." Tolstoy then reproduces the sonnet "A la nue accablante tu," albeit with a bad misreading (*soir* for *sais* in line six), as typical of the poet's inscrutability. In a footnote, Aylmer Maude, the English translator, says tersely, "This sonnet is too unintelligible for translation." When Mallarmé sent a brief, ironic response to *Le Gaulois*, the editor put in his two centimes' worth: "M. Stéphane Mallarmé is an exquisite writer and a distinguished poet, but why in the devil's name does he write so that nobody can understand him?" It is, however, no use wishing that Mallarmé were simpler; as I wrote in my doctoral thesis, "Mallarmé's syntax is his first and last—perhaps also his greatest—metaphor."[3]

And now along comes another optimist—dreamer and hothead—who undertakes a verse translation, no less, of all of Mallarmé's poetry. Henry Weinfield, a self-styled poet who teaches in Notre Dame's Liberal Studies Department, has brought out *Stéphane Mallarmé: Collected Poems*, comprising the poems and facing translations—the rhymed ones in rhyme—followed by extensive commentaries in the back.

The "Introduction" is promising enough. "Speaking metaphorically," Weinfield says, "my primary struggle in this translation has been to render the 'music,' or 'musical essence,' or 'spiritual essence,' of the poetry." He quotes the twenty-year-old Mallarmé: "Everything that is sacred and that wishes to remain so must envelop itself in mystery." And the translator concludes that "Poetry is . . . not only the vehicle but the locus of the sacred for Mallarmé, and in a sense he remains a religious poet even though he loses his belief," a statement befitting one who teaches at a Catholic university. But paradox becomes even more problematic with "Mallarmé is much more of a realist than we have been given to understand, and I would even argue that an essential aim of this poet is toward de-

---

3. *The Prose Poem as a Genre in Nineteenth-Century European Literature*, by John Simon (New York and London, Garland Publishing, 1987).

mystification." Note the sloppy diction: "aim" does not require "toward."

Weinfield is on safer ground with actual quotations, as with "Everything in the world exists to end up [or culminate—'aboutir'] in a book." Or the famous passage from a letter to Cazalis about "my terrible struggle with that old and evil plumage, which is now happily vanquished: God. But as that struggle had taken place on his bony wing which was in death throes more vigorous than I would have suspected," the combat took a dreadful toll. Weinfield fails to derive from this the concept of poetry as a death struggle. This is what Valéry expresses: "as for the world, the totality of the real has no other excuse for being than to offer the poet the chance of playing against it a sublime game, lost in advance."[4]

On the other hand, Weinfield is right to call attention to Mallarmé's revisions of his earlier work, "so the stylistic propensities of the early poems often reflect the poet's later development." Equally correctly, he notes that, at least in the early work, there is concern with social and political issues. Social more than political, I would say. I wish Weinfield could have resisted jargon such as "intertextual meta-narrative" and "semiotic displacement," while he justly recognizes Mallarmé's basic untranslatability. "I did it anyway," Weinfield concludes, brushing aside acknowledged obstacles.

With what results, though? One can turn to any one of these translations to inspect his almost complete failure. In the earlier, easier poems, there may be a glimmer of success here and there; in the later, tougher ones, all is fiasco. But let's start with an early poem, "Apparition." For Mallarmé's pure rhymes—*pleurs-fleurs, violes-corolles*—we get such shabby approximations as "tears-flowers," "violas-corollas," which do not work even as slant rhyme. "S'enivrer savamment" is far more elegant and eloquent than "imbibed its wisdom." And can a near-rhyme be more cacophonous than Weinfield's "them-then"? Can we tolerate, for "tu m'es en riant apparue," "suddenly you happened to appear"? Or for "laisse / La cueillaison d'un Rêve au coeur qui l'a cueilli," the feeble "Which . . . dreams we gather . . . / Distill within the heart that gathers them"?

---

4. *Ecrits divers sur Stéphane Mallarmé*, by Paul Valéry (Paris, Gallimard, 1950).

To get a better idea of the Weinfield minefield, let us examine the entire early sonnet "Angoisse" ("Anguish"). It begins

Je ne viens pas ce soir vaincre ton corps, ô bête
En qui vont les péchés d'un peuple, ni creuser
Dans tes cheveux impurs une triste tempête
Sous l'incurable ennui que verse mon baiser.

I come not to ravish your body, O beast,
In whom the transgressions of multitudes flow,
Nor to rouse a sad storm in your tresses unchaste,
By the incurable ennui my kisses bestow.

Note immediately the metrical confusion: the first three verses are in tetrameter; the fourth is a clumsy pentameter. "Tresses" is a dubious poeticism, and "tresses unchaste" the kind of Victorian inversion unacceptable in a modern translation. It is wrong to render the simple French word for boredom, *ennui*, with the same word in English, where it strikes a fancy, affected note. To continue:

Je demande à ton lit le lourd sommeil sans songes
Planant sous les rideaux inconnus du remords,
Et que tu peux goûter après tes noirs mensonges,
Toi qui sur le néant en sais plus que les morts.

I ask but a dull dreamless sleep from your bed,
Swathed beneath curtains oblivious of remorse,
Which you who know more about nothingness than the dead
Can taste when your falsehoods have run their dark course.

Here we are solidly ensconced in pentameter, but "swathed" is hardly the same as *planant*, and "oblivious of remorse" is much weaker than the text's "unknown [*inconnus*] to remorse." Again, it is strategically wrong to put the great climax of the original not at the end of the quatrain, but, anticlimactically, into line three. Besides, "Which you who know more about nothingness than the dead" loses its lapidariness through that "Which," and the verse is further diluted by the unwieldy "nothingness," where both scansion and fidelity would have been better served by "the void."

To save space, I reprint the final tercets as one sestet:

Car le Vice, rongeant ma native noblesse,
M'a comme toi marqué de sa stérilité,
Mais tandis que ton sein de pierre est habité
Par un coeur que la dent d'aucun crime ne blesse,
Je fuis, pâle, défait, hanté par mon linceul,
Ayant peur de mourir lorsque je couche seul.

For Vice, having gnawed at my innate nobility,
Has marked me like you with a sad sterility:
But while you with your stony breast are the frame
For a heart that the tooth of no crime wounds with shame,
Obsessed by my shroud, I flee, pale, undone,
Afraid of dying when I sleep alone.

Now, alas, we are back to tetrameter again and in lines one and two in the worst kind of singsong thanks to that foul, facile rhyme "nobility-sterility," where the inconsistent dactylic ending, moreover, reinforces the jingling, jarring quality. The breast as a "frame" of the heart is a particularly infelicitous image—something three-dimensional does not frame, it contains—and is there patently and painfully for the rhyme. "Obsessed" is wrong for *hanté* (haunted): it suggests fussy concern rather than unrelieved dread. The last verse would be fine, but the *rime riche* of *linceul-seul* is poorly conveyed by the half-rhyme "undone-alone."

Consider next the famous first and last lines of "Brise marine." "La chair est triste, hélas! et j'ai lu tous les livres" becomes "The flesh is sad, alas, and there's nothing but words!" The second hemistich is a disaster: it does not suggest the profound *Weltschmerz* of the bookish shut-in, but some sort of trivial chitchat or altercation, predicating someone not even alone in his study. And what a loss in music vis-à-vis the original with its alliteration and feminine ending! The last verse, "Mais, ô mon coeur, entends le chant des matelots!" dwindles into "But oh, my heart, listen to the sailors sing!" Here the rich assonance, "entends le chant," is gone, and the sharp masculine ending of "sing" lacks the languorous seduction of the trisyllabic *matelots.*

There are also serious misreadings. Take this from "Toast funèbre": ". . . la mort ancienne est comme pour Gautier / De n'ouvrir pas les yeux sacrés et de se taire." This comes out as "the task of ancient death for Gautier is to close / His sacred eyes and keep his secrets." This utterly misses the point, which is that for Gautier, who, as he said, was "a man for whom the external world exists," not to see and speak was a particularly horrible deprivation.

In the later, more difficult poems failure proliferates. "Surgi de la croupe et du bond / D'une verrerie éphémère / Sans fleurir la veillée amère / Le col ignoré s'interrompt" becomes "Sprung from the crupper and flight / Of an ephemeral vase, / The neck stopped short and forgotten must pause / Without flowering the long, bitter night." First, that ugly and misleading "crupper," which could make you believe it means the leather strap attached to a saddle, whereas, in this sensual description of a vase without a flower in it, *croupe* is, of course, the animal's rump, the globular lower part of the vase. *Bond* is the upward leap of the narrow neck of the vase, which does not fly or flee (take flight) but strains upward in vain. "Ephemeral vase," besides naming the thing, which Mallarmé deliberately avoids, has none of the onomatopoeic charm of "verrerie éphémère," the high vowels sounding like tingling crystal. The translation's third line forsakes the trimeter of the first two and crawls into a soggily shapeless pentameter. Again, by reversing the order of the last two verses, the climactic effect of the original's fourth is frittered away; besides, the neck of the vase doesn't pause, it is conclusively interrupted: the yearning for a flower is foiled by the absence of one. And the poet speaks of a bitter vigil of two lovers, not of some abstract, generalized bitter night. Moreover, to complete the confusion, after trimeter and pentameter, verse four is in tetrameter.

Or take the violence done to the next sonnet, "Une dentelle s'abolit." Let me point out one glaring absurdity. In order to get his pitiful rhymes in, Weinfield commits the following visual and rhythmic aberrations:

> Lace sweeps itself aside
> In the doubt of the ultimate Game
> Only to expose profane-
> ly
>   eternal absence of bed.
>
> This white and undivid-

ed
   garland's struggle with the same
Blown against the ghostly pane
Floats more than it would hide.

I leave it up to you to find the many other flaws of this octet, but I must call attention, in the sestet, to how the lovely "Au creux néant musicien" becomes "The hollow core's" (Mallarmé would never write, in English, "core's" for "core is"!), which is meant to rhyme with "Filial, might have been born." Aside from being no rhyme, this is a dimeter line supposed to balance a tetrameter one, making mincemeat of Mallarmé's comely, regular octosyllabics.

Why go on? In the Introduction, Weinfield says that "the poems have come to exist for me simultaneously in English and in French," which he claims "should be taken neither as immodesty nor as a sign of incipient madness." But what else can it be taken as? Well, maybe abject benightedness.

The commentaries on the poems, however, are quite decent and helpful. Weinfield has clearly boned up on the available exegeses, which he often quotes or makes other use of, while also contributing explications of his own. The purchaser of this book, then, would be well advised to rip it in two, throw away the first half, and keep the second. To replace what he disposed of, he might acquire the *Mallarmé* in the Penguin Poets series, edited with nice bottom-of-page prose translations by Anthony Hartley, worthier than Weinfield's versions, though they, too, come a cropper with "crupper."

Lest it be thought that I have some special animus against Mr. Weinfield, let me adduce the disappointing aspect of Gordon Millan's enterprise as well. It is inconceivable to me how a Glaswegian university professor can write such poor English. To give only a modest sampling of the simpler errors, let me note "enormity," for "enormousness," "infer," for "imply," "verbally" for "orally," "reported back" for "reported," "comprised of" for "consisted of," "intriguing" for "fascinating," and "mutual friend" for "common friend." But at least Millan has written an otherwise readable book.

Amazingly, neither Millan nor Weinfield catches the essence of Mallarmé nearly so well with many words as others have managed with a few. Herewith a little anthology.

Paul Valéry: "Ordinary literature seemed to me comparable to an arithmetic, that is to say to the search for specific results, where one cannot properly distinguish between precept and example; that which [Mallarmé] conceived seemed to me analogous to an algebra, for it presupposed the will to display, to conserve through thoughts, and to develop for their own sake the forms of language." And again: "Consequently, syntax, which is calculation, resumed the rank of a muse."

Jean-Paul Sartre: "[Mallarmé] chooses the terrorism of politeness; with things, with men, with himself, he always maintains an imperceptible distance. It is this distance that he first wishes to express in his verse."

Maurice Blanchot: "[Mallarmé's] is perhaps the last vestige of a language that effaces itself, the very movement of vanishing, but it appears even more as the material emblem of a silence that, to allow itself to be represented, must make itself into a thing, and so remains the scandal of language, its insurmountable paradox." And again: "A pure intellectual act, capable of creating everything by expressing almost nothing."

Francis Ponge: "[Mallarmé] has an exalted idea of the power of the poet. He betrays noise by noise. . . . A poet not to express silence. A poet to cover the other encroaching voices of chance."

Albert Thibaudet: "Anacoluthon and syllepsis are, for Mallarmé, not rhetorical figures, but the very condition of language; not the ruptures of an order, but the form of a freedom." And again: "Poetry, for Mallarmé . . . constitutes itself against two adversaries; it has, Nietzsche would say, two impossibilities: the one Parnassian, that is to say description; the other Romantic, that is to say oratorical inflation."

Pierre Beausire: "What is probably most original and most surprising in his work is this coexistence of mystery and lucidity, this strangeness joined to rigor, this precise and calculating will connected to chance itself."

Robert Graves: "Mallarmé . . . turned the act of suggestion in poetry into a science. He found the tradition of French poetry so exhausted by sterile laws of prosody that he had to practise poetry as a science to avoid malpractising it as an art."

And this from Stefan George, one of Mallarmé's followers, and himself a major poet (incidentally the only one whose verse translations of Mallarmé really work): "For this reason, O poet, do your comrades and disciples so gladly call you master: that you can least be imitated and yet had such power over them; that all strove for the highest perfection of meaning and euphony in order to pass muster in your eyes—because you still preserve a secret from them and allow us the belief in that beautiful Eden that alone is eternal."

As for me, I consider Mallarmé the supreme modern poet because he achieved a transcendence of his own subjectivity into something deceptively close to an objective absolute; because his poetry was the first—and best—to be self-referential in a way permitting us to participate in the creation of the poem; and because of his willingness to accept pure sound—music—*if artfully deployed,* as a surrogate meaning. Mallarmé stood for—or even initiated—all of these. Without him, there would be no modern poetry as we have it today.

1995

Rimbaud, the Anarchic Demiurge

ARTHUR RIMBAUD was the begetter of modern poetry. For it to come to pass, a Rimbaud was required. It did not have to be A. Rimbaud; it could have been a Rimbaud of some other name, in some other place. But in the event, it was this Jean Nicolas Arthur Rimbaud, born in Charleville in the Ardennes on October 20, 1854, and dead on November 10, 1891—in pain and wretchedness, with one leg and all his hopes amputated—that is the fountainhead of modern poetry as we know it. (But we must not forget Stéphane Mallarmé, about whom I wrote elsewhere.) And he did it all before he fully grew up, after which he rejected literature, his own and everyone else's, forever.

Between the ages of sixteen and somewhere between twenty and twenty-five, Rimbaud conducted all the experiments, made all the discoveries, raised all the questions modern poetry needed to accost. We are still stumbling along in his deep footprints in this year of 1991, when you cannot walk a few blocks in New York City without seeing the name of Mozart, another *Wunderkind* and anniversary boy, plastered all over: Mozart this and Mozart that. But where is Rimbaud in evidence—in books or bookstore windows, magazines or newspapers, lecture halls or cabarets—where?

In France, as might be expected, the situation is somewhat better. Thus the April 4–10 issue of *Le Nouvel Observateur* was a special

Rimbaud number, containing several informative articles, critiques, inquiries, and even a quiz and a news story from Japan, where Rimbaud was helping advertise Suntory whiskey. One of the most useful pieces was the last one, a selection of quotations from nine distinguished and concerned writers looking back at Rimbaud—or, in the case of Mallarmé, across, for the two were contemporaries. The quotations are suggestive, although short and, in most cases, undated, which makes it harder to assess their literary-historical significance. I shall, however, use them as points of departure and reference in a further survey of Rimbaud's achievement and influence, both from my own and other observers' vantage points.

The best way to start, however, is with another item in the *Observateur*, a mini-interview given by Michel Butor, "le maître du nouveau roman." Butor tells how, already as a *lycéen*, he was inspired by Rimbaud first to write "spontaneous poetry," later also "constructed texts." "My verbal alchemy [*alchimie du verbe*, Rimbaud's famous phrase]," Butor says, "stems from the *Illuminations*. Thanks to it, I wrote what I would never have dared to write before."

Rimbaud has, indeed, been an influence not only on subsequent poets, but also—and this is extremely rare, perhaps unique—on prose writers. His contribution was to go from formal verse, often in alexandrines, to newer and looser forms of rhymed verse, thence to *vers libre*, which was an innovation even though, in America, Walt Whitman had published *Leaves of Grass*, his version of free verse, as early as 1855. But though samples of this had been published in French by the 1870s, Whitman did not make himself felt as an influence in France till after Rimbaud. Finally, Rimbaud moved on to his most important achievement, the poems in prose of *Les Illuminations*, putting the prose poem as an art form indelibly on the map.

To be sure, the prose poem as a conscious poetic genre had existed since Baudelaire's *Le Spleen de Paris*, published posthumously in 1869; as an unconscious manifestation, it dates back to the works of Louis (Aloysius) Bertrand and Maurice de Guérin, from *circa* 1830 and 1835, respectively. But what Rimbaud produced, most likely between 1873 and 1875, was something very idiosyncratic and different even from Baudelaire's well-behaved little poetic anecdotes and sketches in their only slightly heightened prose. For—need I remind you?—Rimbaud set out to realize a bold literary and existential program that he formulated in two famous letters of May 1871—at age sixteen! According to it, the poet has to turn himself into a *voyant* (seer) by "a long, immense, and systematic *dérèglement* [derailing, disarray] of all the senses," whereby, at enormous personal cost, he becomes "the great invalid [*malade*], the great criminal, the great damned soul [*maudit*]—and the supreme Scientist."

Why scientist? Because, delving into the unknown, the poet brings back what he has seen there, formed or unformed, as he found it. The goal would be nothing less than a universal language of soul to soul. The program included the liberation of women, too, into poet-seers; and poetry would no longer merely translate action into rhythms: it would *be out ahead* (italics Rimbaud's). While awaiting this, we should demand from the poet the *new* in ideas and forms, but not the way the Romantics understood this. As Rimbaud said in *Une Saison en enfer,* "One must be absolutely modern."

The last and most mature works of Rimbaud's, then, are the prose poems of *Les Illuminations,* a title that did not mean for him mystical illuminations (he had gotten over that stage), but, as in English (he was in England then), medieval illuminated initials, or simply colored plates. Just how did Rimbaud work this, his last and best *alchimie du verbe,* to use the term he coined in his autobiographical and transitional work, *Une Saison en enfer?* The easiest way to convey it is by transcribing one of the shortest and loveliest poems from the *Illuminations,* "Départ" (Departure).

Assez vu. La vision s'est recontrée à tous les airs.
Assez eu. Rumeurs des villes, le soir, et au soleil, et toujours.
Assez connu. Les arrêts de la vie.—O Rumeurs et Visions!
Départ dans l'affection et le bruit neufs.

I translate:

Seen enough. The vision met itself in all airs.
Had enough. Rustle of cities, in the evening, in the sunlight,
    and always.
Known enough. The stoppages [decrees?] of life.—O Rustlings
    and Visions!
Departure amid new affection and noise.

This, by the way, is one of the tamer and easier pieces of the collection. Its *versets* (as the French call lines that are longer than single verses normally are, but shorter than prose paragraphs) are brief enough for *vers libre* rather than prose poetry. But we can see here clearly some of the Rimbaldian strategies and innovations. First, a very stripped-down language, a sort of telegraphese. (The opposite—baroque—can also be found in Rimbaud.) Second, a prevailing ambiguity because words in a vague, even cryptic, context do not have single indisputable meanings. Thus the *airs* of line one can mean (1) weather, breeze, atmosphere; (2) tune, melody; (3) facial expression, demeanor. In this particular instance (1) seems likeliest, but even here one cannot be sure; besides, Rimbaud may have wanted to play on two, or all three, meanings. In line three, *arrêts* is a word with four principal meanings: (1) stops, stoppages; (2) decrees, judgments; (3) seizures, impoundings; (4) arrests. Given the rather nebulous context, any one may be right, though, again, (1) seems likeliest.[1]

Clearly, this is a poem that creates more mood and music than meaning. Still, as an example of the things people project onto Rimbaud, consider Robert Greer Cohn in his *The Poetry of Rimbaud* (Princeton, 1973): "The title has the transparent sound of *ar*, echoed in the 'airs.' . . . It is like the airy space over railroad tracks as one is about to go away," etc., all of which is pure hogwash. Wallace Fowlie (*Rimbaud's Illuminations*, London, 1953) thinks that the poem is "the announcement of the new mystical experience, the 'affection' . . . that of pure being, and the 'noise' . . . the wings of the new power of movement." Unsupported and arbitrary daydreaming. Far more sensible is the view of H. de Bouillane de Lacoste (*Rimbaud et le problème des Illuminations*, Paris, 1949) that the poem "in its laconism, announces a change of existence on which the poet congratulates himself." The late scholar Suzanne Bernard merely observes that the poem seems to mark Rimbaud's trip to London; this time, let me add, not with the tiresome old lover Verlaine, but with a new

---

1. Benjamin Britten has beautifully set eight of Rimbaud's poems in his *Illuminations*, Opus 18. I have compared the translations of "Les arrêts de la vie" in the booklets of my four CD versions of the work. Two have "Life's decrees," one "Life's constraints," one "Life's sentences." Wallace Fowlie, in his translation of the *Illuminations*, offers "Life's haltings."

friend—perhaps platonic, perhaps not—the painter-poet Germain Nouveau.

But for all the "reality" in the poem, there is also a great deal of deliberate obscurity. What is this vision that has met up with itself in all airs? And just what would make an inveterate city dweller say he has had enough of the murmur of cities? Why, in fact, is sound described as a possession? Although the poem seems deceptively simple, Suzanne Bernard is quite right to insist (in her splendid doctoral thesis, *Le Poème en prose de Baudelaire jusqu'à nos jours*, Paris, 1959) that this poem, for all its relative coherence and conformity, is still much closer to the rest of the collection than to academic poetry: "The concentration, the terse formulations of 'Départ,' its sudden cessation with two accented monosyllables [most unusual in French], all this displays Rimbaud's trademark—and what stylist would dare write 'Assez eu,' would dare bracket 'l'affection et le bruit neufs'?"

In the same year (1959) that Mme Bernard submitted her thesis to the Sorbonne, I handed in my much more modest one to Harvard's Department of Comparative Literature. Mine, *The Prose Poem as Genre in Nineteenth-Century European Literature*, was a mere 721 typewritten pages, and was not published until 1987, by Garland Publishing, in facsimile. Mme Bernard's 797 Royal Octavo pages in ten-point Long Primer (not to mention the proliferating footnotes in seven-point Minion) were published immediately and deservedly. About "Départ," she doesn't have much to say, yet this piece, to return to the *Observateur*, is clearly what inspired Butor. In the *Illuminations*, he explains, "it is not the end that repeats, but the beginning: rhyme is reversed. . . . This repetition, combined with a perfect typographical alignment, produces a strong visual impression. Sentences are thus concatenated, like variations. Like Schoenberg. . . . In *Passing Time*, to frame the text and facilitate its reading, I introduced a system of *versets*. I divided every sentence into several paragraphs that begin the same way, like Rimbaud. . . . One can even say that *Mobile* was one single giant sentence. . . . The composition of *Mobile*, then, is inspired by the prosody of *Illuminations*."

But about that initial rhyme: it does not occur anywhere in the forty-odd pieces of the *Illuminations* except in "Départ." Even anaphora, the repetition of an opening word or words, is rare, occurring only in three or four other poems here. Yet this device so impressed Butor that he perceived it as a major component of Rimbaud's style. But, then, such is Rimbaud's spell that even his less frequent strategies can deeply affect a sensitive reader. Certainly those -*u* rhymes are striking; I'd like to think that they inspired Mallarmé's "A la nue accablante tu." And, as Mme Bernard notes, "Assez eu" is very much out of the ordinary.

Most immediately striking about "Départ," though, is that it contains no imagery. There is no simile, no personification, no metaphor even, unless "La vision s'est rencontrée à tous les airs" is one. But it must be grasped that *vision* can mean "my faculty of sight" or sight in some general sense, involving all the people of the city or, just as readily, some manner of hallucination (but what, exactly?), or it can be Rimbaud's visionary capacity as such. It is safest to paraphrase the opening sentence as "I have had enough of seeing: there has been so much of it that the air has become stale from all my looking, that my own eyes are looking back at me from every point." This would constitute hyperbole; but is it really what Rimbaud meant? There is not enough context to corroborate or negate it.

Next, could "rumeurs de la ville" have a relatively positive value, as in the English "babbling" of both brooks and people content at their outdoor *badinage*, the latter being the metropolitan equivalent of country sounds: in the evening, at sidewalk tables; in the sunshine, as the citizenry rattles about; and then that casual afterthought, "et toujours," and always, anytime. (But certainly not Fowlie's poeticizing "forever," which, in any case, would presuppose "à jamais" in the original.) This could then lead into "les arrêts de la vie"—the dawdlings of life, the evenings of getting drunk, the noons when one is sacked out. And then the capitalized "O Rumeurs et Visions!"—perhaps glimpses of a new life elsewhere with a deeper meaning.

And the new affection and sounds? Well, yes, it could be Germain Nouveau, a new companion with whom Rimbaud was uncomplicatedly comfortable, rather than sadomasochistically embroiled, as with Verlaine. Thus far in the poem sounds were *rumeurs*; now they are *bruits*, something more assertive and virile—a more masculine relationship perhaps. And affection of any kind might well be a new thing for Arthur, whose strongest emotion hitherto had been his hatred for his strict, miserly, fanatically pious mother, a hypocrite and worldly-success-craving peasant, Rimbaud's curse and—muse. For without the need to escape Vitalie Cuif Rimbaud, as his father did when Arthur was still a small child, and without the equally compelling urge to flee the oppressively bourgeois atmosphere of Charleville, Rimbaud might still conceivably have become a poet, but not *this* poet.

Now to an early voice in the *Observateur*'s collage. In 1912, writing the introduction to an edition of Rimbaud's poems, Paul Claudel, who was converted to Christianity by his reading of Rimbaud, calls him "Un mystique à l'état sauvage," a mystic in the savage (primitive) state. For most of the Catholic literati—Claudel, Mauriac, Rivière, Daniel-Rops—Rimbaud's deathbed conversion to Christianity was a fact, on the authority of Isabelle, who nursed her big brother Arthur through his final phase. But Isabelle was, like her mother, a peasant, as Rimbaud, though he once called himself so, was not. And Isabelle, pious like her mother, was desperate to whitewash Arthur in the eyes of God and the world.

Yet hardly any serious scholar now believes in that conversion. In his agony, with one leg amputated, the cancer spreading through his body, the pain intense, the mind unclear, Rimbaud muttered all sorts of things. As Pierre Petitfils explains in his authoritative *Rimbaud*, hydrarthosis was aggravated by remnants of syphilis, and rheumatism degenerated into synovitis, then into sarcoma and, in due time, carcinoma: "It is probable that by the time he left Harar, Rimbaud was already beyond cure: the disease met no resistance in that undernourished, overworked, exhausted organism." But Arthur never received extreme unction because, as Alain Borer reminds us in his *Observateur* essay, he kept spitting at and accusing the hospital orderlies and even the nuns of choice abominations.

In any case, as Borer points out, Rimbaud's life and work radically defied any religion preaching salvation and an afterlife. Yet even the Muslims have made a bid for Rimbaud's soul because, dying, he muttered some Mohammedan formulas. And it is also true that during his years as a trader in Africa, he adopted some Muslim ways—names, clothes, manners (such as squatting to urinate)— which were the means to prosperity, indeed mere survival, in those parts. Instead of "mystique à l'état sauvage" Claudel should have said "mystique *de* l'état sauvage," the mystic of the savage state, the fellow whose passion for naïve and wild ways elevates them into a kind of mystique. The boy who wrote "Merde à Dieu" on the walls and benches of Charleville lost all interest in God when he became a gunrunner in Abyssinia, and indifference is a more potent weapon than hatred.

The Surrealist Tristan Tzara summed it up neatly: "Rimbaud is childhood expressing itself by means of violating [*transgresser*] its condition."[2] That *transgresser* is a superb choice: transgress with a hint of transcend about it. And Tzara elaborates: "He has seen, through the oblivion of each one of us, the possibilities of infringing the laws of gravity of thought, spoiled by the hardening of age . . . and that only violence can give meaning to freedom." Such mysticism has no truck with God. One of the *Observateur*'s nine sages, André Suarès, in a long-unpublished but immediate reply to Claudel & Co. (the date in the magazine, 1955, is that of posthumous publication; Suarès died in 1948), wrote: "When they dare to show us God cutting off Rimbaud's leg in order to teach him how to walk straight, and to forsake the paths of paganism to enter those of the Church, they are not only caricaturing God, they are also depicting a Rimbaud who was a stranger to Rimbaud." Which might give yet another meaning to Rimbaud's most celebrated utterance, "Je est un autre" (I is another). It is revelatory that Michel Drouin (again in the *Observateur*) quotes a 1966 article by René Etiemble stating that if Suarès had published his views back then in 1912, "I would not have had to write *Le Mythe de Rimbaud*, I would not have had to spend thirty years of my life fighting against these lies."

But Etiemble's work—comprising most significantly the two-volume *Mythe de Rimbaud* (1952 to 1970, counting various importantly revised editions); *Nouveaux Aspects du mythe de Rimbaud dans le monde communiste* (1964); the book devoted to the famous "Sonnet of the Vowels," *Le Sonnet des voyelles* (1968); and the critical study *Rimbaud*, co-written with Etiemble's wife, Yassu Gauclère (1936, but

---

2. From the introduction to the 1948 Lausanne edition of Rimbaud's works. Cf. Bernard's "the art of Rimbaud consists . . . in knowing how to preserve his childlike sense of wonder from the sterilizing intellectual work of the adult, who, with his 'notions,' kills the fairy world."

reissued with radical revisions in 1950 and 1966)—is not a mere demolition of the Christian myth. Rather, it is an attack on all Rimbaud myths. That is why Petitfils's dismissal of Etiemble, ". . . the 'Rimbaud myth' in which nobody ever believed but which a distinguished professor at the Sorbonne saw fit to demolish with the sledgehammer of 3000 printed pages," is not fair. But there is something to it. In his determination to make a kind of rationalist—or, at least, not an irrationalist—out of Rimbaud and deny him any sort of, even lay, metaphysics, Etiemble went too far. He and Gauclère speak, for example, of "the influence of choice, of intelligence, of rhetoric at the service of the passions." And, to give only one typical instance, they explain much of the *Illuminations* as recollections of the theater, "by which we gain access to the imaginary. . . . [T]he multiplicity of possible décor opens up innumerable perspectives." So if Rimbaud speaks in "Enfance III" of "a lake that rises" (*un lac qui monte*), he is thinking of a stage backdrop, where perspective is achieved by making a painted lake seem to go upward.

True, but Etiemble and Gauclère disregard that *explication de texte* (which I, too, devoutly espouse) proceeds in the opposite direction from poetic creation, and that explaining is not the same as explaining away. In other words, textual explication retraces the poet's steps back to the mundane beginnings of the poem, the preoyster grain of sand. But creation proceeds inversely toward the fabulous, the finished, the pearl. It is helpful to show whence the miracle of the poem came, but that does not do away with the undefinable, inexplicable miraculousness of it.

Which brings me to the first item in the *Observateur*'s chrestomathy: "The *Correspondence* starting with Cyprus [the first place where, having chucked poetry, Rimbaud made a sustained effort at a career in business] appears in general, to lovers of good literature, badly written, disappointing, unworthy of so great a writer. . . . We find that this style without elegance, niggardly, flat, has the same extraordinary dryness as the other, but on the plane of banality, from which one does not see why he should have deviated in writing, since such, henceforward, was his mode of life." This is from *La Part du feu* (Paris, 1949), by the important critic and novelist Maurice Blanchot. But though the statement is useful in reminding us that the so-called hallucinatory style of Rimbaud's poetry is

also purposeful, polished (rather than automatic writing), "dry"—
and that, in a sense, there is no break between the poet Rimbaud and
the merchant Rimbaud—there is something misleading here. For
Blanchot, in that same *Part du feu*, also writes, "He has pushed to the
farthest extreme ambiguity, which is the essential movement of po-
etic activity." And earlier, in *Faux Pas* (Paris, 1943), Blanchot called
Rimbaud "he who, *par excellence*, is the poet whose poetry welcomes
the ineffable [*inexprimable*], who gave language the assurance of not
being limited to language. . . ." If that is dryness at all, it is surely
dryness of a very special kind.

And that leads us to another of the nine quoted views, this one
from the poet René Char, in a prose poem first published in 1947
and reprinted in *Fureur et mystère* (1948): "You did well to leave,
Arthur Rimbaud! Your eighteen years antagonistic [*réfractaires*] to
friendship, to the malevolence, to the silliness of Parisian poets, as
also to the murmurings, worthy of sterile bees, of your slightly de-
mented Ardennes family, you did well to scatter them to the four
winds, to throw them under the blade of their precocious guillotine.
You were right to abandon the boulevard of the lazybones, the tav-
erns of the poetry-pissers [*pisse-lyres*], for the hell of the stupid
[*bêtes*], the commerce of the cunning, and the greetings [*bonjour*] of
the simple." But a second quotation from Char offers only the con-
firmation that Rimbaud made a complete break with the past. It
might have been better to quote the ending of that poem from
Fureur et mystère: "You did well to leave, Arthur Rimbaud! There are
some of us who believe without proof that happiness is possible with
you." Or perhaps "who believe with you that happiness is possible."

However that conclusion is to be read, Char is here on the verge
of a major insight: that the same pursuit of happiness made of
Rimbaud in turn a poet and a gunrunner. Thus Tzara perceived in
Rimbaud's poetry "a fevered desire to fill in *une absence*"—a lack, ab-
sence, void, or deprivation. The consistency that Blanchot detected
in Rimbaud's style Char and Tzara find also in his break with the
past. I submit, however, that the consistency, which many who mar-
veled at Rimbaud's self-contradiction failed to catch at all, is of a
rather different nature from what even its perceivers perceived.

Rimbaud, the child genius whose self-expression, freedom, ac-
complishments were suppressed by his antipathetic mother and mi-

lieu, was—always was—in search of power. Power was his true objective—a hunger, a lust for power. Only the method of acquiring that power kept changing. The first tack was that of the poet as seer, as magician or magus, to quote from that famed section of *Une Saison en enfer*, "Alchimie du verbe": "Weeping, I saw gold—but could not drink." The alchemist's pursuit is gold (potable gold in this case), which is wealth and, in turn, power. The alchemist is the supreme magician, the supreme possessor: "I bragged of owning all possible landscapes." He becomes "the god of fire," his life is "a celebration [*fête*]." Power over words, over poetry is a way to conquer the world.

But when that power was denied him, when the small edition of *Une Saison en enfer* that he had printed at his expense was destroyed, partly by himself in disgust and partly by the printer for nonpayment of costs, power had to be sought elsewhere. Still, self-contradictory as he was, and under the brief but apparently steadying influence of Germain Nouveau, Rimbaud tried once more to write poetry, hence *Les Illuminations*. But he gave the manuscripts away and headed for the diametrically opposite method of acquiring wealth and power: commerce. Yet there is a very real sense in which opposites are the same thing—*les extrêmes se touchent*. Thus Rimbaud's preparations for material success were similar to his poetic preparations. He studied foreign languages (for which he had a prodigious talent) to make business dealings easier in much the same way he had studied French and classical tongues for his poetry; he studied scientific books and technical manuals the way he had devoured mystical and historical works; and he traveled in search of job opportunities just as he had journeyed in search of experience, discovery, knowledge.

Movement was essential to Rimbaud. Clinically, this has been diagnosed as dromomania. More lyrically, Verlaine called his lover *l'homme au semelles de vent* (the man with soles of wind), and Mallarmé dubbed him *ce passant considérable* (this passerby of parts). But even movement, the title of one of Rimbaud's *vers libre* poems, is power: no person, no place, no entanglement can hold you so long as you keep moving. Quite rightly, in another *Observateur* piece, "Rimb on the Road," François Cavignoli compares him to real and fictional travelers, Gambetta and Phileas Fogg, and perceives in him

the honcho of the Beat generation, the big brother of William Bur-
roughs, Jack Kerouac, and Neal Cassady. He was, we are told, the
inventor of hitchhiking, of being publicly funded (e.g., enlisting in
the Dutch army to get to Java, then promptly deserting), of taking
on odd jobs to support oneself while bumming around. More im-
portant, he taught the Beats a literary style and some thematics.
Take, for example, this, from Allen Ginsberg's "Howl": ". . . who
sweetened the snatches of a million girls trembling in the sunset,
and were red eyed in the morning but prepared to sweeten the
snatch of the sunrise. . . ." Doesn't this remind you of "Aube"
(Dawn): "I have kissed the summer dawn. . . . One by one, I lifted
her veils. . . . Dawn and the child tumbled to the bottom of the
woods . . ."? And Ginsberg's enumeration—the catalogue as a liter-
ary device—is very much out of Rimbaud ("Devotion" or "Sale," for
example).

But unlike the Beats, Rimbaud did not keep moving merely to be
one jump ahead of failure. Henry Miller, another of the *Observa-
teur*'s pundits, remarks, "Whatever he did, it was always too good.
They seem to have reproached the bohemian for being too bo-
hemian, the poet for being too much a poet, the pioneer for being
too much a pioneer, the businessman for being too much a busi-
nessman, the gunrunner for running guns too well. . . ." I wonder,
though, who were "they"—these carpers who objected to Rimbaud's
excessive skill at everything? Miller's etiology is off, but there is no
doubt that Rimbaud provoked resentment for being dirty and
slovenly, though his poverty had much to do with that; for being ar-
rogant and insulting, though being an underappreciated genius
could sour your disposition; for being brutal and sadistic, though he
had had a pretty rotten childhood.

Rimbaud's sadism does not come out only in his life—his enjoy-
ment of games in which he could plunge a knife in another player's
outstretched hand, or his carving up his lover's thighs to the point
where Verlaine had to make up stories about his limp on the occa-
sion when he met Victor Hugo. It is there also in his poetry, in the
way it mocks, misleads, leaves the reader stranded. Consider the fa-
mous *verset* from "Barbare," "Le pavillon en viande saignante sur la
soie des mers et des fleurs arctiques; (elles n'existent pas)." *Pavillon*
has two meanings: pavilion and flag. Since the line, like the entire

poem, is obscure, either interpretation makes as much, or as little, sense as the other. Both readings have had their champions. Still, I propose: "The flag made of bloody meat on the silk of the seas and the arctic flowers; (they don't exist)." But there are further ambiguities here. Are both the seas and the arctic flowers silken, or only the seas? Are only the flowers nonexistent, or do neither the flowers nor the seas exist? The line tortures the reader, especially with that palinode that does not make clear just how much it retracts. Yet what a challenge to try to make some sense of it, even if, as Suzanne Bernard warns, in Rimbaud criticism everything is only hypothesis.

Nothing that Rimbaud wrote or did was as much resented as his irruption on the Verlaine household, taking Paul away from his young wife and baby, and flaunting his relationship with the older poet as the two wandered, drank, and fought all over western Europe. This brings us to the much disputed question of Rimbaud's homosexuality, which some commentators revel in, others reject, and still others embrace with major reservations. It is a matter relevant both to his poetry and to his posthumous influence.

The rejecters don't have much of a case; there are too many texts by both Rimbaud and Verlaine that spell things out. Most outspoken is Verlaine's sonnet ending with "Vers toi je rampe encore indigne. / —Monte sur mes reins et trépigne!" (I crawl toward you still unworthy. / —Mount on my loins [back] and prance!) As Petitfils ironically comments, "M. André Fontenas has some difficulty persuading one that this sonnet describes a stained glass window in which the Archangel Michael is—temporarily—brought to the ground by the devil." This is the same Verlaine who wrote to Rimbaud imploringly from London: "Je suis ton *old cunt, open* ou *opened,* je n'ai pas mes verbes irréguliers."

The tendency nowadays is to assert that, whereas Verlaine, however clandestinely, was a true homosexual, Rimbaud threw himself deliberately, programmatically into homosexuality by way of practicing the seer's disorder of the senses. Whether this is so, or whether (as I and many others believe) he was truly homosexual—and in Africa either heterosexual or bisexual—doesn't much matter. The nineteenth century was no more ready to forgive reckless displays of homosexuality in Rimbaud's France than, a bit later on, in Wilde's England. It is shocking to read that a man and writer as enlightened as Anatole France voted against admitting a submission from Verlaine to the new *Parnasse contemporain* of 1875: "the author is unworthy," France declared.

On Rimbaud's homosexuality, the *Observateur* quotes the prominent contemporary French poet Yves Bonnefoy, specifically his monograph *Rimbaud par lui-même* (Paris, 1961; English translation, by Paul Schmidt, New York, 1972): "It is certain that his homosexuality was deep-seated, and although it is also true that he did not consider it a moral flaw, he nevertheless described it, not without distress, as the fiasco [*catastrophe*] of the other [i.e., heterosexual] love. . . . Homosexuality remains, in his view, a negative passion, a deprivation, a defeat." (My translation, slightly different from Schmidt's.) If Bonnefoy is right, we have yet another factor that skewed Rimbaud's vision—felicitously—even as the need to escape his background did: the sense of dissatisfaction with the self, and so the urge to flee from the enemy within as well as from the one without. To the need for power is added the need for flight, the two combining into some of Rimbaud's richest poetry.

One escapes from oneself *into* poetry and hopes it will make one famous, rich, and powerful; when this fails to happen, one escapes *from* poetry—into commerce or science—with the same expectations. Or, as Bonnefoy puts it elsewhere in his book (known simply as *Rimbaud* in English): "Rimbaud stopped writing when the end of childhood, more compelling than any intellectual decision, deprived him of the hope that he could *change life*." (Translation Schmidt's, italics Bonnefoy's.)

No, he couldn't change life, but he could and did change poetry. The Surrealists recognized him as their precursor, mentor, and presiding divinity until André Breton, their pope, reversed himself in that famous encyclical, the Second Surrealist Manifesto, in a passage included among the *Observateur*'s critical texts: "Rimbaud erred, Rimbaud tried to trick us. He is guilty in our eyes of having allowed, of not having rendered wholly impossible, certain tarnishing [*déshonorantes*] interpretations of his thought, of the Claudel variety." This is misleading. For a long time, Breton revered Rimbaud. It is possible, though, that just as the poet's annexation by a rival church infuriated Breton, Arthur's manifest homosexuality also displeased the very heterosexual Surrealist. Ironically, the pope's new god, Lautréamont, may well have been even more homosexual. But he was discreet about it: the celebrated passage about pederasts in *Maldoror* is grotesque and elegiac by turns, and not at all realistic like certain passages in *Une Saison en enfer* and *Les Illuminations.*

It is entirely possible that the radical loosening up of French poetry by Rimbaud—like the analogous process initiated in America by Whitman—has much to do with the poet's sexual orientation. If one studies "Délires I" in *Saison* and "Vagabonds" from the *Illuminations* carefully, one can see the connection between the "drôle de ménage" Rimbaud-Verlaine and the kind of poetry that emerged from it. It didn't have to, of course; Verlaine's was never radical. But it could—did—from Rimbaud's particular genius. Consider this from "Vagabonds," about Rimbaud's escaping from one of Verlaine's late-night recriminations to the window, where "Je créais, par delà la campagne traversée par des bandes de musique rare, les fantômes du futur luxe nocturne." (I created, beyond the countryside streaked with scrolls of rare music, the phantasms of a future nocturnal splendor.) This, the poem continues, constitutes a "distraction vaguement hygiénique." Unless one interprets the passage as a mere scene of masturbation, one can view it as an escape from sexual problems into a hygienic activity, a relaxation and release—the creation of the poetry of future splendor, of *vers libre* and the prose poem, of the freedom of unfettered self-expression and damn all conventions, social, sexual, or poetic.

Sure enough, Rimbaud was to be, in times to come, often taken up by poets precisely because of his homosexuality (just as Whitman was)—most obviously by the Beats. A number of scholars and critics, too, have been drawn to him for that reason, most conspicuously those who carry on about his supposed "angelism." Some angel, Arthur Rimbaud!

Yet Rimbaud cannot reasonably be blamed for what others, imitators or interpreters, do to him, although even Claudel, as he wrote Gide, was to be revolted by the detritus littering Rimbaud's heritage—"like a beautiful, artistic place," Claudel complained, "where one finds empty sardine cans." But, as I have said on many an occasion, Claudel was just as guilty of leaving not a few empty holy-water bottles lying about. Nevertheless, the work of sundry commentators is not unhelpful, especially if one admits with Blanchot—and my thesis—that, on top of the obscurity, there is much deliberate ambiguity in Rimbaud. This was also recognized by Gide in the *Feuillets d'automne*, where he endorses not only divergent but also downright contradictory interpretations. Etiemble promptly takes issue with this, there being among the French a great need to *believe* in rationality, Cartesian clarity, unequivocalness even in their poets, even if such a belief in Rimbaud's case requires Olympian mental gymnastics. Thus Yves Bonnefoy, years ago, after sympathetically exploring my then views on Rimbaud, disagreed, claiming that ambiguity was something very un-French, and had not entered French poetry until Valéry, who got it from foreign sources. More recently, during a very brief chat with Bonnefoy, he seemed to indicate that he had somewhat modified his position, though we did not get a chance to pursue the matter.

What further clouds the Rimbaud inheritance is that it has often been betrayed by translators, and not only where it is impossible to know just what Rimbaud meant, but also in the instances where his meaning ought to be unmistakable. Thus the poem "Dévotion," which catalogues various kinds of devotion and dedication, ends with "A tout prix et avec tous les airs, même dans des voyages métaphysiques.—Mais plus *alors*." (At all costs, and with all airs [?], even on metaphysical journeys.—But no longer *then*.) Clearly, these devotions must be pursued to their metaphysical consummations. But then there can be an end to it. Yet Wallace Fowlie translates, "But no more *thens*," for which the French would have to be "mais plus d'*alors*." And Louise Varèse has "but even more *then*," which would require "mais encore plus *alors*" in the text. There is, to be sure, something obfuscatory about this curious ending with its odd italicization of one word; no wonder the worthy Bouillane de Lacoste exclaimed that it "smells of mystification a mile off." Still, that is no excuse for mistranslations, which unfortunately abound in renderings of Rimbaud. Etiemble adduces veritable Tartar hordes of them, often on the order of "jalousie pour les mendiants" (envy of beggars) Englished as "venetian blinds behind which beggars are hiding."

Let us consider one more, short but typical, piece from the *Illuminations*, "Antique," which can mean antique or antiquity:

Gracieux fils de Pan! Autour de ton front couronné de fleurettes et de baies tes yeux, des boules précieuses, remuent. Tachées de lie brune, tes joues se creusent. Tes crocs luisent. Ta poitrine ressemble à une cithare, des tintements circulent dans tes bras blonds. Ton coeur bat dans ce ventre où dort le double sexe. Promène-toi, la nuit, en mouvant doucement cette cuisse, cette seconde cuisse et cette jambe de gauche.[3]

The assumption is that Rimbaud is describing the statue of a satyr seen in a museum, and that he mistakenly supposed that, what with their goat's feet, satyrs were descended from Pan. The revolving eyes seem to prefigure modern sculpture (Pol Bury), but are presumably self-induced hallucinations. "Spotted with brown dregs" suggests, perhaps, a painting rather than a sculpture; but "joues se creusent" may well be an echo effect, a rhyme on "boules précieuses." Fauns do not have fangs, but Rimbaud's savage imagination creates them, with the sound of "lie brune" and "creusent" leading into "crocs" and "luisent." I doubt if a satyr's chest would look like a zither, but Rimbaud, excelling in classics, may have been thinking of Mount Cithaeron, where Actaeon was torn to pieces by the fangs (*crocs*) of his own hounds, and Cithaeron then suggested "cithare." The rippling muscles would evoke tinklings; the brown lees, by contrast, blond flesh. The heart (emotion) is to be conjoined with sexuality, hence heart and genitalia meet in the middle ground of the belly. The belly also suggests a drum for the heart to beat on. Is androgyny implied by "double sex"? Or is it that the phallus and the scrotum, sculptured, look like the same organ in duplicate? If Rimbaud is visiting a museum, he may imagine the statue coming to life after dark, when no one is around. Or he may extend to all day the god Pan's famous noontime siesta. The three legs may have to do with Rimbaud's looking (as Pierre Arnoult put forward) at a

---

3. Graceful son of Pan! Around your brow crowned with flowerlets and berries your eyes, precious balls, move. Spotted with brown dregs, your cheeks are hollowed. Your fangs glisten. Your chest resembles a zither, tinklings circulate through your blond arms. Your heart beats in that belly where sleeps the double sex. Walk about at night, by gently moving this thigh, this second thigh, and this left leg.

statue of a centaur. Or could the third limb be the penis? Some legs don't tread the ground, they *trépignent* on someone's backside.

"Antique" is more characteristic of prose poetry than "Départ," with which we began: it is printed as an uninterrupted piece of prose. Taken together, the two represent fairly Rimbaud's technique. "Départ" is disjointed, working by discontinuities or leaps; "Antique" seems to hang together, but conveys a figure, a situation that cannot be fully grasped. Each poem shimmers between lucidity and opacity. As Roger Shattuck observed in his review of two of Fowlie's works on Rimbaud,[4] "In the *Illuminations* a totally hallucinated universe becomes indistinguishable from a literally noted sensuous realism." Rimbaud, Shattuck writes, "welded together popular and poetic language at the precise moment when Mallarmé was carefully taking them apart." So of the two great founders of poetic modernism, it was Rimbaud who more or less prevailed, because his mode is, or seems, easier to imitate. Perhaps the best definition of Rimbaud's procedure can be found in Castex and Surer's manual for nineteenth-century studies: "What Rimbaud sees, he transfigures; what he doesn't, he creates."

This isn't to everybody's taste. The novelist and traveler Victor Ségalen (1878–1919) is quoted as follows by the *Observateur*:

> Many pages in Rimbaud's work remain inert for us. Neither the beauty of the vocables nor the riches of cadence [*nombre*], nor the unforeseen in the thrust [*volte*] of the images, nothing manages to move us, even though everything in this prose shivers with sensitivity. Why this impotence? Because among the diverse conceptions of a sentient being, only the *generalizable* givens move us, those to which our own memories can become analogous, attached. The rest, personal evocations, associations of ideas that the life of the mind has created in one brain and never in others, that, in art, is dead letter. And Rimbaud's writings teem with solipsisms of this kind.

So you can consider our poet fatally inconsistent, or, as the less sympathetic Remy de Gourmont dubbed Rimbaud, "a consistently pustulant toad."

---

4. *The New York Review of Books*, June 1, 1967.

Mallarmé's portrait of Rimbaud in a letter to Harrison Rhodes is moving despite the crabbed, tortuous prose Mallarmé unfortunately insisted on. The *Observateur* quotes fairly liberally from it (though not the references to "the stammerings of the last poems" and Rimbaud's hands "like those of a washerwoman"). Most important is the mention of his "very classic" effect, and of the "sumptuous disorder one could only call spiritually exotic." And the image of the "dazzle of a meteor, lit with no other motive than its presence, emerging solitary and extinguishing itself." But Mallarmé is mistaken in saying that "everything would have existed since without this passer-by of parts," though his "special case lives on forcefully." Of course, Mallarmé could not forgive Rimbaud his "frequentation of the cities' vulgar bazaar of illusions." But the account is largely sympathetic and climaxes in a passage (unquoted) about "a unique adventure in the history of art. That of a child precociously and impetuously brushed by the wing of literature, who, almost before having had time to exist, exhausted a tempestuous and magisterial destiny [*fatalité*] without recourse to a future."

Yet that future, posthumously, was to be his. By 1926, Cocteau noted that, "at present, Rimbaud was more of an encumbrance than Hugo"—*the* influence for a young poet to crawl out from under. And today Gallimard, France's leading publisher, reports Rimbaud as the house's number-two seller—after Marguerite Yourcenar! As Suzanne Bernard concludes her chapter on Rimbaud, "The man with the soles of wind has truly beaten new paths through the dark forests of language, and . . . the entire poetry of the twentieth century follows in his tracks." Almost all the major French poets of the first half of the century—Reverdy, Jacob, Char, Michaux, and Eluard—to mention only the most stellar ones, are his disciples; only the delightfully chameleonlike Apollinaire stands apart, and Valéry, of course, is the one true heir of Mallarmé.

And the influence continues. A typical motif in Rimbaud is the melding of earth and sky, of land and sea. Now here is Yves Bonnefoy (translated by Richard Pevear): "They walk, barefooted / In their absence, / And come to the banks / Of the river earth." Or consider Rimbaud's trick of converting violence into peacefulness by a sudden leap in moods. Here, again, is Bonnefoy: "Summer: / This screech-owl / Nailed to the threshold / By the star's peaceful iron

[*Le fer en paix de l'étoile*]." And in his afterword to Bonnefoy's *Poems 1959–1975*, from which I have been quoting, Jean Starobinski duly invokes Rimbaud.

Philippe Jaccottet, though Swiss-born, has become one of France's preeminent poets. Recall Rimbaud's way of intertwining the world of gods and magicians with that of mortals—his. Here is Jaccottet: "A brief thing, the time of a few footsteps outside, / but stranger yet than the mages and the gods." Rimbaud has "a white ray, dropping from the high heavens, abolishes this comedy." Jaccottet writes: "a light that leaps over words as if wiping them out." Isn't Jaccottet's "And draws from the invisible water / where invisible beasts perhaps drink still" akin to Rimbaud's "silk of the seas and arctic flowers; (they don't exist.)"?

And what about such an older poet of considerable stature as Francis Ponge? In an early poem (1922), "Sunday, or the Artist," he begins: "Brutally, at noon, the clamor of posters, the publicity of advertisers, plants its barbarous hatchet in the body [*masse*] of Paris. / It severs with one blow a hundred great green and red walls. It cleaves streets where nervous rails grind to the quick, it quarters wheel-broken, dismembered crossroads. Hoot, discordant trumpets! Collapse, railroad stations!" This could almost be a parody of Rimbaud; but here now is a passage from a 1943 text included in Ponge's *Proêmes:* "Of course the world is absurd! Of course, the meaninglessness of the world! / But what's tragic about that? / . . . Ontological suicide is the act only of a few young bourgeois (incidentally likable). / Let there be placed against it birth (or resurrection), *metalogical creation* (POETRY)." Here is the Rimbaldian repertoire of mysterious italics, orgies of capitalizations, exclamation points and parentheses galore.

Clearly, I can provide no systematic survey here, only a spot check, a butterfly's view. Take Germany and Austria, where Rimbaud's influence is everywhere. We find it in two of the most prestigious poets of the early twentieth century, Georg Heym and the Austrian Georg Trakl. Both died young and tragically, like Rimbaud. Talking to Heym in a Berlin café in the winter of 1910–1911, Paul Zech, poet and translator of Rimbaud, noted "his extraordinary predilection for Rimbaud, who in those days was hardly known in Germany." Formally, Heym does not resemble Rimbaud, except perhaps the early, rhymed poems, but thematically he is extremely close. Trakl, on the other hand, is close formally, too, as in the beginning of the prose poem "Metamorphosis of Evil."

> Autumn: black pacing along the woods' edge; minute of mute destruction; suddenly listening [*auflauscht*] the brow of the leper under the bare tree. Long-past evening now sinking along the stairway of moss; November. A bell rings and the shepherd leads a troop of black and red horses into the village. Under the hazel bushes, the green huntsman eviscerates some game. His hands steam with blood and the animal's shadow moans in the foliage above the man's eyes, brown and silent; the forest. Crows that scatter; three. Their flight resembles a sonata, full of faded chords and masculine melancholy . . . etc.

Many Rimbaldian touches here! The inconsistent landscape: bare trees and foliage; the strange grammar: *auflauscht die Stirne* (literally: up listens the brow); the summation of paragraph or sentence in a tacked-on word at the end: "November," "the forest," "three." (Cf. Rimbaud's "Métropolitain.") The unstable reference: does "brown and silent" go with the foliage or with the hunter's eyes? (Recall the *verset* from "Barbare," where we couldn't tell where silkiness stopped or how far nonexistence extended.) And these black and red horses *à la* Franz Marc, relatives of "the great blue and black mares" in Rimbaud's "Ornières." Even the crows flying in sonata formation seem not unrelated to the bridges in "Les Ponts" that are "minor chords crisscrossing and taking off."

It is well known that the young Brecht was influenced by Rimbaud, both in his early poems and in his first plays. In *Baal*, the characters of Baal and Eckart are almost certainly modeled on Rimbaud and Verlaine. And in his journal (October, 1921), Brecht notes: "I thumb through the Rimbaud volume and borrow from it. How glowing it all is! Luminous paper! And he has shoulders of brass.— Whenever I work, when the lava flows, I see the West in lurid fires and believe in his vitality." And am I alone in encountering Rimbaud in that most magical of later twentieth-century German-language poets, Paul Celan? Take, for example, this from "Windgerecht" (Windrowed): "Later: / Snow-growth through all the casings, free / one single field, / numbered by a light ray: the voices."

It is no different in Italy, where Rimbaud, again, is much in evidence. A major Italian poet who wandered the earth, went mad, and died young, Dino Campana (1885–1932), was a self-declared Rimbaldian. Consider George Kay's translation of "Ship Under Way": "The mast swings, beat for beat, in the silence. / A faint white and green light falls from the mast. / The sky clear to the horizon, loaded green and gilt after the squall. / The white square of the ship's light on high / Illuminates the night's secret: from the window / The ropes from above in a gold triangle / And a globe white with smoke / Which does not exist like music / Above the circle with the muted beating of the water." Here, again, the something that doesn't exist, the story-book colors, the mighty leaps from the visual to the auditory and back, the sense of mystery without any noticeable straining to be mysterious, the indeterminate references: what doesn't exist, the globe or the smoke?

Already as a boy in Alexandria, Giuseppe Ungaretti was reading Rimbaud; here, in a prose translation by Joseph Cary, is his "The Buried Harbor": "The poet arrives there / and then ventures to the light with his songs / and scatters them / / Of such poetry / remains to me / this nothing / of the inexhaustible secret."[5] As Cary points out, this is really a version of Rimbaud's *lettre du voyant.* But even such a very different poet as Eugenio Montale is not unaffected by Rimbaud. In a 1949 essay, he compliments Mozart, Bellini, and Verdi on setting "a clear and neutral discourse to which they could do violence." He begins another essay, on an old mentor, the poet Camillo Sbarbaro, by quoting him: "Rimbaud was the addiction of my adolescence." Now read a Montale poem such as "Eastbourne," and see if you are not reminded of Rimbaud; isn't, for example, the personalized goodness of *una bontà* rather like the reason of "A une Raison"?

Moving over to Greece—and remembering that Rimbaud, whomever else he castigated, unfailingly upheld classic Greek poetry—what do we find? Here is "Thanks," by Yannis Ritsos, as translated by Edmund Keeley: "You heard your voice saying: *thanks* / (so unexpected, dumb naturalness)—you were certain now: / a large piece of eternity belonged to you." This, again, is the pri-

---

5. The double slash indicates one line's space. The period at the end is mine.

vate incident given over to the poem without mediation, without any care for universality. And, again, the italics, the parentheses, the laconism, even the unorthodox punctuation.

Now over to Hungary, for an actual prose poem (part of a sequence, as often in Rimbaud) by the marvelous János Pilinszky (1921–1981):

> Then at night we went on dreaming the battle, and that was like a stage image, which begins by coming to an end. The guests leave the table, the room empties out. A girl sweeps away the crumbs. Makes order. Night falls.
>
> From here on in everything attacks and everything flees: the inadmissible fates, the inadmissible situations, the inadmissible species of animals. And in the morning, we wakened to war as to order itself, as if with gunfire eternal peace were nearing the world.

True, this is much more coherent than a Rimbaud poem tends to be, but the theatrical trope, the chamois leaps of the imagery, the sudden changes in sentence length, with a two-word sentence summing up a paragraph, the basis in paradox—these are truly Rimbaldian.

An influence, then, that could be traced in all Western literatures. One could find it in Wallace Stevens, a supposed pure Mallarméan, in Geoffrey Hill, in Thom Gunn as in Ted Hughes, Sylvia Plath, and all the Beats and beat-derivatives. "Rimbaud was the last great poet that our civilization will see," declared Hart Crane in 1926; in 1923, Ezra Pound had already pronounced, "The actual writing of poetry has advanced little or not at all since Rimbaud."[6]

Mallarmé may be in the bloodstream of all modern poets, whether they know it or not. He gave the word, beyond its meaning or meanings, over and above its sound, its shape on the page. A word became not a pictogram but a pattern in black on a white background that framed it in different ways with more or less surrounding whiteness, with companionship or isolation. More than that: words assumed the character of precious jewelry fitted into sonorous

6. It may be worth a footnote to mention that the intellectually slumming academic off whose protagonist Sylvester Stallone made his second fortune based his hero's name, Rambo, on Rimbaud.

bracelets, necklaces, belts made up of precious stones in precise yet arcane combinations. Phrases became multivalent, forming strange, recondite, chiseled yet unstable relationships, proffering signification with one hand, withholding it with the other. The high priest was behind each verse, an abstruse smile on his lips, an intoxicating music in his chant. It is the music, in the later poems, of the emperor's nightingale brought to its highest mechanical perfection, inferior to the warblings of the real one only for those who prize folk poetry above all other, who hold Anonymous to be the greatest poet of all.

Rimbaud, too, is in every poet, and more visibly: like the rabbit inside the python, a bulge in the snake's middle. He reaches us sometimes through the mediation of the Surrealists, with their modifications; sometimes undiluted, neat. (I realize that this usage is British, but I can't say "straight," can I?) His words, individually and in conjunction, seem to be chosen carelessly. They appear to be effusions, gushings; they are a moment's recklessness caught in amber, a form that imitates formlessness to perfection. As Jacques Barzun puts it in *An Essay on French Verse*, "The form of these prose pieces ... is itself an invitation to giving up the rational mind. ... [T]he poem mirrors the unreality of what is."

Rimbaud is the poet of a world gone irrational—ours. As the Pole Tadeusz Rozewicz (born 1921) expressed it in a lyric, translated here by Stanislaw Baranczak and Clare Cavanagh: "... Season in Hell / what a glorious age / hell heaven / / The metaphor still living / bloomed within / metaphysics / / letters and words / appeared in miraculous color ... / / Poetry began from that moment / to rave deliriously. ..." Rozewicz goes on to say that the bedeviling colors Rimbaud assigned to vowels are preferable to the post-nuclear-holocaust color scheme: everything simply white, a white desolation. I agree with Suzanne Bernard that Rimbaud was an anarchic demiurge, and would add only that he could exult in disorder because *he* could still feel himself its creator. *We* are its creations.[7]

1991

---

7. Regrettably, this was written before the publication of Graham Robb's *Rimbaud*, which supersedes all previous biographies. My review can be found in *Washington Post Book World* (November 26, 2000). Better yet, seek out the book itself.

A Great, Baggy Monster:
Rilke's "Duino Elegies"

THE LONG POEM, if we rightly exclude the dramatic, comes in three varieties: narrative, including epic; philosophical, including existential; and metaphysical, including religious. And, of course, in any combination of the above. When we, here and now, think "long poem," we usually mean Homer, Virgil, Dante, Milton, maybe Blake, and probably Yeats and Eliot. What is perspicuous is how much most of these depend on plot: how many nonacademics push beyond the *Inferno* or plod on to *Paradise Regained?*

Yet the plot is not a basic constituent of the poetic, except perhaps as a hurdle. Prose can do its job, with some minor losses, much better. Homer resorted to verse as a mnemonic device in a largely preliterate age. Others followed because it was the tradition, and because the novel in prose had not yet caught on. Once it did, it was goodbye, epic poetry. As a nonheroic narrative, the long poem is even more cumbersome: think of those shipwrecked Robinsons, Edwin Arlington and Jeffers, whom no one now thinks of rescuing.

The philosophical poem, too, is easily outdone by prose; even Lucretius reads nicely in a good prose translation, and can you imagine anything worse than Heidegger in verse? The same for metaphysics. The great religious or quasi-religious poems—think Donne, Herbert, or Hopkins; Verlaine, Claudel, or Francis Jammes; Matthias Claudius, Hölderlin, or Novalis—are short. The lyrical impulse refuses to be stretched thin. So it seems that Poe was right; there are no long poems. I for one have always preferred Eliot before he started playing quartets, and there are any number of Rilke's poems I'll take over *The Duino Elegies*, near-universally acclaimed as the poet's magnum opus.

Yet now, all at once, we have three new translations of *The Duino Elegies:* in a separate volume, as part of a selected works, or as the crowning conclusion to what concerns me here, William H. Gass's *Reading Rilke: Reflections on the Problems of Translation*, which deals with a lot of things, but gravitates toward the *Elegies*. There have been many English translations of this work of roughly thirty pages and in ten parts, but people still keep trying; poetry is hard to translate, and this late work of Rilke's especially so.

To what extent that work has preoccupied the poetry world can be learned from the three-volume study of it, the so-called *Materialien*, a kind of anthology edited by Ulrich Fülleborn and Manfred Engel, to which I will abundantly but tacitly refer. It reprints or excerpts just about everything conceivable up to 1964—and not only in German—in three volumes of three to four hundred pages each (inception, variants, publishing history, letters, utterances, reviews, interpretations, evaluations, reevaluations, and bibliography)—a trilogy of which Gass seems to be unaware.

More damaging is his not taking into account Rilke's *Testament*, first published in 1974. Rilke had been struggling with the unfinished *Elegies* for ten years, and put together this slender, handwritten volume in 1920, as he abandoned hope of termination. It was intended for his then major mistress (Rilke had a handful of major, and a legion of minor, ones), the painter Elisabeth Dorothee (Spiro) Klossowska, mother of the painter Balthus, and known as Mouky to her friends, Merline to Rilke, and Baladine to herself. She was, it seems, the chief inspirer of the *Elegies*, and the thirty-page *plaquette* was made up of poem fragments and unfinished letters to the beloved.

Of course, it was also a self-justification, eventually, to the world for Rilke's inability to finish the great work, the unchivalrous reason being proffered that loving deflects too much from working on one's poetry, the poet's ultimate purpose in life. This theme runs through much of Rilke's work, and Gass is, obviously, not unaware of it. Yet the poet never sums up this predicament as tersely as Pierre Costals, the novelist-hero of Montherlant's *Les Jeunes Filles*, in the passage about the two faucets, work and life, between whose respective turnings on and off the writer uneasily fluctuates.

Reading Rilke elicits from me an intense love-hate: it is often dazzling and, almost as often, infuriating. The book is, first, a concise psychobiography of Rainer Maria Rilke (1875–1926), and offers a fine sense of this complex, devious, vain, mock-humble, surpassingly sensitive, and frequently insensitive man. We get the biographical data not in chronological order, but subsumed by a free-floating meditation on Rilke's work, of which this is a compelling critical study. Gass mixes biography and criticism, specific analyses and speculative generalizations, with considerable dexterity.

But this is also an essay on the problems of translation, of Rilke's poems and poetry in general, not lacking in astute observations. Two of them I find most interesting: that translations need not make a poem sound as if it were written yesterday, and that "one is generally wise to render the poem as the poet wrote it, and let the poet's poem explain itself." Unfortunately, Gass the translator often ignores Gass the critic's wise precepts. For yes, *Reading Rilke* is also a selection from Rilke's poetry translated by Gass, sometimes reproducing Rilke's rhyme scheme, sometimes more freely. Gass has some genuine successes here, as well as resounding failures.

The book is, further, a kind of omnium gatherum, with many an excursus on what fascinates Gass, such as a lengthy parallel between the modus operandi of Rilke with that of the mathematician Henri Poincaré, which does little for me. These digressions can be highly stimulating as well as annoyingly self-indulgent. More disturbingly, Gass yields at times to the urge to equal Rilke's poetry with Gassian, not to say gassy, prose. Most valuable, however, are extended line-by-line comparisons of numerous English translations of the *Elegies*, with usually judicious assessments of their achievements and shortfalls, incidentally providing a close reading of the text, with many a welcome insight for readers who have no German. Alas, Gass's own translations of these passages, sometimes even in several versions, often fall below those of previous translators. The culmination of *Reading Rilke* is Gass's complete Englishing of the *Elegies*, imperfect and not even quite honest: it fails to provide the original on facing pages (or anywhere else), making it much harder to detect the translator's traducings. But at least Gass does not attempt to boil down the *Elegies* to some limp formula: the traducer is not a reducer.

Let me proceed to some of my observations while reading *Reading Rilke*. Gass nicely evokes the bad luck and unhappiness that dogged the marriage of Rilke's parents, and Rilke's mother dressing the boy as a girl (a not all that uncommon practice then—think Wilde), with the possible bad effect this had on the grown man. But promptly Gass becomes *outré* describing the household: "Kid, Kitchen, Kirk, Koffee in which to dip a Kookie: they add up to Komfort." This is soon redressed by an elegant trope: "Contradiction paves every avenue of feeling, and we grow up in bewilderment like a bird in a ballroom, with all that space and none meant for flying, a wide shining floor and nowhere to light [sic for *alight*]." Nicely put, as is this about Rilke's involvement with the formidable Lou Andreas Salome, as formative as it was unsettling: "Meeting your match may make for a doubled flame, but it will certainly result, quite soon, in two burnt ends." In this case, it was only René Maria Rilke, who at Lou's urging became Rainer Maria, who got burned.

Gass aptly evokes Rilke,

> the lover and letter writer, a man drawn to women like a bee who, heavy with their honey, soon returns to his hive; or one might remark Rilke's career as a social climber, as the accomplished cultivator of those who may prove of some assistance to Art—occasionally artists, critics, editors, and poets, but generally people of wealth, position, and comfortable estates; or take note of the "inspired one," who is attacked by the Muse from time to time the way storms lash rocky coasts . . . with sudden stiff onslaughts of both poetry and prose . . . Rilke is the traveler who passes through places the way others pass their years.

This is often censured in Rilke: his pretensions to nobility and his playing up to aristocratic ladies and, more rarely, gentlemen, who could provide him with the odd palazzo, castle, or tower—and requisite servants—in which to live in heroic isolation in the fawning company of women falling on their faces (or, too often, over backward) before such incomparable sensitivity and insight. Irritating is not so much the parasitism of all this as its influence on the work, which doubtless found being wistful, ethereal, and unremittingly elevated conducive to steady patronage. Rilke had to sing and swing high for his supper, "a professional melancholic and castle-dweller" as that fine poet Wilhelm Lehmann called him. Or, as Gass drolly puts it, Rilke "had realms" in which he "dwelt."

Even better is this:

> The course of life was . . . marked and marred by weakness, by giving in, by disappointment, as he ate, loved, schemed for advancement, groveled for money or employment, worried about a roof over his head, while trying to keep that head in the good clouds where it belonged.

And again: "Rilke liked to display his allegiance to the simple life by eating greens and taking barefoot walks." Many passages evoke Rilke's existential shenanigans with wry humor—but also often with show-offy, cluttered imagery. Particularly effective are the descriptions of Rilke as Rodin's amanuensis, and of the dying poet "refusing narcotics in order to keep a clear head, the better to confront his illness."

Sadly, though, Gass mistranslates part of one of Hölderlin's finest poems: "With yellow pears hangs / And full with wild roses / The land in the lake." This should be "into the lake." The poem is "Hälfte des Lebens" ("Half [or mid-point] of Life"), where what was hangs toward the lake and is reflected by what is to come: the same, only in reverse—a great, tragic image for what the future holds. With "*in* the lake," which bypasses the confluence of inverse doubles, all is lost. No less annoying are hyperkinetic Gassian tropes such as "The sonnet shape is as powerful as a right-wing religious group . . . conservative to the core, and snooty to boot," by way of discussing the difficulties of translating formal verse. But need there be such mistakes as when Gass translates "und ohne Füsse kann ich zu dir gehn" as "walk without feet to where you were," which flubs the needed point of "where you *are*," to say nothing of producing the jingle *where-were*.

Next comes the book's invaluable part: the minute, line-by-line comparison of selected passages from the *Elegies* as rendered by a dozen or more translators, with sound assessments of what they got right or wrong. The only trouble is that, as noted, we get Gass's own versions, quite often as faulty as any, sometimes even in bad English, e.g., "that completer existence."

Gass's interpretation of the much-debated Rilkean Angels is as good as any:

> The Angels are what the poet would be if he could free himself from human distraction, if he could be indifferent to the point of divinity, absorbed in himself like [sic] all noumena are, and at one with the work and the world of the work, its radiant perfections.

If the sentence stopped here, all would be well, but our author seldom leaves well enough alone, and embellishes with trifling tropes and mannered minutiae—smidgens in the Gass, alas—so the sentence staggers on: "like those twice luminous worms which [preferably *that*] glow with the added glory of their own phosphorescence: the lower light flouncing outward like a shout—that rare instreaming Rilkean light—swirling toward its source like water softly down a drain."

Gass's version of "Ein jeder Engel ist schrecklich," "Every Angel is awesome," is awful. We read: "'Awesome' is also a word being given the teenage treatment, but I think it's still possible to say 'awesome' and not mean the noise from an electrolouded band." Think again, Gass; *awesome* is as coopted as *gay*. But he is right to remark, "Many translations do not bother to understand their texts. That would interfere with their own creativity and with their perception of what the poet ought to have said." An admirable caveat, regrettably overlooked by Gass the translator. Before you buy this book, check out Gass at his most verbose on pages 70–71. If that is too much for you, as it almost is for me, you had better desist.

Gass, indeed, can be pretty opaque, as when he glosses "ich . . . verschlucke den Lockruf dunkelen Schluchzens" with "the cry is held back because the fear itself is a fear we worship out of frightened gratitude," which I defy an Angel to explicate. Although he is funny about the failings of other translators ("As we advanced into the elegy as into some movie Africa, the weaknesses of our company became increasingly manifest: the heat is getting to them, the rotten gin, the drums, the flies"), he is not funny when he allows himself five shots at translating one short passage: that is translating with a spray gun, and even so he manages to miss the target.

Gass is often overfancy, as when he imputes the German *gelösten* (loosened) "its twin suggestions of 'listen' and 'loosen,'" the first of which is utter nonsense. His writing can also be slatternly: "Language of incredible musicality." But Gass is again provocative in his disquisition of what a translator must preserve at all costs, and what he can sacrifice if he must, something different for every poet. In Rilke, he says,

> the poetry of idea must come first, the metaphors he makes out of the very edge and absence of meaning, the intense metaphysical quality of his vision . . . while [sic] tone and overall effect would be next.

Well, yes, if you have those, you have just about everything, but Gass himself usually fails on both counts.

He correctly asserts of the *Elegies* that "Their Being was to be beyond the poem," but is that a virtue? I think it's better for the essence to remain inside the poem. Again, Gass goes cryptic: "Rilke's *Elegies* will end when happiness falls." What? "Mouth them . . . for these poems are the most oral I know . . . they must be spoken—not merely by but for yourself." This strikes me as pure cant, and it continues, "the voice-making quality of these lines goes beyond their music. They are an utterance." Of what good poetry could you not say all the above? Beyond the poem, beyond the music—this surely is metacriticism.

But Gass is good at conjuring up Rilke's frustration from writer's block, and cogently lists all the things bothering the poet, including "those migraines that troubled one end of him and the hemorrhoids that pained the other." Yet he has to spoil it:

> Rilke was as restless as one who hoped to leave his pain in the parlor when he enters the dining room, and his worries in the bedroom when he comes down for breakfast, only to find them spread over his toast and clouding every view.

That metaphor is not just mixed; it's as scrambled as the eggs that go with the worry-buttered toast.

Eloquence possesses Gass on the subject of the death of young women, which so excited Rilke, as it did Poe. Gass writes:

> Certainly such a death . . . had obsessed Rilke during nearly his entire life. Not only did it seem that a girl had to die to make room for him [a reference to his parents' first child, dead in infancy], but it also seemed that this sad prematurity preserved the child's possibilities along with her innocence.

Furthermore,

> lovers who loved and lost but who continued more devotedly to love, like Gaspara Stampa . . . were his sort of saint [sic]. . . . Rilke's jilted ladies (and all were left in some sort of lurch) ought to love him the more for his resistance. And they did.

Gass gives all kinds of reasons, but neither he nor anyone else, to my knowledge, has raised the possibility of some sort of Rilkean sadism. Thus the reveling in the death of the young women, thus the jiltings, thus one very curious passage in *Malte Laurids Brigge*, which this is not the place to examine.

Sloppy syntax again: "Laws . . . exist in the realm of number, where the pioneer, like a verdant valley, finds them." This passage is about mathematics, but even mathematical pioneers tend not to resemble verdant valleys. We get a very unconvincing passage trying to explain why Rilke was unable to finish the *Elegies* during their first onrush at Duino in 1912, and why completion had to wait until 1922 at Muzot. Another terrible Gass trope concerns the breakup of Rilke's marriage, which the poet claimed to have "reached a higher plane." "Actually," Gass goes on, "the couple's plane had crashed, and they were scattered about like baggage on incongenial ground." We have here, all at once, a poor pun, a nonexistent word (for *uncongenial*), and a ghastly simile. This from the jacket copy's "admired essayist, novelist, and philosopher"?

Gass is good at communicating Rilke's betrayal of his friend, the fine painter and human being Paula Modersohn-Becker, to whose tragic death the poet indirectly contributed. In that way, however, he could produce what he was so good at: a moving requiem on the death of a youngish woman. Gass quotes an affecting entry from Paula's diary that is almost as poetic, and certainly more humane, than most of Rilke's prose. He notes that the "Requiem for a Friend," one of Rilke's best poems, begins "I've had my dead, and I let them go, and was surprised to see them so consoled, so soon at home in being dead."

This brings up death as a main theme of the *Elegies*, as well as in much of Rilke's other work. The poet renounced Christianity, and stipulated that there be no priest at his deathbed. But, as Gass correctly observes, there are more saints, Christs, and Virgin Marys in Rilke's poetry than you could squeeze into a major cathedral. And, of course, Angels. To me, this smells both of fear of death and of hedging your bets. Rilke's chief way of dealing with that fear was to incorporate the dead as variously participating in life. About the above quotation, Gass wryly comments, "The *Elegies* will argue otherwise, deciding that 'it's difficult to be dead.'"

It seems to me allowable for the dead to have as conflicting feelings about death as the living have about life. But only if you assume that the dead have any feelings at all, which looks to me like cheating in the poet's fundamentally nonreligious scheme of things. Yet there are more participatory stiffs in Rilke's poetry than there are in ghost stories and horror movies. I find them even more inappropriate than the Angels—always, of course, with a capital *A*, although in German all nouns are capitalized. The meaning and existence of Angels can be argued about; the dead are palpably plain dead.

It would be different if this afterlife of the dead were conceived figuratively, as some kind of symbol. But no, these dead are all over the place, disporting themselves more energetically than many of the quick. Which can ultimately have only one explanation: the attempt to allay *timor mortis* by denying rigor mortis. This strikes me as more bizarre than another debatable Rilkean trait, frequent in the *Elegies* and elsewhere: interpreting the feelings of animals in anthropomorphic terms, while also stressing the animals' differentness from, indeed superiority to, human beings.

There is, then, overassertiveness to combat doubt. Or, as Gass aptly puts it, "Whenever a poem of Rilke's seems to admonish the reader, openly with 'You must change your life,' or tacitly, through the poem's example, we can be certain that Rilke has failed the

charge," just as he failed Paula Modersohn-Becker by not support-
ing her well-earned disinclination to rejoin her unworthy husband,
with fatal consequences for her—a death unjustified by whatever
great poetry it occasioned.

On the other important subject in the *Elegies*, love, Gass has this
curious statement: "We kiss with our eyes closed because there isn't
much to see. And if there were, we wouldn't want to see it." Are
there no better explanations for this by no means universal phe-
nomenon, such as Rilke's relentlessly advocated need for interior-
ization?

Yet there is redemption in Gass's excellent disquisition—no
mere digression—on the *objet trouvé* as art, specifically on the urinal
(*Fontaine*) of Marcel Duchamp—alas, misspelled as "Duchamps"
throughout, copy editors being even more extinct than the dodo.
Gass then proceeds to dispute Rilke about animals being more in-
stinctively at one with the world than we are, although Gass's argu-
ments based on animals' alertness to danger signals or becoming
habituated to human beings surely cut both ways.

On the subject of Rilke's beloved *Weltinnenraum*, clumsily trans-
lated as "innerworldspace," Gass is reasonable when he explains that
the invisible signal emitted by objects lands "in an inner space, not
the space between our ears, but the space between where our ears
hear." The Ninth Elegy asks, "What, if not this deep translation, is
your ardent aim?" whereupon Gass makes two of his best observa-
tions. First,

> Contemplation was possible for Rilke—but it was more likely to
> occur in front of a Cézanne. Most of the revolutionary "new"
> poems [i.e., *Neue Gedichte*], supposed to demonstrate this saintly
> openness to objects, are about animals in zoos and flower beds
> in parks, photographs in books, works of art in the shelter of
> their museums, figures in myth, icons of the church.

In other words, second-hand contemplation. And good, too, Gass's
telling conclusion: "I feel obliged to say, when we perceive fully, we
do ourselves a favor, not the world." So all this gathering of mes-
sages from animals and objects is really a matter of, however en-
lightened, self-interest, and not the selfless fulfillment of a sacred
obligation.

While expatiating on the Rilkean doctrine that, by using them, time inscribes on things and people their history, Gass again lapses into cuteness: "Rust destroys, but it creates character more surely than most playwrights. Aging delights in lines," with a desperate pun on *lines*. And further: "For Rilke, the world has an expressive surface, and its 'looks' should not be ignored." True enough, but of how many scrupulous writers is this not equally true? Then, more pirouettes: "According to the *Elegies*, we are here just to utter. To sew concept to referent like a button on a coat . . . a button meant not to button but to be." Well, if that isn't cute as a button!

Gass does, however, get at what makes many impatient with Rilke, his

> emphasis on Being rather than Doing, on relinquishment rather than retention, on acceptance rather than on revision; it smacks more of moral indolence than saintliness to them; and its radical subjectivity is offensively antisocial and indifferent to the collective.

This view was splendidly expressed in 1946 by Franz Blei in a generally favorable appraisal, wherein, however, he remarked cannily, that "the ship Rilke steers by a compass that points toward the iron of the ship," and, perhaps more disputably, that "there is not a single true love poem by Rilke—so lonely in the soul was he." Lonely or self-absorbed? The critic Friedrich Sieburg noted in 1949 that "an immeasurable religious need has seized people—with the greatest ineptitude for religiosity. In this tension, the message of . . . *The Duino Elegies* ensconces itself."

In 1975, the distinguished journalist-critic Joachim Kaiser wrote that "it is not only from the all-too-sifted words of this most carefully selective poet that the impression of a taste-monger derives. Alienating was and is the thoughtless deliberateness of his God-fixation, his tendency toward the aristocratic, his lyrical-prophetic *Gefunden-Haben*," which sounds terrible when Englished as "having-foundness." In 1979, the essayist-biographer Peter Wapnewski spoke aptly of Rilke's "mythical code devised for him who contrived it."

Now, it is equally true that, as early as 1926, the good lyric poet Peter Gan praised Rilke's "arduously wrested, incomparable ability to voice finenesses, uniquenesses, nuances of feelings and thoughts that hitherto were lost in the ocean of the ineffable," a perception echoed in 1975 by Marcel Reich-Ranicki, Germany's leading critic, as Rilke's "triumph in the struggle with the unsayable." Something similar was expressed even better back in 1925 by the eminent poet-critic Oskar Loerke, for whom Rilke "increased with all his words the treasure of silence." Loerke also averred that philosophy could express itself better through associations than through ratiocination, which quickly exhausts itself.

Contrariwise, in 1929, Baron Börries von Münchhausen, Germany's most popular poet and specialist in ballads (and yes, of the same clan as the Great Liar), though variously appreciative of Rilke, berated him for his rather close imitation of late Hölderlin, for his "substantivitis, a festering of the living verb into the desiccated noun," and for the *Elegies* being, as Rilke himself states at their outset, a self-portrait, far removed from the concerns of the common man. Wilhelm Lehmann took Rilke to task in 1966 for "not taking sensory phenomena very seriously," and seeing them "with a preconception about whether a way from them led 'inward.'" Thus Lehmann: "So he opined that the fig tree bore fruit without first having to bloom, and promptly became a symbol. His work was full of speculativeness, of which the lyric sicklies." Reading Rilke compelled Lehmann "to defend things against this interiorization: trees are so fulfilled in their creatureliness that apprehending them requires none of this heavily talked-about 'innerworldspace.'"

The most succinct screed against the *Elegies* comes from a letter by the distinguished poet and prose writer Albrecht Schaeffer in 1924, who read them

> almost with a shudder. This now is the most hapless blather; an endless, dulcet rustling of the rarest words and phrases, all of them babbling away as sweetly as children's questioning. For this pious, this sanctimonious man, who converses only with God and Angels, nothing is sacred, and he now rips to shreds . . . hexameters . . . the noblest creation of the noblest folk . . . into his free rhythms. . . . It is impotence turned lyrical drivel, all sucked out of nihilism. . . . All is nothingness, only the Angels exist, a little, as if by mistake. . . . For he is unstable,

everything slips through his fingers, it is all mere associative prattle . . . rags.

Something comparable was stated by Hofmannsthal, Rilke's friendly rival (the only other one, Stefan George, was less friendly) in a letter of 1927: "The *Elegies* I believe, are simply not good—they lack that rarest rhythmical inspiration, which alone can legitimize this highest poetic mode."

But back to Gass, who describes Rilke's psychological pattern as follows:

> First, he expects of ordinary life far more than it can possibly produce. . . . Second, he consequently enters a state of dismay and disappointment. Third, he requires of the poet . . . an elevated life anyway. Fourth, the poet, in order to lead that elevated life, is forced to accept and praise the same ordinary world he began by disdaining.

And Gass proceeds to illustrate this practice with wit and insight. In short, "Rilke takes away with one hand, and gives with another . . . what he gives is always a task."

And then the women: "Orpheus did not fare well at their hands, hands which tore him to pieces. So unless the women are both young and dead, the poet will not praise—he'll blame." Again: "Irony might save some of these poems, but Rilke is rarely ironic." Then another grammatical whopper in Gass's rendering of the Eighth Elegy: "one of those Etruscan souls who has [sic] flown from the corpse." Indeed, by way of putative interpretation, Gass writes his own poem:

> Show the Angel a billfold that has ridden in the rear pocket on someone's rump, the creases it now contains, where money and credit cards once slid in and out, as oiled and stained as a fielder's glove . . . or a mohair sofa, shiny where the man wearing that billfold sat, or the cat curled, or love was made.

Elsewhere in overlong sentences on pages 181–182, Gass explicates away fulsomely, sometimes in Kantian terms, and is hard to follow.

Yet his final apotheosis of poetry, Rilke's and others', is eloquent enough for extensive quoting:

The poem is thus a paradox. It is made of air. It vanishes as the things it speaks about vanish. It is made of music, like us, "the most fleeting of all" yet it is also made of meaning that's as immortal as immortal gets on our mortal earth; because the poem will return, will begin again, as spring returns: it can be said again, sung again, is our only answered prayer; the poem can be carried about more easily than a purse, and I don't have to wait, when I want it, for a violinist to get in key, it can come immediately to mind—to my mind because it is my poem as much as it is yours—because, like a song, it can be sung in many places at once—and danced as well, because the poem becomes a condition of the body, it enlivens our bones, and they dance the Hardy, the Hopkins, the Valéry, the Yeats; because the poem is a state of the soul, too (the soul we once had), and these states change as all else does, and these states mingle and conflict and grow weak or strong, and even if these verbalized moments of consciousness suggest things which are unjust or untrue when mistaken for statements, when rightly written they are real; they themselves *are* as absolutely as we achieve the Real in this unrealized life—*are*—are with a vengeance; because, oddly enough, though what has been celebrated is over, and one's own life, the life of the celebrant, may be over, the celebration is not over, the celebration goes on.

So what hath Gass wrought? Not a biography or a work of criticism. He has written an extended freeform essay circling around his subject, bringing in biography and criticism wherever it suited him. Quite aside from how one feels about specifics, his book, qua genre, is commendable down to its agreeable length: not counting the complete *Duino Elegies* at the end, 180-odd pages.

But what about the *Elegies* themselves? Ten longish poems about so many diverse things: the poet, fear, the Angel, the Saint, the Hero, Death, women (early deceased or jilted), the dead in their afterlife, not according to any known religion. Can the center hold when there is no center? Despite some fine passages, there is no whole here. There could have been more or less of it with much the same effect. A great, baggy monster.

Yet Rilke was a real poet, and I'll adduce one of my favorite quatrains of his from an uncollected poem, one of two written for Marthe Hennebert, a wretched working-class girl he picked up in the summer of 1911 on a Paris street.

Befriedigungen ungezählter Jahre
sind in der Luft, voll Blumen liegt dein Hut
und der Geruch aus deinem reinen Haare
mischt sich mit Welt als wäre alles gut.

Appeasements of innumerable years
are in the air, your hat lies full of flowers
and the scent from your pure hair
mingles with world as if all were well.

Thus speaks the poet to his momentary girl in a *Grande Jatte* setting.

No one in German handled sound and rhyme better than Rilke. We should note the *u*'s in lines two and three, the *i*'s in line four, the alternation of well-chosen feminine and masculine rhymes, the inner rhyme of *deinem reinen*. Also the progression from peace, through idyllicism, to the quietly devastating *as if*: as if all were well. Four simple German words exude the impermanence of joy, the sense of human transience, the skull that lurks in Arcadia.

Let me conclude by comparing Gass's and two other recent translations of the *Duino Elegies*. I pick, almost at random, this from the "Seventh Elegy": "Hiersein ist herrlich. Ihr wusstet es, Mädchen, *ihr* auch, / die ihr scheinbar entbehrtet, versankt—, ihr, in den ärgsten / Gassen der Städte, Schwärende, oder dem Abfall / Offene." I translate: "Being here is resplendent. You knew it, girls, *you* too / who seemed to do without, who sank—, you, in the most wretched / streets of the cities, festering, or rife for the refuse heap." In Edward Snow's new, properly bilingual and annotated edition, this reads: "*Life* here is magic. Even *you* knew that, you girls / who seemed deprived of it, who were trapped in the city's vilest streets, festering there, or cast aside / for rubbish." In Galway Kinnell and Hannah Liebmann's attractive *The Essential Rilke*, this becomes: "Being here is glorious. You knew it, you girls, you, also / who seemed left out, who sank—you, into the most squalid streets of the city, festering, open to / garbage." And finally Gass: "It is breathtaking simply to be here. Girls, even you / knew, who seemed so deprived, so reduced, who became / sewers yourselves, festering in the awful alleys of the city."

Obviously, the original is best. *Hiersein ist herrlich* is untranslatable in its simplicity, directness, cadence, and music. Equally clearly, Gass's chatty, prolix way with it is too prosaic, and "who became sewers yourselves" is offensive. But Snow's version is either too grandiose or too colloquial. Kinnell's *glorious* is correct but a bit flat; his *into* for *in* is plain wrong. *Garbage*, though correct, has taken on other, unwanted English meanings. *Rubbish* is better. Gass's "awful alleys" suggests back streets of crime rather than mere squalor. Snow's *trapped* is less imaginative than *sank*.

Even in this short fragment Gass comes off worst, and he can also be downright incorrect, as when, in the "Fifth Elegy," he renders the *selten zärtliche Mutter* (which Kinnell rightly translates as "seldom tender mother") as "one seldom allowed to be your mother," though here Snow's "your remote mother" is rather too weak as well. A trying business, translation; but, all the same, it must be tried.

2000

Death Fugues:
The Poems of
Paul Celan

POETRY IS the meeting point of parallel lines—in infinity, but also in the here and now. It is where the patent and incontrovertible intersects with the ineffable and incommensurable. It can be as complicated as Mallarmé or Paul Celan, or as simple as Heine or Verlaine, but something about it, however strongly it is felt, surpasses comprehension. It is what, when thought of, made A. E. Housman's face bristle, and his razor inoperative; it is what made Emily Dickinson's whole body so cold no fire could ever warm her.

There is a wonderful story I. A. Richards used to tell that I remember only imperfectly. It seems that word got back to the University of Chicago that young Robert Oppenheimer, who had been given a grant to pursue his scientific studies in—Vienna, was it?—was writing poetry instead. So a great scientist, his mentor (I forget his name, alas), was deputized to restore him to his senses. Poetry or science, the disciple remonstrated, it's really all the same. Not so, rejoined the master: science is saying in language that everyone can understand things nobody knew before; poetry is saying what everyone knew all along in language that nobody can understand. At this point, Ivor Richards would draw himself up and sound and look even more vatic than usual, and declaim: "He was absolutely right:

poetry is saying something everyone always knew in language that passes all understanding."

The great modern poets, starting with Rimbaud and Mallarmé, were striving to push utterance to its limits, to where it approached or attained the unutterable. The rest, of course, is silence. As the decades wore on, however, the problem became somewhat different: how to wrest meaning, perhaps even beauty, from a language that had been used and abused by dictatorships and their propaganda machinery and concentration camps quite literally to death. For poetry in German, the problem was especially acute. It is understandable how scarcely and accidentally surviving victims of genocide mistrusted or even rejected the language of the mass murderers. Yet the rejection had to be couched in the selfsame tongue. Or did it? Theodor W. Adorno had proclaimed repeatedly and influentially that, after Auschwitz, no poems could be written. It has always amazed me how wide an acceptance this profoundly mistaken notion was to gain.

Poetry, though, kept being written—even by survivors—and fairly soon after the war a generation of younger poets acquired imposing stature. The most important figures were Karl Krolow, Walter Höllerer, Heinz Piontek, and Paul Celan, to be followed a little later by Ingeborg Bachmann and Hans Magnus Enzensberger. Older poets enjoying longevity also contributed to the renewal and vindication of German verse; in the end, even Adorno had to retract his sweeping pronouncements, while George Steiner and others were still mouthing them elsewhere. Among all these poets, the one who was to achieve the greatest international resonance was Paul Celan (1920–1970).

Let me skip ahead and across to the Anglophone world, where Bruno Bettelheim wrote about Celan's "Todesfuge": "It was this poem which immediately established [Celan] as Germany's—and probably Europe's—most important poet of his generation." And George Steiner (in *After Babel*, 1975) announced that Celan was "almost certainly the major European poet of the period after 1945." In Germany, Rolf Hochhuth published his provocative play *Der Stellvertreter* ("The Deputy") in 1963. It contained mini-treatises in its stage directions, in one of which we read about the dangers, at least in drama, of "proceeding in the manner of, say, Paul Celan in his masterly poem 'Death Fugue,' which has translated the gassing of Jews entirely into metaphors." Because, Hochhuth continued, "great as is the power of suggestion that emanates from word and sound, metaphors inevitably hide the hellish cynicism of this reality." Contrariwise, the distinguished poet-essayist Hans Egon Holthusen had praised Celan's ability to "sing the Holocaust in a language that, from first line to last, is true and pure poetry, without a trace of reportage, propaganda and argumentation." He extolled "Death Fugue" as "one of the most magnificent occasional poems [*Zeitgedichte*] we possess." This essay, published in Holthusen's collection *Ja und nein* (1954), infuriated the hypersensitive Celan, whose paranoia where German critics were concerned was boundless.

"Todesfuge" is indeed a major poem of our century, reaching the acme of fame by being reprinted in its entirety in *The New York Times Book Review*, along with condign praise, in conjunction with the appearance in English of Celan's *Speech-Grille and Selected Poems* (1971, translated by Joachim Neugroschel), a full year after the poet had committed suicide by leaping into the Seine. There have been books about Celan even in English, notably Jerry Glenn's *Paul Celan* (1973); Israel Chalfen's important and beautifully written 1979 account of the poet's early years was brought out in translation here in 1991.[1] Nevertheless, it is *Paul Celan: Poet, Survivor, Jew*, by John Felstiner, that makes the most inclusive attempt at criticism and biography thus far published in English. Felstiner, a professor of English and Jewish studies at Stanford, has also written books on Neruda and Max Beerbohm, revealing him as a scholar of catholic taste. His knowledge of Judaica in both Hebrew and Yiddish was especially useful for a study of Celan and the writings about him; it goes without saying that Felstiner also knows his German. His book is a significant achievement that, unlike many such endeavors, is at least as much criticism as biography; in a mere 344 pages, Felstiner analyzes most of Celan's important works in both verse and prose—if not in full, at least in generous part.

The first, and probably most debatable, characteristic of the

---

1. *Paul Celan: A Biography of His Youth* by Israel Chalfen (New York, Persea Books, 1991).

book is that it reproduces the overwhelming majority of poems dis-
cussed only in the English of Felstiner's translation. Although we are
told otherwise, this may well have been the publisher's way of saving
space, and it strikes me as unfortunate. To be sure, in exceptional
cases the original is included, but with a poet whose effects are so
idiosyncratic, and whose meanings so elusive, the original text must
always be given, if only in fine print at the bottom of the page. True,
Felstiner includes in his analyses phrases and words of Celan's Ger-
man—and sometimes, I repeat, the whole poem—but that is not the
same as allowing readers with knowledge of German (or even with-
out it) to get the full sense (or at least sound) of what the poet wrote.
Would one want a critical biography of a composer without quota-
tions from his music?

As for the quality of Felstiner's translations, it is generally high,
just short of what a major poet-translator could offer. Felstiner ago-
nizes over getting the meaning, sound, and ambiguities of the text
right. Where he has to take liberties, he explains them; sometimes
he even admits to total bafflement. Now and then he also adduces a
rival translation. All this is splendid, but has its disadvantages as
well. At times, Celan's life gets shortchanged in favor of the work.

To be sure, not everything about the poet's private life is avail-
able, despite an ample correspondence and a profusion of memoirs
by intimates and not-so-intimates. Felstiner has spoken to everyone
who could be interviewed, whenever possible face to face. He has
enjoyed the full cooperation of Celan's widow, Gisèle Lestrange
Celan (since deceased), and son, Eric. But two lacunae immediately
hit us: though the book is illustrated, there are no pictures of Gisèle
or Eric, or of the women in Celan's life. Indeed, least to be had from
the book is information about the poet's marriage and love life.

A useful biographical précis is provided by Felstiner himself in
his introduction to the correspondence between Celan and his fel-
low poet Nelly Sachs:[2]

> Paul Celan's parents came from Galicia and Bukovina, the "east-
> ernmost" reach (he emphasized) of the Austrian empire. His up-

---

2. *Paul Celan-Nelly Sachs: Correspondence*, edited by Brenda Wiedemann and trans-
lated by Christopher Clark (Riverdale, N.Y., Sheep Meadow Press, 1995).

bringing, though it entailed moderate religious observance and a Bar Mitzvah, would still have left him more-or-less comfortably engaged, like countless other Jews, with western European culture. But Celan underwent a drastic education: Iron Guard anti-Semitism, Soviet occupation, Nazi invasion, ghetto, forced labor, overnight deportation and loss of both parents in Transnistria. Toward the war's end he abandoned Czernowitz (renamed Chernovtsy), spent two years in Bucharest, fled to Vienna, and in 1948 settled in Paris, becoming a translator and above all a poet writing against the grain of a mother tongue the murderers had brutally abused.

What other salient facts need mention? Celan was born Paul Antschel, in Romanian transliteration Ancel, which, for purposes of euphony, he anagrammatized into Celan. He had no use for his stern and uncultured father, but worshiped his refined and literate mother, who adored her only child. It was she who insisted that only High German be spoken in the house, and it was only relatively late that Paul, a remarkable linguist, evinced interest in Yiddish and Hebrew, with both of which he became conversant. It was this intense closeness to his mother that kept his relations with girls (even the charming Ruth Lackner and the beautiful Rosa Leibovici, both, as Chalfen relates, very much in love with him) apparently platonic. Not until his late twenties, in his Bucharest years, did he lose his virginity to the capital's prostitutes, though (as Chalfen also reports) he complained that they were "dreadfully primitive." He did, however, have close relationships with young men, mostly fellow students, although there is no evidence of anything more than comradeship.

Celan was, for the most part, withdrawn and aloof, sometimes remaining silent during an evening's party. Yet there were also periods of entrancing merriment, when he would do sparkling impersonations, vivid enactments of scenes from plays (notably Shakespeare), and spellbinding poetry readings—though never of his own poetry, which he kept secret. Crucial experiences of his youth were nineteen months in various unspeakably vicious labor camps, and the loss of his parents under particularly guilt-inducing circumstances. Paul had left home in a huff to hide out elsewhere one weekend—the usual time for deportation roundups—and, returning home, found the door locked and his parents gone. Deported to Transnistria, his father died of typhus; his beloved mother, too weak to work, was shot in the back of the head. Paul could never quite get over the probably mistaken notion that, had he been there, he could have shielded his parents in the camp, and somehow brought them back alive.

Celan was always passionate about botany, and knew the names of flowers in many languages. Besides German, he had perfect Romanian (in which he wrote some fine poems and prose), French (for a year, he had studied medicine in Tours), Hebrew, Russian (he translated officially approved Russian writers into Romanian), Ukrainian (more translations, providing desperately needed funds), English (a visit with an aunt in London enabled Paul to see Shakespeare at the source), and also a command of Italian, Portuguese, and some Spanish (which he must have studied on his own). Throughout his life, translation, especially of poetry, was of great artistic and financial importance to him, as were studies of Romance and English literature. In Paris he studied philology and German literature at the prestigious Ecole Normale Supérieure, where he later taught.

Of particular meaning in his later years was his correspondence with the German-Jewish poet Nelly Sachs (1891–1970), then living as a refugee in Sweden. The two poets admired each other's work, and cheered each other up in their ever-increasing depression. Both were to win major awards in Germany, which they were hesitant to collect—but collected anyway—and both, especially Sachs, spent time in mental hospitals and received shock treatment. They sent each other their poems—Sachs rather more than Celan—and received hearty mutual encouragement and admiration, even though Sachs's later work was pretty poor. They saw each other once in Zurich, and, a bit later, in Paris, where Sachs briefly visited at the Celans' invitation. Sachs was religious, Celan was not; yet they shared two quasi-mystical experiences involving a special sort of light sighted on the water in Switzerland and on a wall of the Celans' Paris apartment.

Late in his short life, Celan made it to Israel, where he had further opportunities for agonized soul searching about why he did not relocate there, as so many of his Bukovinian co-religionists did.

With one of them, Ilana Shmueli, he conducted a love affair during his relatively short stay in Israel, then corresponded with her until his death. On or about April 20, 1970, he threw himself into the Seine, and, although a strong swimmer, drowned. His body wasn't found until several days later, and was buried on the very day his dear Nelly Sachs died.

During the last part of his life, Celan was living apart from his spouse; he was, as Felstiner writes, "a sick man, sometimes violent and even suicidal." It is not clear how complete the break with his wife was. She had been Gisèle de Lestrange, member of an aristocratic French Catholic family that intensely disapproved of her marriage to a Jewish refugee. Her mother, widowed late in life, became a nun, with whom her family could converse only through a grille, most likely the speech-grille that became the title, first of a poem by Celan, and later of an entire collection. Indeed, most of Celan's collections took their titles from a poem or phrase in a previous collection, presumably as a conscious or unconscious reaching for continuity in the poet's fragmented life. Gisèle was a graphic artist, whose work was, we are told, highly regarded, though what reproductions of it I have seen leave me cold. The titles of her—usually very abstract—works were often supplied by her husband.

Why the suicide? Obviously, there was much in Celan's past that painfully clung to him. Yet he also had good times with his wife and son, and to some extent enjoyed the success of his poetry, which earned him the respected Prize of the City of Bremen, and the coveted Büchner Prize of the City of Darmstadt. But Celan always imagined that prizes, publications, invitations to read or lecture had to do with attempts by Germany to assuage its bad conscience, rather than with genuine recognition of his work. Thus even essentially laudatory articles about it by such prominent critics as Holthusen and Günter Blöcker struck him as patronizing, if not downright insulting. Typically, he resented it equally when no mention was made of his early masterpiece, "Todesfuge," and when it was singled out after he himself felt he had surpassed it. Even its inclusion in the curriculum of many German schools failed to appease him.

What hurt him most, though, was the Goll affair. Yvan (or Ivan) Goll was an Alsatian Jewish poet living in Paris, writing mostly sur-

realist poems and plays in German and French, often in collabora-
tion with his wife. Claire Goll had in her youth, though Felstiner
doesn't mention this, been Rilke's mistress, a thing that could go to
any woman's head. I myself visited with the Golls at the American
Hospital in Neuilly during Ivan's terminal illness, and found the
couple most stimulating. So, no doubt, did the young Celan when
he was asked to translate some of Goll's French poetry into German.
As Felstiner notes, Celan translated "three collections, which went
unpublished because, Claire Goll later claimed, they bore too
closely the 'signature' of Paul Celan." Now, it is true that Celan was
a rather free translator—though nowhere near so free as, say, Robert
Lowell; nevertheless, the result was almost always impressive and,
ultimately, undamaging to the reputation of the originals.

So it was most ungracious of Claire Goll to launch, later on, an
attack on Celan in a German magazine, asserting and trying to doc-
ument that the younger man's poetry plagiarized that of her late
husband. This envy-motivated accusation had some repercussions,
but both the German Academy as a body, and most leading poets in-
dividually, rallied to Celan's defense. Still, given his overdelicate na-
ture, Celan was to nurse this grievance to the utmost, and it became
perhaps the chief goad of his paranoia. (It is worth noting how many
poets in all languages ended up more or less insane; one could not
begin to match their numbers among painters, composers, and
prose writers.) So it was that Nelly Sachs, during one of the bad
phases of her persecution mania, which is what ailed Celan as well,
summoned Paul to her sanatorium bedside, then countermanded
the summons in a telegram that arrived too late. In Stockholm,
Celan was either not admitted to Nelly's room, or, more likely, not
recognized by the older poet.

Still, why suicide? Clearly, terrifying depression. I can visualize
Celan jumping off the very Pont Mirabeau (near which he lived at
the end of his life) that inspired Apollinaire's famous poem "Le Pont
Mirabeau," from which Celan quoted in one of *his* poems. Apolli-
naire's poem stresses not only our sad transience, experienced espe-
cially keenly watching the river flow beneath the bridge ("Ni temps
passé / Ni les amours reviennent"), but also our burdensome,
anxiety-ridden existence ("Les jours s'en vont je demeure"). Kinesis
and stasis can be equal enemies to the poet. This may well be the

source of what the Yugoslav writer Danilo Kiš has noted in his book *Homo Poeticus:* "Yes, the defining factor in the literature and thought of Central Europe is just that: ironic lyricism. Perhaps it's a combination of Slavic and Hungarian lyricism, with the ironic part, like a grain of salt, coming from the Jews." A grain of salt, Kiš might have added, that could as easily turn into a grain of sand inside a poetic oyster.

It is indicative that, of Celan's favorite poets—Hölderlin, Rilke, Trakl, and Mandelshtam—one died mad, and two prematurely, in war or the gulag. And his favorite prose writer, Kafka, was a Jew and perennial imaginary victim, whose defense mechanism was, precisely, Central European ironic lyricism. Celan, who translated a good deal of Mandelshtam, also rendered into German the narration in Alain Resnais's hallucinatory documentary *Night and Fog.* It is not hard to imagine how much that first and best film about Auschwitz must have possessed the poet's mind. Not only must the translator have relived the horrors of the Holocaust, he must also have endured a recrudescence of his guilt at surviving. This, in turn, might have become aggravated by remorse about his love affair with Ilana—more traumatic for a habitual nonwomanizer—and torment at his separation from wife and child.

"Of course survivors sustained deep damage," observes Terrence Des Pres in *Writing into the World*, "but let us . . . consider, despite the damage done, the strength revealed." Celan's work is a lasting memorial, "an example worth knowing when we contemplate the darkness ahead." Perhaps the best short definition of Celan's poetry comes from the literary historian Hans Mayer, who knew the poet; it is a summation that all writers on Celan have formulated in not dissimilar terms. Mayer calls it a "poetic practice *des gestalteten Verstummens*," which English can render only clumsily as "the embodied falling silent." Celan himself has evoked it in two verses from "Strähne" ("Strand") singled out by Karl Krolow in *Aspekte zeitgenössischer deutscher Lyrik*: "Dies ist ein Wort, das neben den Worten einherging, / ein Wort nach dem Bild des Schweigens." ("This is a word that went about alongside words, / a word in the likeness of silence.") And, again quoting, Krolow continues: "The word is then '*ein kleines unbefahrenes Schweigen*' [a small trackless silence]."

Here it behooves us to give examples of Celan's poetry, starting
with a relatively early, 1950 poem in elegant rhyme, which, as Fel-
stiner notes, uses a stanza form borrowed from German baroque re-
ligious verse:

So bist du denn geworden
wie ich dich nie gekannt:
dein Herz schlägt allerorten
in einem Brunnenland,

wo kein Mund trinkt und keine
Gestalt die Schatten säumt,
wo Wasser quillt zum Scheine
und Schein wie Wasser schäumt.

Du steigst in alle Brunnen,
du schwebst durch jeden Schein.
Du hast ein Spiel ersonnen,
das will vergessen sein.

In translating this lyric, the usually sober and conscientious Fel-
stiner permits himself a game that should be forgotten: together
with one Melissa Monroe, he renders the piece into a rhymed
pseudo-Dickinson poem, which he boasts of having passed off as a
Dickinson original. But the poem is not much like Dickinson
(whom Celan later came to admire and translate); rather, it is in the
best German lyric tradition, with added Celan characteristics. Here-
with my own, non-Dickinsonian version:

So then you have become
as I have never known you:
your heart beats everyplace
in a country of wells

where no mouth drinks and no
shape [figure] borders the shadows,
where water springs into gleaming [semblance]
and gleam foams like water.

You descend into every well,
you float [sway, hover] through every gleam.

You have thought up a game
that wants to be forgotten [seeks oblivion].

Bukovina is a country of wells, and one might easily take this for a poem of landscape and love, except that Celan, uncharacteristically, revealed it to be about his vanished mother. The rhymes and near-rhymes are sinuously incantatory, yet a vague unease prevails. Even that the dedicatee of such a quasi-amatory poem is the mother is somewhat disquieting. The ghostly mother figure blends with the landscape in a sort of matriarchal pantheism. There are the resplendent compounds, *Brunnenland* and *allerorten*, but most of the key words are pared-down monosyllables. Alliteration in *sch-* flows through the poem: the murmur of wavelets.

The mother haunts the depths of wells from which no one drinks—graves?—and where no shape (or figure, or body) borders (or edges, or hems) the shadows (or shades)—which must be the realm of the dead. Yet in these shadowlands water springs into sunlight or gleaming, or, via its German homonym, semblance. So the shadows are really unbordered by human forms that would cast them (a typical Celanian reversal or paradox), and the life-giving water is only an illusion. Yet even such a semblance can foam, can bubble up in memory: the dead mother is recalled, ebulliently alive.

So the mother has both descended into the dark and risen into gleaming day. And then those mysterious, multivalent verses: "You have thought up a game / that wants to be forgotten" (or "seeks oblivion"). Is that game the teasing, tormenting haunting of the son? Or is it merely a sneaky kind of death? And by whom or what does the game want to be forgotten? In any case, a terrible game, but still only a game. An indefinable irony blends with the sadness.

Now for a somewhat later poem (1952), again to the mother, but more characteristic of the poet's mature mode:

Zähle die Mandeln,
zähle, was bitter war und dich wachhielt,
zähl mich dazu:

Ich suchte dein Aug, als du's aufschlugst und niemand dich
    ansah,
ich spann jenen heimlichen Faden,

an dem der Tau, den du dachtest,
hinunterglitt zu den Krügen,
die ein Spruch, der zu niemandes Herz fand, behütet.

Dort erst tratest du ganz in den Namen, der dein ist,
schrittest du sicheren Fußes zu dir,
schwangen die Hämmer frei im Glockenstuhl deines
    Schweigens,
stieß das Erlauschte zu dir,
legte das Tote den Arm auch um dich,
und ihr ginget selbdritt durch den Abend.

Mache mich bitter.
Zähle mich zu den Mandeln.

As translated by Felstiner:

Count up the almonds,
count what was bitter and kept you waking,
count me in too:

I sought your eye when you glanced up and no one would see
    you,
I spun that secret thread
where the dew you mused on
slid down to pitchers
tended by a word that reached no one's heart.

There you first fully entered the name that is yours,
you stepped to yourself on steady feet,
the hammers swung free in the belfry of your silence,
things overheard thrust through to you,
what's dead put its arm around you too,
and the three of you walked through the evening.

Render me bitter.
Number me among the almonds.

Felstiner tries as hard for the rhythm as for the meaning, which
is admirable, but can distort what the poem is saying from the very
start. Thus "Count up" renders the disyllabic *Zähle* but puts an un-
welcome spin on the meaning, which is simply "count." "Der Tau,

den du dachtest" is not quite "the dew you mused on." For *dachtest*, literally the past tense *thought*, I would prefer *imagined*. The pitchers, I would say, are *guarded* or *preserved*, rather than *tended*. I would translate the next line as, "Only there did you wholly enter the name that is yours"—shades of Mallarmé on Poe: "Ainsi qu'en lui-même enfin l'éternité le change." *Strode* would be better than *stepped*. And, please, not "things overheard" and "what's dead," but "the Overheard" and "the Dead," with capitals to drive home the personification. Finally, that "render me bitter." True, it gets across the disyllabic verb, but it has to resort to the more elaborate *render*, instead of the simple *make*, and incurs a slight singsong with the repeated *-er* ending. As for the suggestive echo in *Mache* and *Mandeln*, no one could get it in English.

In his comments on the poem, Felstiner is characteristically perceptive and thorough in adducing the significance of almonds in Hebrew and Yiddish literature, and even operetta, as well as in Celan's work. He is also sedulous in rounding up possible allusions in the poem, including "*Zählappell*, a head count in Nazi camps." The associative zeal, though often suggestive, can carry him too far afield. He writes: "It's possible, though only just, to think here of the smell of almonds given off by Zyklon B, the gas the SS used." Here that cautionary "only just" seems almost overscrupulous. In other places, where it might be more appropriate, it is absent. For example, Felstiner labors valiantly, but I think in vain, to establish parallels between Celan and Marianne Moore. Elsewhere, in the poem "Blume," he will link "The stone in the air, which I followed. / Your eye as blind as the stone" with the famous passage in "Death Fugue," where, at Auschwitz, "we shovel a grave in the air"—about as far from the stone in the air as one can get.

Even more bizarre is Felstiner's finding in these verses of a late Celan poem, "die Offenen tragen / den Stein hinterm Aug" ("the Open ones carry / the stone behind their eye"), something that "reminds me of the statue in Rilke's 'Archaic Torso of Apollo': 'for there is no place on it / that does not see you. You must change your life.'" One sometimes gets the feeling with Felstiner that the things farthest apart are only a stone's throw away. This reaches the heights of the ludicrous when, for Felstiner, Celan and his wife, Gisèle, become "Lan-celot" and Guinevere.

One more example. Discussing Celan's Büchner Prize accep-
tance speech, Felstiner writes (note, by the way, the dangling con-
struction): "Along with the pervasive 'Allow me,' Celan studs his
talk with *Meine Damen und Herren* ('Ladies and Gentlemen') eigh-
teen times over, with a spate toward the end. While this honorific
keeps the poet conversant [sic] with his listeners, it also impugns
their honor, as Jerry Glenn suggests, and even—who knows?—
evokes the politeness the SS used." This is very strange. It seems far-
fetched, though not preposterous, to endow the repeated rhetorical
apostrophe with irony, but it is absurd to invoke the politeness of the
SS, assuming that such politeness there was.[3]

But to get back to the almond poem. Here, as on occasion else-
where, Felstiner does not come to grips with the real interpretive
difficulties. What is the secret thread with its putative dew? What is
the unheard word? What are those pitchers? And so on. It appears
to me that line four, about Paul's mother's opening her eyes wide
with no one looking at her, refers to the moment when she was shot
from behind. The secret thread is Paul's empathy, which allows the
mother's dying thoughts—a benison that her gentleness exudes even
in death—to be collected like dew into the pitchers of memory. The
son's recollections preserve an utterance that found no destination—
except that Celan, once again, paradoxically inverts the statement. It
is the utterance that preserves the memory rather than vice versa:
the rememberer is sheltered by what he remembers.

There—in death and in her son's memory—the mother becomes
fully herself. In life, she was repressed ("the belfry of your silence"),
but now her essence rings out loud and clear. The Overheard—what
she hinted at—joins the solid contours of finality (the Dead), and to-
gether with Mother they walk into the dark. Felstiner's "the three of
you" is feeble for *selbdritt*. "You walked, a threesome [or, better yet,
triune], through the evening." There remains only for the son to

3. For the useful translation into English of Celan's sparse but not unimportant
prose, see *Paul Celan: Collected Prose*, translated by Rosmarie Waldrop (Riverdale, N.Y.,
Sheep Meadow Press, 1996). The translator aptly remarks, "For Celan, whose poems
moved ever closer to silence, prose was too noisy a medium." Unfortunately, Miss Wal-
drop reduces the decibels overmuch, as when, in a particularly poetic passage, she renders
"überflogen von Sternen, die Menschenwerk sind" as "with manmade stars flying over-
head."

achieve full identification with mother by absorbing all her suffering, by inheriting her bitter fate.

I point out my differences with Felstiner hesitantly, impressed as I am with the thoroughness of his research, the care that went into his translations, and the sensitivity with which he evaluates the achievement. If, at times, he is overindulgent with certain recurrent devices and excessive obscurities, these foibles are an earnest of the devotion and effort needed for an undertaking as arduous as this book. Yet Felstiner does not address Celan's exaggerated tendency to invert relationships, noted by Holthusen, who remarks on how the poet "quite simply stands the real world on its head. 'The sea above us,' he says, 'the hill of the deep,' 'the stars of noon.'" And again: "At several climaxes of his poetry, paradox becomes the punch line (*Pointe*) of the statement . . . 'we part intertwined' or 'a hanged man strangles the rope.'" This conceit is so compulsive in Celan that it almost merits the stern word *trickery* that Holthusen employs. It goes so far (as Felstiner notes but does not comment on) as to deliberately misquote another poet. Where Verlaine, in *Sagesse*, writes simply, "Ah! quand refleuriront les roses de septembre!," Celan gives us the intentional inversion, "Oh quand refleuriront, oh roses, vos septembres," which strikes me as excogitated and even unfair to Verlaine.[4]

In his last phase, Celan could be overwhelmingly opaque, but, on occasion, also magnificently pellucid. As an example of the former, take this poem in its entirety:

Mandelnde, die du nur halbsprachst,
doch durchzittert vom Keim her
dich
ließ ich warten,
dich.

Und war
noch nicht
entäugt,
noch unverdornt im Gestirn

---

4. To be sure, this happens not in a translation of Verlaine but in Celan's own comic poem "Huhediblu."

des Lieds, das beginnt:
Hachnissini.

What are we to make of this, one of the rare poems Felstiner re-
produces with text and translation facing each other?

> Almonding one, you half-spoke only,
> though all trembled from the core,
> you
> I let wait,
> you.
>
> And was
> not yet
> eye-reft
> not yet enthorned in the realm
> of the song that begins:
> *Hachnissini.*

Thus Felstiner, who also explains that this was written for a young
woman Celan knew in Czernowitz, of whose survival in Israel he be-
came joyously cognizant. But he does not say whether this was Ilana
Shmueli, with whom the poet was soon to have an affair on his trip
to Israel. Felstiner does, however, note that Celan "has turned the
obsolete verb *mandeln* ('to yield almond kernels') into . . . the noun
Mandelnde, 'almonding woman,'" and that for Celan "that oval-eyed
sweet or bitter fruit had signaled Jewishness."

Felstiner further reminds us that the poet's mother (surprise!
surprise!) "also hovers near this almonder, along with the Shechi-
nah, the female presence of God." He dubiously asserts that the
coinage *entäugt* can mean both *dis-eyed* and its exact opposite. "Both
senses feed into a blinding which is visionary truth, as the Shechinah
in exile wept out her eyes. . . . Celan's 'enthorned' also wrests a Jew-
ish destiny out of Jesus' crown of thorns. Whatever the poet has 'not
yet' become—'eye-reft,' 'enthorned'—ties pain to hope."

He then explicates *Hachnissini* ("Identified easily enough," he re-
marks cavalierly and overoptimistically) as "a Hebrew imperative to
a feminine singular, 'Bring me in,'" and as the opening of "a popu-
lar 1905 lyric by the first modern Jewish poet, Chaim Nachman Bia-
lik . . . 'Bring me in under your wing, / and be mother and sister to

me. . . .' " Felstiner rightly concludes, "Celan had no sister, had lost his mother, and sought them both in a beloved." He ends by adducing Bialik's, and thus Celan's, biblical sources, and how the erotic element stands for "a return from homelessness," i.e., conversion to true Judaism. All this is admirable elucidation, but stops short of full explication and evaluation; the poem strikes me as a total failure. Like so many of Celan's lesser efforts—I think that he published far too much—it is a doodle: the skeleton of a poem that remains unfleshed-out.

Yet this is not to say that other short pieces of Celan's do not score, or that the poet, even in his last and most self-destructive phase, did not have moments of serendipitous aptitude to write a gorgeously translucent poem. Such a one is "Es stand," which also rates parallel German and English in Felstiner. As he explains, the "Danish skiff" (really a *ship*) refers to a monument erected in North Jerusalem to the ships in which the Danes in 1943, secretly and gallantly, ferried Jews across to the safety of Sweden. The monument is surrounded by pines, and Celan viewed it with Ilana, his mistress on the trip to Israel (a trip he, characteristically, cut short):

Es stand
der Feigensplitter auf deiner Lippe,

es stand
Jerusalem um uns,

es stand
der Hellkiefernduft
überm Dänenschiff, dem wir dankten,

ich stand
in dir.[5]

Felstiner helpfully points out the biblical significance of the fig, and of the "standing" of Jerusalem, although he is unclear when he writes "both Hebrew versions say the same"—versions of what? The poem, of course, works better in German. First, the lovely com-

5. Felstiner translates: "There stood / a splinter of fig on your lip, // there stood / Jerusalem around us, // there stood / the bright pine scent / above the Danish skiff we thanked, // I stood / in you."

pound words—*Feigensplitter, Hellkiefernduft, Dänenschiff* (a ship Fel-
stiner, out of excessive concern with sound, renders as *skiff*). Then
the fine alliteration in *d*, culminating in *dir*. Next, the various mean-
ings of *stand* (stood), repeated as a kind of litany cum anaphora, and
climaxing in that last *stand*, which, besides its metaphorical meaning,
has a literal one: Paul and Ilana seem to have made love in that pine
grove.

The four or five kinds of standing take on vivid life. The splin-
ter of fig sensuously adhering to the beloved's mouth; the whole big
city of Jerusalem protectively encircling the lovers; the scent of
bright green pines in the air that surrounds the earthy surroundings,
translating them to a higher, heavenly plane; and, lastly, the lover
erect inside the beloved, also in the figurative sense of sheltered,
supported in a woman's maternal and sisterly love. Even the gener-
ous white spaces between the brief strophes contribute their sug-
gestive power.

But neither Ilana's love nor anything else could keep Celan
going. Felstiner quotes from one of the poet's last letters to Ilana,
shortly before the suicide: "The doctors have much to answer for,
every day is a burden, what you call 'my own health' is probably
never to be, the damage reaches to the core of my experience. . . .
They've healed me to pieces! (Man hat mich zerheilt)." That
coinage, *zerheilt*, is superb and tragic, whether or not it is strictly
true. It is of a piece with the daring language of Celan's poetry and
some of his prose. But the prose could also be touchingly simple, as
can be seen in the letters to Nelly Sachs, for example. These contain
only one remotely "literary" passage, when Paul writes Nelly on
May 30, 1958: "All the unanswerable questions in these dark days.
This ghostly mute not-yet, this even more ghostly and mute no-
longer and once-again, and in between the unforeseeable, even to-
morrow, even today." Otherwise, everything in the letters is plain
and unconcerned with posthumous publication.

The poetry, however, can be difficult. Felstiner quotes Samuel
Beckett: "Celan me dépasse" (Celan is beyond me). Beckett at least
is honest. Others, including some of the most vociferous admirers,
often misunderstand what they read. Thus Felstiner cites George
Steiner's mistaking for Yiddish a Middle High German passage from
Meister Eckhart incorporated in a Celan poem. Thus in "Shibbo-

leth," where Celan quotes the rallying cry from the Spanish Civil War, "No pasarán" (though unaccountably omitting the accent), Jacques Derrida perceives a relationship between that slogan and Socratic aporia. Bruno Bettelheim managed to misinterpret the shattering "black milk" of "Todesfuge"—the black ash from the crematoriums imbibed by the as yet living inmates—as "the image of a mother destroying her infant."

Felstiner himself can be on shaky ground. In the poem "Es war Erde in ihnen" ("There was earth inside them"), Celan evokes the Auschwitz inmates digging, endlessly digging. The powerful poem ends, as Felstiner translates, "O you dig and I dig, and I dig through to you, / and the ring on our finger awakes." He comments: "Now the digging leads to a ring and an awakening: is it the Nibelungs' ring of buried gold? If so, what of the rings pulled from the fingers of Jews about to be slaughtered?" This is all perfectly otiose. Finally Felstiner gets it right: "Celan's ring seals the bond with those who dig." But why didn't he throw out those useless bits of free association?

Never mind, though. He has accomplished what he promised in his subtitle: given us Celan the poet, the survivor, the Jew. Partial survivor only, for the aftereffects of persecution and loss, time-bomblike, induced delayed death by suicide, as they did for others like him. "It is no coincidence," Felstiner writes, "that Jean Améry and Primo Levi also took their own lives. Nor that Celan's loyal friend and brilliant critic, Peter Szondi, another survivor, drowned himself the year after Celan." But incomplete survival in life does not preclude full survival in death. Celan's work lives on undaunted, undented by time. To this survival, Felstiner's book makes its modest but invaluable contribution.

1996

Anna Akhmatova

❦ "POETRY IS what gets lost in translation," observed Robert Frost, and was only partly right. The thrust and sweep of epic poetry translates well enough: there is no dearth of decent translations of Homer, Virgil, Dante. Philosophical poetry also survives quite well: Eliot's *Four Quartets*, for example, has been successfully rendered into a number of languages. Lyric poetry is the one that has the most to lose.

There is, obviously, the problem of rhyme. Unrhymed poetry fares much better in translation: Walt Whitman reads just about as well (or poorly) in French or German. Even as delicate an unrhymed lyric as Leopardi's "L'infinito" has thrived in English. But rhyme is a killer. With elaborate rhyme schemes, tricky rhyming words, and short lines (dimeter, trimeter), the difficulty increases exponentially. Think of Byron's *Don Juan*, or this, from Heine: "Sie sassen und tranken am Teetisch, / Und sprachen von Liebe viel. / Die Herren, die waren ästhetisch, / Die Damen von zartem Gefühl." Verses 2 and 4, with their masculine rhymes, are no problem: "And talked about love and such" and "The ladies who felt so much." But 1 and 3 are impossible: the splendid joke lies in rhyming, femininely at that, *Teetisch* and *ästhetisch*, "tea table" and "aesthetic." Failing this, you've got nothing.

But there are poems untranslatable not because of their intricate rhyme scheme, rich rhymes, or fancy prosody. There exists something even more basic. In my doctoral dissertation, I quote from the journal of Jules Barbey d'Aurevilly for September 19, 1836: "[Maurice de] Guérin est venu. Causé de la poésie des langues, qui est toute autre chose que la poésie des poètes." I commented: "Languages have their intrinsic poetry, a poetry they yield to the proper touch with gracious forthrightness." This is the kind of *objet trouvé* that certain words or sequences of words offer up to the poet, as blocks of marble supposedly suggested to Michelangelo the figures he would hew from them.

Take the last lines of the beautiful "Járkálj csak, halálraitélt" (Keep walking, condemned man) by the great Hungarian poet Miklós Radnóti, which, after giving the contemporary poet various ways to live, concludes with "S oly keményen is, mint a sok / sebtöl vérzö, nagy farkasok." Literally: "And as toughly, too, as the from many / wounds bleeding, great wolves." (The Hungarian "s," by the way, is our "sh.") What is a translator to do, confronted with these darkly resonant sounds? Shoot the poem in the foot, or himself in the head? There is no way "great wolves" can render the mighty rumble of *nagy farkasok*. (*Nagy*, incidentally, is a monosyllable, not unlike our *nudge*.) This is the *poésie des langues*, the poetry inherent in the sounds of a language's words, and it is this more than anything that makes a poet such as Anna Akhmatova virtually (virtually? totally!) untranslatable into English.

Consider the opening quatrain of a three-stanza poem of 1921, which the poet dedicated to her friend Natalya Rykova. The "literal" prose translation in Dimitri Obolenski's *Penguin Book of Russian Verse* runs: "All has been looted, betrayed, sold; death's black wing flickered [before us]; all is gnawed by hungry anguish—why then does a light shine for us?" Peter Norman's translation reads: "Everything is ravaged, bartered, betrayed, / The black wing of death has hovered nearby, / Everything is gnawed through by hungry gloom, / Why then did we feel so light of heart?" Stanley Kunitz manages to get one rhyme into his translation: "Everything is plundered, betrayed, sold, / Death's great black wing scrapes the air, / Misery gnaws to the bone. / Why then do we not despair?" With all due respect, Kunitz would never have published such poetry under his own name. Finally, here is the version of Walter Arndt, one of our principal rhyming translators from the Russian: "All is looted, betrayed, past retrieving, / Death's black wing has been flickering near, / All is racked with a ravenous grieving, / How on earth did this splendor appear?"

This seems passable at first glance, but look now at the original: "Vsyo rashishchenyo, predano, prodano, / Chernoy smyerti mel'kalo krilo, / Vsyo golodnoy toskoyu izglodano, / Otchega zhe nam stalo svetlo?" There is no way the sonorities of that very first line can be conveyed in English, especially the play on *predano, prodano*. And not even the supposedly literal version does justice to the simplicity of the last: "Why then did it become light for us?" with *stalo* and *svetlo* again creating an echo effect. Russian poetry is a poetry of sound effects *par excellence*, because Russian is a sonorous, declamatory language; this is what those latter-day stadium-filling poets—the Yevtushenkos, Voznesenskys, and Akhmadulinas—called "pop poets" by Akhmatova, were to exploit to her disgust.

And yet she, too, benefited from big public readings at various times in her life. For Russia is that rare country in which poetry is loved by the masses, a country where simple folk quote poetry at one another and discuss it as people here do a football game. Because they often declaim in huge auditoriums and stadiums, Russian poets have adopted a vatic mode of recitation: part hieratic, part histrionic, loud and singsongy. It was Mandelshtam who reproached one of the most stentorian perpetrators with, "Mayakovsky, stop reading your verse. You sound like a Romanian orchestra." But the vatic mode is still with us, and even such a Westernized poet as Joseph Brodsky, Akhmatova's dearest disciple and protégé, subscribes to it wholeheartedly. This vatic mode, in turn, battens on the "poetry of languages," as the Acmeists, the group of poets to which Akhmatova belonged, certainly did. The Poets' Guild, as the Acmeists called their splinter group from the Symbolists, believed, as Max Hayward puts it, that "language was like any other material, and in fashioning poetic artifacts from it, one had to take account of its natural qualities and limitations."[1]

1. From the very useful introduction to *Poems of Akhmatova*, selected, translated, and introduced by Stanley Kunitz with Max Hayward (New York, Atlantic Monthly Press, 1973). For my purposes, the two most important collections of source material in English are *Anna Akhmatova: My Half Century, Selected Prose*, edited by Ronald Meyer (Dana Point, Calif., Ardis, 1992), and *Anna Akhmatova and Her Circle*, edited by Konstantin Polivanov and translated by Patricia Beriozkina (Fayetteville, University of Arkansas Press, 1994).

Anna Andreyevna Gorenko was born in Odessa in 1889, but was moved as a tot to St. Petersburg, living mostly in Tsarskoye Selo, the delightful suburb whose most famous inhabitant had been Pushkin, to whom the future poet was to dedicate many searching critical-historical studies. Her father was a naval engineer; she was the third of five children. One brother was killed in the Revolution, another committed suicide; both beautiful sisters died of tuberculosis, from which only a thyroid condition saved Anna.

When Papa Gorenko bemoaned that the tomboyish girl would become a poet and thus besmirch the family name, the seventeen-year-old changed her name to Akhmatova, as having descended on her mother's side from the Tartar ruler Akhmat, himself a descendant of Genghis Khan, and the last leader of the Golden Horde. As Joseph Brodsky writes in his essay "The Keening Muse" (1982),[2] "the five open a's of Anna Akhmatova had a hypnotic effect and put this name's carrier finally at the top of Russian poetry." In 1905, Anna's parents divorced, and she finished the gymnasium first in Yevpatoria on the Black Sea, then in Kiev. A crush Anna had on a handsome student at St. Petersburg University remained unrequited. She herself quit her law studies and eventually yielded to the persistent and protracted wooing of the poet Nikolay Gumilyov (1886–1921), whom she married, lovelessly, in 1910. The marriage lasted three years, and produced Anna's only child, Lyov.

It was a strange marriage, with infidelity on both sides, but also real love from Gumilyov. Nikolay at first dismissed his wife's verse as insignificant, advising her to become a dancer instead. But upon his return from a lengthy trip to Africa, he was genuinely impressed by Anna's new poems, and told her she must publish a volume. Soon Gumilyov, Akhmatova, and Osip Mandelshtam became the mainstays of a new movement that a hostile critic dubbed "Acmeist." Gumilyov was executed in 1921 for his alleged part in a counter-revolutionary conspiracy, an affair that remains opaque; Mandelshtam died in the gulag in 1937. Akhmatova survived—often precariously—till 1966, and never renounced Acmeism, indeed becoming more Acmeist as she grew older. It was a poetry of the here

---

2. Collected in *Less Than One: Selected Essays* by Joseph Brodsky (New York, Farrar, Straus & Giroux, 1986).

and now, eschewing both the mysticism of the Symbolists and the radicalism (often, but not always, political) of the Futurists.

When Anna left Gumilyov after three years, it was because she had fallen in love with Vladimir Shileiko, an Orientalist of stature. Being married to him meant becoming his research assistant while also holding down a librarian's job at the Agronomic Institute. Needless to say, this impeded her own writing. Nevertheless, her verse collections, *Evening*, *Rosary*, and *White Flock*, made the young Akhmatova one of the most popular poets of Russia, and this reputation was confirmed by *Plantain* (or *Wayside Herb*, the Russian word carries both meanings), and *Anno Domini MCMXXI*, to say nothing of such later masterpieces as *Requiem* and *Poem Without a Hero*.

What did she look like? There are many likenesses of her by various artists. Too bad that of Modigliani's sixteen drawings (Anna and Amedeo had a touchingly innocent flirtation when she was honeymooning in Paris with Gumilyov) only one survives. The poet Georgy Adamovich writes: "When people recall her today, they sometimes say she was beautiful. She was not, but she was more than beautiful, better than beautiful. I have never seen a woman whose face and entire appearance—whose expressiveness, genuine unworldliness, and inexplicable sudden appeal—set her apart . . . among beautiful women anywhere. Later her appearance would acquire a hint of the tragic: Rachel in *Phèdre*, as Osip Mandelshtam put it. . . ." Or, to quote Ronald Meyer, "Virtually every account refers to the poet's grandeur, regal bearing and stately demeanor. The adjective *velichavaya* (stately, majestic, regal) functions as a code word for Akhmatova." And he quotes an eyewitness, a woman who saw her in 1910 in the poet Vyacheslav Ivanov's literary salon: "Lithe, tall, and svelte, her head wrapped in a floral shawl. The aquiline nose, her dark hair with the short bangs in front and held in place in back with a large Spanish comb. The small, slender mouth that seldom laughed. Dark, stern eyes. [Others call them bright gray.] It was impossible not to notice her."

"A fine, unpretentious woman" Pasternak called Akhmatova in a letter to his cousin Olga Freidenberg. Yet the unpretentious woman was justly proud of her looks, as when she told Natalya Roskina that "sculptors had no desire to sculpt her because she wasn't interesting to them: nature had already done it all." Her nose, by the way, was not aquiline but, even more imposingly, shaped like a big fleshy "S." And consider this tribute from the great satirist Yevgeny Zamyatin, commenting on Annenkov's painting: "The portrait of Akhmatova—or, to be more exact, the portrait of Akhmatova's eyebrows. Like clouds, they throw light and heavy shadows on the face, and in them, so many losses. They are like the key to a piece of music; the key is set, and you hear the speech of the eyes, the mourning hair, the black rosary on the combs."[3]

After the breakup with Shileiko (another three-year marriage) in 1921, Anna moved in with two Petersburg friends, the composer Artur Lurye (or Lourié) and the famous actress Olga Glebova-Sudeikina, a great beauty. (A "sex-bomb," Nadezhda Mandelshtam contemptuously called her.) This may well have been a sexual *ménage à trois*; at any rate, it induced a creative outburst in Anna. Years later, her longest and most renowned work, *Poem Without a Hero*, was to take off from the 1913 suicide of Vladimir Knyazov, a young cadet whom Anna loved, but who loved and was rejected by Olga.

Her fame having peaked around 1921–1922, Anna was due for a reaction. Blok died after a painful illness, and Gumilyov was executed for his alleged counterrevolutionary activities, both in 1921. Akhmatova's fifth volume, *Anno Domini MCMXXI*, appeared in 1922, after which she published no other book till 1940. Attacks on her multiplied, and there was a ban on publishing her. Lurye and Sudeikina emigrated to Paris and, like other friends, urged Anna to follow suit. She refused and, in one of her finest poems, explained why. Instead, she moved back in with Shileiko, from whom she was divorced, but who traveled much, and whose St. Bernard needed looking after.

The poet's health was precarious: tuberculosis plagued her, and, later, heart attacks. While convalescing in a pension in Tsarskoye Selo, she met again Nadezhda Mandelshtam, ten years her junior, with whom she was to be linked in lifelong friendship. She also met

---

3. *A Soviet Heretic: Essays by Yevgeny Zamyatin*, edited and translated by Mirra Ginsburg (Chicago, University of Chicago Press, 1974), page 90. The "rosary on the combs" refers to the little ornamental spheres on the diadem-like comb, and also alludes to the title of Akhmatova's second volume, *Rosary*.

Nikolay Punin, the critic and historian, who was to become her third husband, though the marriage was never officially registered. Although she was to stay with him fifteen years ("fifteen granite centuries" she calls it in a poem), the marriage as such probably didn't last longer than the usual three years; but where else was she to go? This despite that a previous Punin wife and, later, a subsequent one inhabited the same house. And as with Shileiko, Anna became an amanuensis to Punin, helping him with translations and lectures. Arrogant and promiscuous, he treated her worse; yet when asked later on which husband she loved most, she implied that it was Punin.

After the Central Committee's unpublished but binding resolution that she was no longer to be printed, Akhmatova worked on her unsubsidized Pushkin studies and on translations, which were allowed her. The Thirties were dominated by Stalin and Yezhov's Great Terror. Anna was staying with the Mandelshtams in 1934 when Osip was first arrested; soon Punin and Lyov, Anna's son, were imprisoned too. They were released upon Akhmatova's petition to Stalin, who liked her poetry, which may eventually have saved her own life. Lyov was to be in and out of prison for much of his life; Mandelshtam, re-arrested, died in the gulag in 1937, as Punin did later on.

Between 1939 and the outbreak of World War II, Akhmatova's fortunes were low indeed. The critic Korney Chukovsky noted that she didn't even have a warm coat, or, often, enough money for the streetcar. It was at this time that Chukovsky's daughter, the writer Lydia Chukovskaya, met Akhmatova and became her Boswell. She kept *The Akhmatova Journals,* three volumes in the original, of which we now have the first, 1938–41, as translated by Milena Michalski and Sylva Rubashova, with fifty-four poems—those mentioned in the text—Englished by Peter Norman.[4]

There is something very unsatisfying about having to read these journals on the installment plan. An important character such as Vladimir Garshin, a physician and professor of medicine, and at this time Anna's lover, will appear frequently in these pages, but a foot-

4. *The Akhmatova Journals, Volume I, 1938–41* by Lydia Chukovskaya (New York, Farrar, Straus & Giroux, 1994).

note on page 21, barely identifying him, concludes: "For more details on him, see *Journals*, vol. 2." Yet the reader should know more. When, like other artists in wartime, Anna was evacuated to Tashkent (whither she traveled clutching the precious manuscript of Shostakovich's Seventh Symphony), she conducted a loving correspondence with Garshin, although he wrote relatively infrequently and then often about other women. Finally, however, he proposed marriage. Anna not only accepted but even agreed to his request to drop her own proud name and become merely Garshina. When she arrived in, as she put it, "the hungry and cold city of post-blockade Leningrad," Garshin met her at the station and chillingly asked where she wanted to be taken. She named the old Punin apartment. "He took me there, said goodbye at the entrance, and kissed my hand. We never saw each other again. . . . I know very well how relationships are ended, and thank God, I've done it myself a thousand times. But this was simply incomprehensible." Garshin, it turned out, was already married.

There are other problems with Chukovskaya's notes. When a new figure appears, a footnote directs you to an endnote. But it is often not the endnote you expect, which should be, let's say, number 19. Instead, you're directed to look ahead to, say, note 64, where this person is dealt with more extensively. Thus later, when you legitimately get to note 64, you find yourself rereading what you've already read. It is fortunate that the publisher, at the last minute, added a glossary, as it were annotating Chukovskaya's notes. But confusion thrives in other ways, too. The *dramatis personae* appear in three guises: with their full names, i.e., first name, patronymic, and last name; or, thereafter, first name and patronymic; or, often, nickname only—or diminutive of the nickname. So when on a given page a Nikolay Ivanovich (i.e., Khardziev, the poetry specialist and historian) jostles a Nikolay Nikolayevich (i.e., Punin), and then a Nikolay Stepanovich (i.e., Gumilyov) pops up, it's hard to keep them apart. When we next hear the nickname Kolya, it might take even a Russian reader a while to figure out which Nikolay is meant. Of course, it turns out to be yet another: Kolya Demidenko.

Still, one should not be put off. *The Akhmatova Journals* begins with a moving prologue in which Lydia Chukovskaya tells about how she lost her husband to the gulag; how she, too, might have lost

her life but for a friend's warning phone call; and how her having a
husband in the camps brought her closer to Akhmatova, who had a
son there. The conversations she doesn't dare report in her journal
are the many ones about these and other cherished prisoners; in-
stead, there is much talk about writers and writing, and about the
trivia of daily life. Especially poignant is the evocation of the way
much of Akhmatova's poetry, unsafe to commit to paper, survived:

> Anna Andreyevna,[5] when visiting me, recited parts of "Re-
> quiem" . . . in a whisper, but at home in Fontanny House did
> not even dare to whisper it; suddenly, in mid-conversation, she
> would fall silent and, signaling to me with her eyes at the ceil-
> ing and walls, she would get a scrap of paper and a pencil; then
> she would loudly say something very mundane: "Would you like
> some tea?" or "You're very tanned," then she would cover the
> scrap in hurried handwriting and pass it to me. I would read the
> poems and, having memorized them, would hand them back to
> her in silence. "How early autumn came this year," Anna An-
> dreyevna would say loudly and, striking a match, would burn
> the paper over an ashtray.

But already from the outset of the book, in its English transla-
tion, we see sloppiness creeping in. Thus the code name the women
used for the secret police is given on one page as Pyotr Ivanich; on
the next, as Pyotr Ivanovich. Or there'll be a comment such as "Paul
was murdered in that room," without any explanation in footnote or
endnote. Again, in May 1939, Anna tells us how much she admires
Joyce's *Ulysses*, even though it's a mite too pornographic for her; she
has read it four times. By October 1940, she tells of reading this
"great and wonderful" book six times. Could she have read that dif-
ficult work two more times in seventeen months? Was she given to
exaggeration? Did her mind wander? Chukovskaya doesn't say.

She walked lightly, this fifty-year-old woman who was often
trailed by two secret policemen and who always carried her pocket-
book and a shabby suitcase with her writings with her out of fear

---

5. I transliterate the patronymic as "Andreyevna" rather than "Andreevna," as do the
translators of the book. Throughout my article, I have silently made such changes in an
attempt to achieve consistency, which, even so, may well have eluded me.

they might be secretly searched. But she was terrified of crossing wide streets, even when empty, and would cling anxiously to whoever accompanied her. Although she disliked Tolstoy, and mounts a splendid attack on *Anna Karenina*, she concedes that he could be marvelously *zaum*. (*Zaum* or *zaumny yazik* refers to transrational or metalogical discourse, as invented by Khlebnikov and the Futurists, a distant precursor of *poésie concrète*.) Anna herself preferred established languages, reading Dante in Italian and, after six months of mostly self-taught English, Shakespeare in the original. But for all the various languages she knew, Russian spelling and punctuation were beyond her; she even misspelled the name of her beloved Annensky, the only poet she admitted to being influenced by.

Anna thought poorly of men because there were few to be seen in the prison queues, and perhaps also because none of her husbands ever hung a picture of her over the table. She was unable to judge her own poems until they were old, which is why she avidly recited the new ones to friends, eager for their judgment as well as memorization. She lived in great poverty, often subsisting on potatoes and sauerkraut; sometimes there was no sugar for the tea she'd serve her guests. Here is a characteristic scene, as Anna and her friend, the actress Olga Visotskaya, decide to go queue up in front of the Procurator's office:

> Anna Andreyevna insisted that Olga Nikolayevna should wear her autumn coat (Olga Nikolayevna only had her summer coat here), and she herself would wear her winter coat.
>
> "It will be hard for you to stand in your winter coat," said Olga Nikolayevna. "Better for me to put on the winter coat, and you the autumn coat."
>
> But Anna Andreyevna disagreed.
>
> "No, *I'll* put on the winter coat. You won't be able to handle it. It's tricky. It hasn't had a single button on it for a long time now. And we won't manage to find new ones and sew them on. I know how to wear it even without buttons, whereas you don't. I'll wear the winter coat."

It is piquant to discover Akhmatova admitting to not understanding one of her own poems. She repeatedly declared that she wrote two kinds of poems: those that seemed to come from an external dictation and were easy to write, and those that she willed herself to write and were impossible. She considered Hemingway a great writer, although she hated the cruelty of his fishing. Vyacheslav V. Ivanov, in his "Meetings with Akhmatova," reports that she "approved of observations comparing her early poetry with the prose of Hemingway and describing it as 'novella-like.'" This ties in with something Mandelshtam wrote: "Akhmatova brought into the Russian lyric all the enormous complexity and wealth of the Russian novel. . . . Akhmatova's origins lie completely within Russian prose, not poetry. She developed her poetic form, keen and original, with a backward glance at psychological prose."[6] What it all seems to add up to is straightforwardness, lucidity, and narrative progression, apparently considered more appropriate to prose.

Tom Sawyer, for Akhmatova, was "an immortal book. Like *Don Quixote*." A bold view in its way, but not unusual for her, who, for example, dared place the *Epic of Gilgamesh* above the *Iliad*. Some of her nonliterary ideas were even stranger: "For some reason, she had got into her head that the steps began right outside her apartment door, and I could not persuade her to cross the landing for anything." Poor Akhmatova! She could no longer even pronounce "sh" and "zh" clearly; some of her front teeth were broken. Nor could she, a pariah in the house of Punin, get a pass to the garden of the House of Entertaining Science (!), where they were all living: "He is someone, a professor, but what am I? Carrion."

Her most cherished poems could not be published; her earlier ones she no longer cared for, and couldn't understand why other people liked them. I myself am more than a little puzzled by her own and other people's judgments on her poetry. In one of her autobiographical sketches, Akhmatova writes that of her entire first book, *Evening* (1912), "I now truly like only the lines: 'Intoxicated by a voice / That sounds exactly like yours . . .'" With all allowances made for what gets lost in translation, it is impossible to understand what could make those two verses special. Even more mysterious, though, is the recollection of the poet Georgy Adamovich about the other great modern Russian poetess, Marina Tsvetayeva: "She [had]

6. In *Mandelstam*, by Clarence Brown (New York, Cambridge University Press, 1978), page 97.

just read Akhmatova's 'Lullaby,' and praised it, saying that she would give everything she had written and would write in the future for a single line from that poem: 'I am a bad mother.'" Even if you allow for the context (a father is speaking), how can that line have such value? There is perhaps something even beyond the poetry that gets lost in translations from Akhmatova.

Amusingly, Anna discusses Pasternak's indifference to her work and goes on to comment with wonderful outspokenness: "Haven't you noticed that poets don't like the poetry of their contemporaries? A poet carries with him his own enormous world—why does he need someone else's poetry? When they're young, about 23 or 24, poets like the work of poets in their own group. Later though, they don't like anybody else's—only their own." Vyacheslav V. Ivanov confirms this: "Certainly Akhmatova was not inclined to listen to the praise of other literary figures of the first decade." Her attitude to Tsvetayeva was particularly ambivalent, even though Marina was much more generous: she called her rival "Anna Chrysostom of all the Russians," and her beautiful poem "To Anna Akhmatova" begins "O muza placha, prekrasneyshaya iz muz!" (O muse of weeping, loveliest of muses). This became a metonym for Akhmatova: Muse of Weeping—or, as Brodsky renders it, Keening Muse.[7] Notice, again, the eloquent fanfare of *prekrasneyshaya*; how is an English translator to do justice to that?

Yet there were also times when the Russian language seemed to thwart Akhmatova. There is a droll page in the *Journals* where Anna agonizes to a couple of friends about something she had written: "One line has been vexing me all my life: 'Gde milomu muzhu detey rodila [Where she bore her dear husband children].' Do you hear: *Mumu?!* Can it be that neither of you, both such lovers of poetry, has noticed this mooing?" Whereupon she proceeds to recite Pushkin's "Monument" to her friends—only, as a footnote tells us, it wasn't that at all, but the epilogue to her own *Requiem*; she was trying to mislead those who, she claimed, were bugging her room. But the greater, metaphysical, risks of her profession haunted her most: "The word is much more difficult material than, for instance, paint.

---

7. The poem is handsomely set to music in Shostakovich's *Six Poems of Marina Tsvetayeva*.

Think about it, really: for the poet works with the very same words that people use to invite each other to tea. . . ."

What is the poetry of Anna Akhmatova really like? Here is how Chukovskaya sees it:

> When you first apprehend it, it does not strike you by the novelty of its form as does, say, the poetry of Mayakovsky. You can hear Baratynsky and Tyutchev and Pushkin—sometimes, more rarely, Blok—in the movement of the poem, in its rhythms, in the fullness of the line, in the precision of the rhymes. At first it seems like a narrow path, going alongside the wide road of Russian classical poetry. Mayakovsky is deafeningly novel, but at the same time he is unfruitful, barren: he brought Russian poetry to the edge of an abyss. . . . Akhmatova's little path turns out to be a wide road in fact; her traditional style is purely external . . . within this she brings about earthquakes and upheavals.

Frankly, in struggling with her poems in Russian—never mind the translations—I cannot find the earthquakes. But I do see a poet with an original vision and a personal voice who manages to maintain her individual talent within the tradition. No wonder she admired T. S. Eliot.

Strange where poets come from! As a child, Anna had no poetry surrounding her; "We didn't have any books in the house, not a single book. Only Nekrasov, a thick, bound volume. My mother used to let me read it on feast days and holidays. This book was a present to Mama from her first husband, who shot himself. . . . I have loved poetry ever since I was a child and I managed to get hold of it somehow. At the age of 13, I already knew Baudelaire, Voltaire and all the *poètes maudits* in French. I started to write poetry early but . . . before I had even written a line, all those around me were convinced that I would become a poetess."

If Chukovskaya were doing her job right, she would answer some troubling questions here. But she never mentions Nekrasov as one of the influences on Akhmatova's poetry—perhaps because he was greatly concerned with social issues, which Anna, until much later on, was not. But he was a loosener and modernizer of diction, someone from whom Anna may have learned things. The real question, though, is: How did the thirteen-year-old daughter of Russian bourgeois manage to get hold of Baudelaire? (That she knew French is, in Imperial Russia, believable.) And what of this quaint juxtaposition: Baudelaire, Voltaire? Is the sage there merely for the rhyme? As a lyric poet, he is known only for a few poems of love and friendship, and for some terse, biting epigrams. Could Anna's short poems in *Rosary* (or *Beads*) owe something to the latter? Or could something of the former have influenced the manner of the poetic teenager—say this, to Mme du Châtelet: "On meurt deux fois, je le vois bien: / Cesser d'aimer et d'être aimable, / C'est une mort insupportable; / Cesser de vivre, ce n'est rien"? But the most puzzling bit here is "all the *poètes maudits.*" It seems impossible for Anna to have gotten hold of even Rimbaud in 1902, to say nothing of the lesser *maudits.* Lydia should have asked some important questions here, though, to be sure, they were interrupted by the entrance of an old woman—shades of Coleridge and the person from Porlock.

Akhmatova harbors some pretty radical ideas about poetry: "Only through contemporary art can one understand the art of the past. There is no other path. And when something new appears, do you know how a contemporary should feel? As if it is pure chance that it is not he who wrote it, as if . . . somebody had snatched it out of his hands." And what a country for poets, this Russia! As Lydia and a woman friend leave Anna's place, the following happens: "Tusya walked me right up to my house. On the way she recited Tyutchev's 'Spring' to me . . . which, until now, I hadn't given the attention it deserves: and then together we recited Baratynski's 'Autumn,' to which Shura [another friend] had introduced us. . . . I thought: This may be the best poem in Russian literature." None of these women was a poet; what they were is Russians.

From this derives Lydia's worshipful attitude toward Anna, which at times becomes cloying, as when the biographer comments on Anna's refusal to fight for a paid vacation owed to her, which the poet contemptuously rejects as "the communal scuffle." Comments Chukovskaya: "Oh, how grateful I am to her that she understands so well who she is, that in preserving the dignity of Russian literature, which she represents at some invisible tribunal, she never takes part in any communal scuffle!"

The poet's stoicism was indeed heroic, as the state treated her shabbily. "That's my life, my biography," she allows. "Who can re-

nounce his own life?" Much later on, in 1954, she was to formulate
it more nobly to Lydia's father, Korney: "I have been very famous
and very notorious, and I know now that essentially it's just the same
thing." And to Georgy Adamovich: "My lot was to suffer everything
it's possible to suffer." So you believe it when Lydia reports, "Anna
Andreyevna put the kettle on. We had tea without sugar, with a stale
roll." Amid such misery, Anna would prodigally dispense insight:
"[Vyacheslav Ivanov] was . . . an outstanding poet, but his poems
were often bad. No, no, there is no contradiction here; one can be a
remarkable poet, but write bad poems." Or: "The Modernists did a
great thing for Russia. . . . They handed back the country in com-
pletely different shape from that in which they received it. They
taught people to love poetry once again, even the technical standard
of book publishing went up."

"I don't know any other country where . . . there is a greater
need for [poetry] than here." She was right. In the large, cold, poor,
and often lonely spaces of Russia, poetry came to fill a void. If (as it
is said) sex was for the French the *cinéma des pauvres*, for average
Russians it tended to be poetry. And, of course, gossip. There are
delicious pages here of Akhmatova gossiping, for example, about the
women in Blok's life, in the midst of which she digresses about
Punin: "'But such an accumulation of wives'—once again, she
tapped Nikolay Nikolayevich's wall lightly—'is utter nonsense.'"
She mocks the pettiness of various literary circles, and concludes, "I
am the only one who is indifferent to what people think of my po-
etry." (But here is Korney Chukovsky: "Akhmatova divided the
world into two uneven parts: those who understand her poems and
those who don't.")

All her life Akhmatova remained a firm believer in Christianity,
Russia being perhaps the premier country for practicing Christians
among its artists and intellectuals. A tolerant woman, she was nev-
ertheless repulsed by the homosexual excesses in Mikhail Kuzmin's
poetry. She makes shrewd observations about Dostoyevsky: "These
are all aspects of his soul. . . . In reality, there never was or will be
anything like it." She evokes charmingly her youth as a nervy, un-
conventional tomboy, and sadly admits to her present discombobu-
lation. I find it regrettable that she so dislikes Chekhov, whose plays,
for her, "epitomize the disintegration of theater"; in both his plays
and fiction "everybody's situation is hopeless." In Natalya Roskina's

memoir, "Good-bye Again," Anna is even blunter: "He was short-sighted in his view of Russia. If one looks too closely, all one sees is cockroaches in the cabbage soup."

In her youth, we learn, Anna was seemingly double-jointed; people thought she should join the circus. (No wonder Gumilyov first suggested she become a dancer!) In maturity, it was her mind that became agile and keen, correctly perceiving, say, the influence of Joyce on Hemingway, Dos Passos, and the rest. She had no delusions about fame: "When you're standing in a courtyard, wet snow falling, queuing for herring, and there is such a pungent smell of herring that your shoes and coat reek of it for ten days, and someone behind you recites: 'On the dish the oysters in ice smelled of the sea, fresh and sharp . . . '—that is something else entirely [from her celebrity in Imperial Russia]. I was gripped with such a fury that I didn't even turn around." Yet this strong, proud woman couldn't finish reading *Uncle Tom's Cabin*: "I felt too sorry for the Negroes."

The Akhmatova Journals, Volume I ends with the 1941 wartime evacuation of Anna, Lydia, and other notables, first to Chistopol, then to Tashkent in Uzbekistan, in Central Asia. It was a difficult sojourn, and there is a fascinating episode (relegated to a footnote) where Chukovskaya gushes to Marina Tsvetayeva about how lucky it was for Akhmatova to have escaped at least Chistopol: "She would certainly have died there. . . . After all, she can't do anything for herself." Tsvetayeva interrupts: "And you think I can?" Soon after, the forty-nine-year-old Tsvetayeva hanged herself. Perhaps the last memorable quotation in this volume has Anna reading her beloved Lewis Carroll again in Tashkent and asking, "Don't you think we too are now through the looking glass?"

There is, of course, much more to even this relatively short first volume. But Peter Norman's translations of some Akhmatova poems are not it. Like all other such translations that I am aware of, they do not begin to convey a true poet. What to do? To reproduce some of her poems in Russian would be redundant for those who know the language, and useless for the rest of us. The best I can do is cite some evaluations of her work.

We have many good descriptions of her personality (I particularly like this from the generally odious Walter Arndt: "Young Roland on his way to the dark tower, crossed with a Beardsley Salome"), but few helpful ones of her verse. Zinaida Gippius (or Hippius), the leading poetess of the preceding generation, rated her and Pasternak highest among their generation.[8] Sidney Monas called her "the supreme mistress of the verbal gesture, poetess of tragic love, who became, in her old age, the poetess, too, of endurance and survival."[9] Aleksandr Blok carped at first: "She writes verses as if standing before a man and it is necessary to write as if standing before God." (Ironically, though, Akhmatova remarked to Vyachelsav V. Ivanov that "there was no humility in Blok's poetry, that humility could only be found in orthodoxy.") Later, Blok considered the truest poets to be Mayakovsky and Akhmatova, "whose muse he saw as 'ascetic' and 'monastic.' "[10]

This is a curious evaluation of someone known as a poet of love, but even more curious is that by Anna's close friend Nadezhda Mandelshtam: "Akhmatova was a poet not of love but of the repudiation of love for the sake of humanity." You might think that this refers to the change in Akhmatova's later poetry, but no: "This woman with a zest for life had rejected all earthy things since her early youth."[11] The gap between such contradictory perceptions is perhaps bridged by Brodsky's view: "It is the finite's nostalgia for the infinite that accounts for the love theme in Akhmatova's verse, not the actual entanglements." Which, in turn, should be balanced against the point of Renato Poggioli in a book that Akhmatova, to be sure, disliked: "The muse of Anna Akhmatova is memory, a memory incredibly near in quality, if not in time, to the incidents she records from the exclusive viewpoint of her 'I.' [Or as Akhmatova put it *contra* Browning in her *Pseudo-Memoirs:* "I speak myself and for myself everything that is possible and that which is not."] Yet in what the poetess reports there is no afterthought or hindsight: one would say that she represents objectively a past which has only a subjective reality."[12]

8. See *Zinaida Hippius: An Intellectual Profile,* by Temira Pachmuss (Carbondale, Southern Illinois University Press, 1970), page 381: "Although she admired Akhmatova's achievements in poetic expression, Hippius disagreed with her 'typically feminine approach to love,' devoid of all mystery and sublimation."

9. In his introduction to *Selected Works of Nikolai S. Gumilev* (Albany, State University of New York Press, 1972), page 17.

10. *The Life of Aleksandr Blok,* Vol. II, by Avril Pyman (New York, Oxford University Press, 1980), pages 141 and 363.

11. For the quotations from Nadezhda Mandelshtam, see Polivanov, *op. cit.,* pages 110 and 114.

For what may be the best overview, we must return to Brodsky's "The Keening Muse": "She was, essentially, a poet of human ties: cherished, strained, severed. She showed these evolutions first through the prism of the individual heart, then through the prism of history, such as it was. This is about as much as one gets in the way of optics anyway." But for the effect that Akhmatova had on other people, I go back to Chukovskaya's prologue, entitled "Instead of a Foreword": "Before my very eyes, Akhmatova's fate—something greater even than her own person—was chiseling out of this famous and neglected, strong and helpless woman a statue of grief, loneliness, pride, courage." Short of a reading of her poetry in the original, this will have to do.

And what lay ahead for Anna? It is absurd to summarize so much in a few words, but here goes. After even worse persecution in the Forties under Zhdanov[13] than in the Thirties under Yezhov, expulsion from the Writers' Union and near-starvation (living off the kindness of friends), then ultimate reinstatement, increased economic comfort and various honors, even the power to protect and promulgate others in her profession. Finally trips abroad to receive a major literary prize in Italy, and an honorary doctorate from Oxford—also reunion in Paris with long-lost friends and lovers. It came very late, and was not really enough. But it provides a mellowly bittersweet ending to a life of fantastic ups and downs.

1994

12. In *Poets of Russia*, by Renato Poggioli (Cambridge, Mass., Harvard University Press, 1960), page 231.

13. The notorious cultural commissar Andrey Zhdanov proscribed Akhmatova in a lengthy execration boiling down to her being "half whore, half nun." In his crude way, Zhdanov was right: she was in fact half glorious love poet and half impassioned religious moralist.

Brodsky
in Retrospect

🌿 LAST JANUARY 28, Joseph Brodsky's heart gave out at age fifty-five. The English language has proved hospitable to foreign prose writers as diverse as Joseph Conrad, Isak Dinesen, and Vladimir Nabokov, but Brodsky wrote poetry and that, as we shall see, may require a finer ear. Moreover, he came to the United States at the comparatively advanced age of thirty-two.

In 1964, the Soviets sentenced Brodsky to five years of exile and hard labor in the Arkhangelsk region of northern Russia for "parasitism." Allowed to return to his native Leningrad after serving eighteen months, he continued to be harassed by the KGB and on June 4, 1972, was forcibly deported to Israel via Austria. In Vienna he met W. H. Auden, who deflected his destination westward, and with whom he would form a not unprofitable mutual admiration society.

In this country, Brodsky had affiliations with numerous colleges and universities, and was the Andrew Mellon Professor of Literature at Mount Holyoke. His true home, though, was in Greenwich Village. (Having settled into marriage with an Italo-Russian translator in 1990, he moved three years ago to Brooklyn Heights.) Brodsky published essays and criticism as well as poetry, which he gradually began to co-translate, translate, and ultimately write in English. A history of heart trouble notwithstanding, he had a good life reading and lecturing and round-tabling around the world. He became an American citizen in 1977 and earned, among other honors, the Nobel Prize in Literature, a MacArthur fellowship, the National Book Critics Circle Award, and two consecutive Poet Laureateships. We now have his last personally overseen collections, issued by Farrar Straus Giroux: *So Forth*, poetry; *On Grief and Reason*, prose.

These books confirm my feeling that, at least as he came through in English, Brodsky was better as a prose writer. His poetry in Russian is not for me to judge. Not only because of my merest smattering of Russian, but also because the Russian concept of a poet differs radically from the Anglo-American. Russian poetry to this day is more emotional than intellectual, more conservative than experimental (with some notable exceptions), and, even on intimate subjects, more public. Russian poets read aloud a good deal, performing often in large venues such as sports arenas; they are public figures followed by the masses, somewhat like athletes in America.

Becoming an American poet, then, is especially hard for a Russian. In this respect, even what I view as Brodsky's rather limited achievement must be seen as genuine success. But the great, if not insuperable, problem with all of his writing is its mannerism, its attitudinizing. He wrote prose as if it were poetry, and poetry as if it were prose. His prose is often apodictic and obscure; his poetry, especially the later verse, discursive and diffuse.

On Grief and Reason is a gathering of essays, introductions, speeches, lectures (some to students), and reminiscences. These last, whether of his early days in the USSR discovering the West through such things as Tarzan movies, or of his later years associating with the likes of Stephen Spender, are informative and entertaining. Other subjects range from Horace to Rainer Maria Rilke, Marcus Aurelius to Thomas Hardy, the Muse of history to Robert Frost. Still others include "How to Read a Book" and "In Praise of Boredom." There is a whimsical account of a literary conference in Brazil, and a speculation on what the women who inspired poets may have looked like.

In "An Immodest Proposal" Brodsky advocates selling inexpensive editions of poetry in all sorts of places, thus making it as universal as, he thinks, it can and should be. In a commencement address he tells graduates what to expect and, more pointedly, what not to expect from life. In an open letter to Václav Havel he takes issue with the Czech writer and political leader's optimism about the future. In a talk to the Foundation of Creativity and Leadership he tries to define creativity, especially as it differs in the arts and sciences. We get here both the Nobel lecture and the short acceptance speech. Strangest is a long essay on Kim Philby and the nature of espionage. An odd piece on travel posits a "composite city" of the memory.

A wandering, ever-inquiring mind, you may conclude, that absorbs much and passes it on generously augmented with insight and speculation. Well, yes, but beware of the pitfalls. Brodsky was a bit of a flibbertigibbet, phantast, and showoff. A poet may sometimes indulge in free association, butterfly maneuvers; for the essayist or lecturer seeking to convey apprehensible ideas, orderly flow is superior to capricious flight.

Add to this the desire to astound, to shock, to solicit forced camaraderie. The favorite devices are paradox, the mighty revelation stripped down to catchy but often opaque apothegm, the euphoniously formulaic utterance tailored for memorization instead of comprehension. The omnipresent master idea is that of the poet not creating his language, but being created by it. With this goes the correlative conceit that the inanimate may (*may* because Brodsky usually hedges his bets) be scanning the animate as much as, or more, than the reverse. Otherwise put, the infinite scrutinizes the finite. For Brodsky, that is what poetry is really about.

We read: "The finite [life] always mistakes the permanent [art] for the infinite and nurtures designs upon it. That, of course, is the permanent's own fault, for it cannot help at times behaving like the finite." "It's quite possible that from time's own point of view the murder of Caesar and World War II occurred simultaneously, in reverse order, or not at all." Or take these formulas. On the uses of uncertainty: "It is better to agonize than to organize." On mingling with the multitude: "Try to be more like them than like those who are not like them; try to wear gray. Mimicry is the defense of individuality, not its surrender." On poetry: "It should be as ubiquitous as gas stations, if not as cars themselves. . . . I don't see why what's done for cars can't be done for books of poetry, which take you quite a bit further." And soon, "before literacy is replaced by videocy."

A longer passage tries to epitomize Frost's "Home Burial": "[The poet] was, I think, after grief and reason, which, while poison to each other, are language's most efficient fuel—or, if you will, poetry's indelible ink. Frost's reliance on them . . . almost gives you the sense that his dipping into this ink pot had to be with the hope of reducing the level of its contents; you detect a sort of vested interest on his part. Yet the more one dips into it, the more it drips with this black essence of existence, and the more one's mind, like one's fingers, gets soiled by this liquid. For the more there is of grief, the more there is of reason."

What a hodgepodge! Why are grief and reason the prime movers of poetry? Does love come under either rubric? Does family? Does religion? Would Frost be so much less smart than Brodsky as not to realize the staining power of his curiously bipolar ink? Essence and existence being opposites, what could "essence of existence" be? Why, in any event, would poetry's very quiddity be something deleterious? If grief and reason are poison to each other, why would an increase in one produce an increase, and not a decrease, in the other?

Good observations in a long essay on Marcus Aurelius are undercut by such cryptically gnomic utterances as "A Stoic's life was a study in ethics, since ethics buys nothing except osmosis." That enthymeme could easily pass for a rebus. Again, "Toward the wrong and atrocious, Marcus was not so much forgiving as dismissive. Which is to say he was impartial rather than just and that his impartiality was not the product of his mind's fairness but of his mind's appetite for the infinite; in particular, for impartiality's own limits." This is hairsplitting to do a sophist or Jesuit proud. "You were an island, Caesar," Brodsky apostrophizes the emperor, "or at least your ethics were, an island in the primordial and—pardon the expression—postmordial ocean of free atoms." Add bad puns to the Brodsky repertoire.

"Ideally, perhaps, the animate and the inanimate should swap places," Brodsky opines in "A Cat's Meow." Perhaps the dictionary's definition of creativity as "ability to create," he goes on, "is nothing more (or less) than matter's attempts to articulate itself." Later: "Matter, I believe, comes to articulate itself through human science or human art presumably only under some kind of duress. This may

sound like an anthropomorphic fantasy, but our cellular makeup en-
titles us to this sort of indulgence. Matter's fatigue, its thinning out,
or its oversaturation with time are, among a host of other less and
more fathomable processes, what further enunciates chance and
what is registered by the lab's instruments or by the no less sensitive
pen of the lyric poet. In either case, what you get is a ripple effect.
In this sense, the ability to make is a passive ability: a grain of sand's
response to the horizon."

Note, first, the hedging; those "perhaps"es, that "more or less,"
"I believe," "presumably," and "some kind of." To disprove the no-
tion of "fantasy," Brodsky invokes the equally subjective "indul-
gence." Are "fatigue" and "thinning out" conjunctive or disjunctive
concepts, and how does "oversaturation with time"—whatever it ex-
actly means—enter into the picture? What of that darkly hinted at
host of other "processes"? How does the plural predicate *are* man-
age to refer back to a singular subject? How do we get from this to
"chance" and "a ripple effect"? Either Brodsky is skipping interme-
diate steps of his argument, or he is parading non sequiturs for our
bedazzlement.

There follows "Wooing the Inanimate," where, as with Frost,
Brodsky tries to rehabilitate Hardy through textual explication. But
along with genuine insights, he heaps up overstatement: subtleties
that plainly are not in the text, grandiose assertions that the poems
cannot quite sustain. And plain nonsense, as when Hardy's idiom is
described as "both down-to-earth and metaphysical," and Brodsky
continues: "Well, metaphysics is always down-to-earth, isn't it? The
more down-to-earth it is, the more metaphysical it gets, for the
things of this world and their interplay are metaphysics' last frontier;
they are the language in which matter manifests itself." To declare
the things of this earth metaphysics' last frontier is like pronouncing
Mexico the last frontier of the United States, confusing the first of
B with the last of A.

In addition, we are told Hardy's poems "have the feeling of being
detached from themselves, of not so much being poems as main-
taining the appearance of being poems." First off, poems don't have
a feeling; *we* have it about *them*. Second, how does a poem get de-
tached from itself? Third, if these poems merely have the appear-
ance of poems, are they worth discussing? As for Hardy's language,

Brodsky avers that "There is no such thing as antiquated diction, there are only reduced vocabularies. That's why, for example, there is no Shakespeare nowadays on Broadway; apparently the modern audience has more trouble with the bard's diction than the folks at the Globe had. That's progress for you, then; and there is nothing sillier than retrospection from the point of view of progress."

But, of course, there *is* such a thing as antiquated diction, as we know from some of Shakespeare and more of, say, Chaucer. Does Brodsky want Middle English to be carefully stored in everyone's memory bank? What is that "apparently" greater trouble we have with Shakespeare than "the folks" at the Globe had? There is no "apparently" about it: They were hearing their own language; we hear something four centuries old. And what is that sneered-at "progress" from which it is "silly" to retrospect? For one thing, Brodsky is putting that word "progress" into our mouths; for another, where else can we look back from except from where we are? It is only through such retrospection that we *can* approach Shakespeare.

Next, consider this crucial passage: "Language is capable of arrangements that reduce a human being to, at best, the function of a scribe. . . . It is language that utilizes a human being, not the other way around. . . . Language . . . is ultimately the voice of inanimate matter, and . . . poetry just registers now and then its ripple effect." There's that old ripple effect, and an elaboration: "I am far from suggesting that this is what Thomas Hardy was after in this line [from "The Darkling Thrush"]. Rather, it was what this line was after in Thomas Hardy, and he responded." That, certainly, is a kind of metaphysics: The animate and inanimate, for Brodsky anyway, *did* trade places.

To exalt Hardy, our essayist simply established links—however tenuous and arbitrary—between him and Auden. For what runs through Brodsky's entire critical thinking is rampant Audenolatry, a worship of the benefactor as a kind of Archpoet, toward and from whom all poetry flows. I have a healthy admiration for Auden, but I think he has to share the heights with Yeats, Eliot, and Pound on the grand scale, and, on the smaller one, with such masters of the short lyric as D. H. Lawrence, John Crowe Ransom, Louis MacNeice, and especially Robert Graves. But the way Brodsky keeps quoting him, often referring to him simply as "the poet," and holding him up to us as the paragon, I find untenable.

In an essay on Rilke's "Orpheus. Eurydice. Hermes," we read: "While it's silly to suggest a hierarchy among various realities, it can be argued that all reality aspires to the condition of a poem: if only for reasons of economy." So, although one must not suggest a hierarchy, Brodsky does—with poetry, his thing, at the top. Reasons of economy? Hardly. A prose aphorism is as economical as a verse epigram. And why make economy so important? Our desire for elaboration—or, in the author's case, overelaboration—is equally powerful. These are contrary currents that coexist in us—like grief and reason, you might say.

Brodsky can, to be sure, hit the nail on the head, even if I have emphasized his misses. For example: "On the whole, the representational pattern in myths boils down to the man-is-his-purpose principle . . . everyone is defined by his action. This is not so because the ancients were unwitting Sartreans but because everyone was then depicted in profile. A vase, or for that matter a bas relief, accommodates ambiguity rather poorly." But he promptly falls from perspicacity by asserting that "definitions normally bespeak the presence of an alternative," which is either obvious or absurd. It is interesting to read that a "parenthesis is the typographical equivalent of the back of one's mind," but how does it follow that it is the "true seat of civilization in modern man"?

Weirder still is a discussion of the vowel sounds and caesura in a line about Hermes, "The god of faring and of distant message," where Brodsky finds "quite a lot of 'airing' in 'faring.'" That he should be totally oblivious to this being an English translation is remarkable. Rilke's German, "*der Gott des Ganges und der weiten Botschaft*," contains none of the airy-fairy, or airing-faring, stuff. Yet even had Rilke been writing in English, would there really have been "airing" in "faring"? This kind of manipulative newfangled cleverness is no better than the old-style obtuseness. Neither is his casually tossed-off pseudoprofundity: "Come to think of it, virtue is horizontal." And much as we may enjoy Brodsky's enthusiasm, we bridle at the pronouncement that Rilke's three lines beginning with "She was already loosened" constitute "the greatest sequence of three similes in the entire history of poetry." Windy hyperbole blows neither analyst nor analyzed any good.

How seriously, indeed, can we take an exegete explaining Eurydice's sleepwalking "Who?" as "oblivion's own voice. . . . Because forces, divine powers, abstract energies, etc., tend to operate in monosyllables; that's one way of recognizing them in everyday reality"? The lumping together of that vague threesome ("forces," "powers," "energies") troubles me, as does the slatternly "etc." that may mean anything. More to the point, why in heaven would such "forces" use monosyllables, and who on earth could recognize them thereby?

The cutesiest piece in *On Grief and Reason* is "Letter to Horace." It concerns Ovid, approvingly, and Virgil, disapprovingly, as much as its nominal addressee. Curiously, Brodsky seems to prefer Ovid to Horace, perhaps because Ovid was a womanizer, permitting a fellow ladies' man to wonder whether he looked more like Paul Newman or James Mason. "Time," Brodsky allows, were it to compose a poem, "would include leaves, grass, earth, wind, sheep, horses, trees, cows, bees. But not us. Maximum, our souls." Bizarre as this exclusion is, "maximum" for "at most" makes it more so; and how could a poem about our souls not ipso facto be about us?

The epistle continues: "Next to [Ovid, aka Naso] somebody like the Viennese doctor—never mind not catching the reference—is kindergarten, child's play. And frankly, you [Horace], too. And so is Virgil. To put it bluntly, Naso insists that in this world *one thing is another.* That, in the final analysis, reality is one large rhetorical figure and you are lucky if it is just a polyptoton or a chiasmus. With him a man evolves into an object, and vice versa, with the immanent logic of grammar, like a statement sprouting a subordinate clause. With Naso the tenor is the vehicle, Flaccus [i.e., Horace], and/or the other way around, and the source of it all is the ink pot."

The context being dreams and reality, "Viennese doctor" is plain enough, so why the condescending "never mind not catching the reference"? Or, if such a danger exists, why not "Freud" instead of "good old Ziggy," as Brodsky patronizingly puts it elsewhere? As for "one thing being another," is that not the way all imagery works, with Ovid holding no patent? And even if reality is one large rhetorical figure, why that "you are lucky if it is just a polyptoton or a chiasmus"? Why these two rather than, say, anaphora and praeteritio—are those more difficult? Why, in the first place, rhetorical figures, which are primarily the orator's, rather than tropes, such as metaphor and simile, which are chiefly the poet's? "Tenor" (the thing compared) and "vehicle" (the thing compared to) are terms out of I. A. Richards, whom Brodsky casually co-opts. As for the ink pot as primary source, where else should a poet dip his pen? In his blood?

The closing essay, a tribute to Stephen Spender, is engaging, but once more another poet obtrudes heavily: "If in your undergraduate days you meet Wystan Auden, your self-infatuation is bound to be short." Isn't that true of early meetings with any major poet? How does it bear on Spender? "After this encounter, nothing was easy: neither writing nor living." Isn't that a bit—or a great deal—too much?

I have stressed the weaknesses of Brodsky's criticism as a counterweight to the hero worship that surrounds his figure. My aim is to warn readers, particularly young and impressionable ones, against swallowing this unquestionably intelligent, erudite, and talented man whole. That would seem virtually impossible, however, with his poetry, especially in its later phases. Without indulging in Brodskyan overstatement, I can affirm that the one or two long and 60-odd short poems collected in *So Forth* constitute about as poor a volume of verse as any I have ever encountered from the most minor of poets.

In the liminal poem, "Infinity," a Crusoe-like figure addresses in his mind the natives of his island. He contends that "Islands are cruel enemies / of tenses, except the present one. And shipwrecks are but flights from grammar / into pure causality. Look what life without mirrors does to pronouns / not to mention one's features!" I can see how the island of your shipwreck cuts off the past and the future. But what are "flights from grammar"—which, after all, is not exclusively about tenses—doing here? And what is "pure causality"? Surely not something that dispenses with past and future. What does "life without mirrors" do to pronouns other than, perhaps, the "I"? Very little. Then comes one of Brodsky's familiar crutches, "not to mention," and, finally, what does make sense here, "one's features."

The gain, though, is promptly forfeited as we read on: "Perhaps your ancestors also ended up on this wonderful beach in a fashion similar / to mine. Hence, your attitude toward me. In your eyes I am / at the very least an island within an island." Nothing could be more prosaic than the first two verses here. Is "wonderful beach" ironic? Too facile, in that case. Sincere? Too trite then. I am not sure, either, what a possible ancestral shipwreck has to do with the attitude of the present native population. "An island within an island" is nice, but "at the very least" is merely a filler, like the "not to mention" above.

Next in the volume is the Audenesque "A Song," beginning:

> I wish you were here, dear,
> I wish you were here,
> I wish you sat on the sofa
> and I sat near.
> The handkerchief could be yours,
> the tear could be mine, chin-bound.
> Though it could be, of course,
> the other way round.

The end here echoes all those "vice versa"s we encountered in the essays. Such reversibility is better in a raincoat; and "chin-bound" is too obviously there only for the rhyme.

The alternative is even more pointless in the next stanza, where the lovers might drive off in a car. "We'd find ourselves elsewhere, / on an unknown shore, / Or else we'd repair / to where we've been before." Yes, that's the choice: somewhere new or somewhere old. But the archaic "repair" is unfelicitous, particularly in a car; it suggests engine trouble. Most Audenesque is a transition from lyrical to mundane: "When the moon skims the water / that sighs and shifts in its slumber / I wish it were still a quarter / to dial your number." Is that a plea for lower telephone rates?

The poem concludes:

> I wish you were here, dear,
> in this hemisphere,
> as I sit on the porch
> sipping a beer.
> It's evening, the sun is setting;

boys shout and gulls are crying.
What's the point of forgetting
if it's followed by dying?

"Hemisphere" is a bit weak: If he were, say, in Alaska, and she in Patagonia, the distance would not be diminished. And incantatory as the cadence may be, "beer" is (dare I say it?) pretty flat in a romantic context. Also, if "the sun is setting," don't we know it's evening? Most needlessly puzzling is the conclusion. The poet, reminiscing, is clearly not forgetting, so he must mean "Why *should* I forget"? This presupposes a nearness to death, which does not seem to be the case. Even if it were, wouldn't his *not* forgetting make dying easier, as a surcease from painful remembrance? Do those impressively melancholy closing lines add up to more than a facile paradox, with "forgetting" where you expect "remembering"?

If the best is not at the beginning of a collection, perhaps it is at the end. There we get the poem "Taps." It starts: "I've been reproached for everything save the weather / and in turn my own neck was seeking a scimitar. / But soon, I'm told, I'll lose my epaulets altogether / and dwindle into a little star." What is "in turn" doing there? Who, these days, would think of a beheading with a scimitar rather than with a sword or axe? Only a Turk, or a person who needs a rhyme for "star."

As "a sky's lieutenant" (a rather high rank for someone who lost his epaulets altogether), he will "hide in clouds where thunder roars, / blind to the troops as they fold their pennant / and run, pursued by the pen in droves." Are the troops the lesser stars? They must be his troops, for he couldn't escape so easily from enemy ones. Yet why would such a bad officer command any troops? What sort of pennant may stars fold? Though "pen" echoes "pennant" nicely, what could it mean here?

"With nothing around to care for, it's of no import / if you are blitzed, encircled, reduced to nil. / Thus wetting his dream with the tumbled ink pot, / a schoolboy can multiply as no tables will." Who, I ask again, would conduct deadly warfare in heaven? How does the opaque second half of the quatrain, casually introduced by a "thus," relate to the first half? A wet dream suggests a sexual one; but wetted with ink? Does "multiply" in this sexualized context mean procreate, or does it, mathematically, tie in with "tables"? Either way, the meaning of the stanza eludes me. But rhyming "import" with "ink pot" is cacophonous: Neither rhyme nor half-rhyme, it is a kind of grating three-quarter rhyme.

"And although the speed of light can't in nature covet / thanks, non-being's blue armor plate, / prizing attempts at making a sifter of it, / might use my pinhole, at any rate." Does one covet thanks? No, one craves or demands them. Whereas light could be a valid subject here, "speed of light," a mere attribute, does not work as the necessary agent. I can't see why the "blue armor plate"—the sky—would "prize" being punctured, even by a star. Anyway, how could a star, the poet's heavenly incarnation, be a mere puncture, a pinhole? And why that bathetic anti-climax, "at any rate," for closing? As for meter, the scansion here is scandalous.

The third likely candidate for superior achievement would be the title poem, "So Forth." Consider the first stanza:

> Summer will end. September will come. Once more it's okay to
>   shoot
> duck, woodcock, partridge, quail. "You've grown long in the
>   tooth,"
> a belle may sigh, and you'll cock up your double barrel,
> but to inhale more oxygen rather than to imperil
> grouse. And the keen lung will twitch of a sudden whiff
> of apricots. On the whole, the world changes so fast, as if
> indeed at a certain point it began to mainline
> some muck obtained from a swarthy alien.

"Shoot" and "tooth" will do as a half-rhyme, but "mainline" and "alien" is outlandish—or, at least, phonically phony. One can no longer describe a girlfriend as "a belle," with its antebellum ring. You *cock* your *gun*; you do not "cock up your double barrel"; a "cock-up," Brodsky's specialty, is a blunder or a mess. "On the whole" and "indeed" are deadwood; "at a certain point" is scarcely better. "Muck" as a synonym for junk (heroin) is strictly from hunger. "Swarthy alien," for pusher, is insulting.

The second stanza meanders on to this conclusion: "A train in the distance runs whistling along the rail, / though you will spot no smoke inspecting its inventory. / But in a landscape's view, motion is mandatory." The distant train whistle is perhaps the hoariest of all poetic clichés. In the next verse, after we get past the misleading word order (it is not the smoke but *you* that does the inspecting), we still wonder why and how anyone would inventory a distant train. It turns out the meaning is merely that the train is so far away, we cannot even see its smoke. What a cumbersome, near-impenetrable periphrasis as a smoke-screen for banality.

In the third stanza, "per se" rhymes clumsily with "you see," and, worse yet, "the edge of the forest echoes a rustling junction." But a train junction makes noises far too harsh for comparison with forest murmurs. "And it's not a lump but a hedgehog that fills your throat" is grotesque without being evocative. "An airplane's callous / profile looks odd on high, having lost its haloes" is a trope meant to convey a detail-obliterating distance. Do invisible propellers make a plane seem "callous" rather than sleek? Only to rhyme with "haloes," I fear.

The poem continues, "That's what speed's all about. The belle was right. What would / an ancient Roman, had he risen now, recognize?" The first hemistich sounds like "thats whats peeds" and is grating. But just how was that belle, complaining of dental longitude, right? Is the poet so old as to be a risen ancient Roman—perhaps even our old friend Marcus Aurelius? A bit grandiose, that. As the stanza progresses, it becomes somewhat clearer, albeit not less clumsy: Some folks traveling abroad are like an ancient Roman surfacing today. The poem's final octave is a total jumble, leaving us gasping for breath as we grope for meaning.

Absurdity and risibility dog this collection. A quasi-sequence of five poems about centaurs begins: "They briskly bounce out of the future and having cried 'Futile!' / immediately thud back up to its cloud-clad summit. / A branch bends, burdened with birds larger than space—new style, / stuffed not with dawn or feathers but only with 'Damn it, damn it.'" Note how mechanical it all is. "Future" leads automatically into "futile," though the centaurs should, properly, come from the past. The indicated "stuffed with down" undergoes an arbitrary vowel shift to "dawn." "Summit" wants a rhyme and conjures up the ludicrous double "damn it." "Cloud-clad" is a facile way out of the cliché "cloud-capped," but lands in an overall-literative jingle, even more thudding than the four b's of the next verse, capped with that "burdened-birds" heavy-handedness. In "Centaurs IV," Brodsky comes up with a verse deserving inclusion in any stuffed-owl collection: "This century's serial number matches a rooster's croak."

Capitalizing on the prosiness that current poetasters have apparently legitimized, Brodsky treats poetry like bubble gum, and sticks a line break wherever the gum snaps. His flaccid meters and tortured rhymes resemble crooked teeth topheavily capped, and every so often there are unsightly gaps in meaning. His earlier poetry was better, lending credence to the old saw about hunger being the true muse; the later work, begotten on satiety, mistakes ambition for necessity. But how many artists have been able to recognize that their future was in their past?

1996

On Translation

CERTAINLY literature should be translated, and, of course, it can't be. The work of art is unique (which is not the least of its virtues and may even be the greatest), and though a good translation is unique too, that is a different uniqueness. But this should not deter us from translating. Readers cannot be expected to know many, if any, languages; so here is a case where the mountain must come to Mohammed. Translations of prose can even be accurate; translations of poetry only brilliant.

We are not getting more translations than we can absorb. Readers who really want a fair idea of what Homer sounds like in Greek, but have no Greek, will never consider adding a Fitzgerald to a Lattimore piling Ossa on Pelion. Such readers know that several good translations together form a *gradus ad Parnassum*, and, though the summit is not reached even in that way, every step helps.

There is no great harm in getting some bad translations. They provide good teachers with a useful means of conveying all the riches of the original that even so dedicated a duffer as the translator missed, and they may spur on other translators to do better. They also permit critics to display their superior scholarship and make remarks that may occasionally prove useful. A poor translation is no serious threat to the original unless it is the only one available; even then it is perhaps better to have it than none at all. Moreover, it can be impressed upon the reader that he is getting only one-tenth of what the original offers, though in fact he is getting, let's say, three-fifths. The somewhat exaggerated awe with which he will re-gard the original redounds to its glory—not a bad state of affairs, considering the general indifference to literary works.

I have translated and may translate again. My reasons for desist-ing are, first, that translating takes too much time from a writer who may be struggling to make a reputation as a writer, not as a transla-tor; second, that it is grossly underpaid. I don't mean that transla-tions such as we usually get are underpaid—quite the contrary; I mean that a good translation is worth much more than it now fetches. Both reasons point in the same direction: unless you are a translator first and last, translate *after* you have arrived as a writer. Then you won't have to do so much lesser original work to prove yourself, and, when you do translate, you will command a more nearly decent fee.

A good translation is, to borrow words from Rilke about the uni-corn, an animal of which there isn't any. But, like the unicorn, it ex-ists sufficiently; more than, for example, the Tasmanian tiger, which, though it does exist, does so considerably less for most people than the unicorn. I mean that a near-success in translating a major work is worth more than complete success in writing a minor one. The old adage about translations being like women—the beautiful ones cheat, the faithful ones are ugly—is not true. A beautiful woman who overflows with love yet practices discretion does not cheat; she is merely faithful to two men instead of one.

But what, ideally, would a good translation be? First, one in which the translator serves the author more than himself. This seems obvious, indeed is so, except to a good many translators, par-ticularly famous ones. Second, a good translation is a balancing act: keeping perfect equilibrium between absolute literalness (fidelity to the minutest features of the original) and total freedom (using the translator's language in its most natural, idiomatic way, which is to say in a manner inevitably different from that of the original). How does the translator achieve this equipoise? By tact, which, regret-tably, I cannot define; by immense patience; and by being a good writer, or poet, in his own right. If he is also famous, he will do well to forget it while translating.

Cleverness is not to be despised. Very often, especially in verse but also in prose, equivalents are the only way out—for puns, topical references, etc. This is where ingenuity is mandatory, though highly respected writers may find themselves, when they turn translators, devoid of it. Thorough familiarity with and love for the work to be translated are obvious prerequisites. So, too, is intimate knowledge of both languages, for the good translator must know everything the best dictionary knows, as well as everything the best dictionary does not know. It is true that one must know the language into which one is translating even better; but this axiom has given rise to excesses, such as translations by essentially monolingual celebrities based on trots and counseling. Although this method has yielded some happy results, its current enthusiastic espousal is proving a mixed blessing. Poetry trots themselves, at the bottom of the page as in Penguin poetry editions, have their modest use, particularly for readers who have some knowledge of the original language. Outstanding translations that have dated—like Dryden's Virgil or Pope's Homer—may also shed some light on the original, though they are more valuable as illuminations of the distinguished translator and his age.

All this barely begins to define a good translation. Let me make a desperate stab: A good translation is one that to a sensitive and informed reader—perhaps even an expert—reads, first, like *an* original, and, second, like *the* original. A good translator is easier to define. He is, in that handy German word, *kongenial* (a fellow genius), and, as the English cognate has it, congenial.

1968, revised 2001

Traduttore, Traditore,
or the Tradition
of Traducing

A Longing for the Light: Selected Poems of Vicente Aleixandre. Tr. by Lewis Hyde.

Hours in the Garden and Other Poems, by Hermann Hesse. Tr. by Rika Lesser. Bi-lingual text.

The Storm & Other Poems, by Eugenio Montale. Tr. by Charles Wright.

The Face Behind the Face, by Yevgeny Yevtushenko. Tr. by Arthur Boyars and Simon Franklin.

Nostalgia for the Present, by Andrei Voznesensky. Ed. by Vera Dunham and Max Hayward. Bi-lingual text.

Easter Vigil & Other Poems, by Karol Wojtyla (Pope John Paul II). Tr. by Jerzy Peterkiewicz.

Bells in Winter, by Czeslaw Milosz. Tr. by the author and Lillian Vallee.

The Poems of Catullus. Tr. by Frederic Raphael and Kenneth McLeish.

Poems of Pierre de Ronsard. Tr. and ed. by Nicholas Kilmer. Bi-lingual text.

The First Encounter, by Andrey Bely. Tr. by Gerald Janeček. Bi-lin-
gual text.
Vasko Popa: Collected Poems. Tr. by Anne Pennington.
Homage to the Lame Wolf, by Vasko Popa. Tr. by Charles Simic.

☙ NINETEEN POETS in twenty translations—nineteen poets among
whom there are three Nobel laureates, two matinee idols, and one
pope. Let us start with these palpable celebrities, and take, first of
all, the Nobel Prize–winners in alphabetical order.

Vicente Aleixandre, the 1977 laureate, is represented with *A
Longing for the Light,* a generous selection from his work, early to re-
cent, made by Lewis Hyde. Roughly half of it is translated by the ed-
itor, the other half by W. S. Merwin (unfortunately, one early poem
only), Robert Bly, Willis Barnstone, and eleven others. The politi-
cal credentials of Aleixandre (born 1898 in Seville) are as good as his
poetic ones: poor health and isolation removed him from Franco's
world; he began publishing in 1926 in Ortega's *Revista de Occidente,*
was influenced by Darío, Machado, and Jiménez, and was friends
with Lorca, Cernuda, Guillén, and especially Dámaso Alonso. A
certain vagueness of poetic profile has nevertheless kept him, per-
haps not quite undeservedly, less esteemed than some of his famous
contemporaries. Significantly, Neruda refers to him somewhat pa-
tronizingly as the "poet of limitless dimension"; Jorge Guillén num-
bers him, less than enthusiastically, among the "poets of delirium
and free form."

Actually, Aleixandre's work falls, almost too conveniently, into
those three phases schoolboys love: early, middle, and late. The
early, emerging from a brief dalliance with traditional formalism and
poésie pure, soon takes the shape of free verse and prose poems redo-
lent of surrealism, the lava of the unconscious gushing forth partly
also under the influence of Freud, whom the poet was reading at the
time. Aleixandre called this "poetry as it is born, with a minimum of
elaboration," admitting the prose poems to be, of all his works, the
hardest to read. I find both the prose poems and the *vers libre* of this
period unimpressive—too private, nightmare-ridden, undisci-
plined—which goes, I am afraid, also for three later volumes, up to
and including *Mundo a solas* (1936). From this, I quote one quatrain
of "El árbol" ("The Tree"), in Lewis Hyde's translation:

Immense knee where kisses will never try to act like false ants.
Where the moon won't pretend to be a piece of fine lace.
Because the white foam that might even dare graze it one night
is stone in the morning, hard stone without moss.

This excerpt exemplifies Aleixandre's early strategy of evasion, of describing things that are not rather than things that are. "Now the sun isn't horrendous like a cheek that's ready: / it isn't a piece of clothing or a speechless flashlight. / Nor is it the answer heard by our knees, / nor the task of touching the frontiers with the whitest part of our eyes," we read in "With All Due Respect," and I respectfully submit: "Don't tell me what it isn't—tell me what it is!" (Stephen Kessler translates *esa dificultad* (this difficulty) as "the task" and *linterna* (lantern) as "flashlight," out of that kind of perverse, translatorish self-importance that runs through this volume.) The sun, we learn forthwith, "has already become truth, lucidity, stability," which isn't much help either in fixing it in our consciousness.

When it is not outright negation, the game is the tenuous equivocation of either-or. A poem in *The World by Itself* is entitled "Guitar or Moon," and an entire collection of 1935 is named *Destruction or Love. Or*, even more than *not* or *nor*, is Aleixandre's poetic prop. "In front of me, the dolphins or the sword . . . ," "Like that final longing to kiss the shore good-bye, / or the painful footprint of a hermit or a footstep gone astray . . . ," "Bull made of moon or honey . . . ," "A horn or a sumptuous sky . . . ," "An upward impulse wants to be moon, / or calm, or warmth, or that poison of a pillow in the muffled mouth. . . ." These fragments represent only the most flagrant *or*'s from four poems from *Swords Like Lips* printed consecutively in *A Longing for the Light*. It is, throughout the earlier works, a pitiless proliferation that contributes to their haziness.

With the collections *Shadow of Paradise* (1939–1943) and, especially, *Heart's Story (Historia del corazón)* of 1945–1953, the middle period gets under way and things look up. These are mostly reminiscences of the poet's childhood in Málaga and love poems; in them, Aleixandre achieves a blend of verdant innocence and lush description of nature, as well as perceptions of love expressed with a very personal *conceptismo*—perhaps a synthesis of Rubén Darío's wildness and Machado's restraint. The rhythms are meticulously

balanced, and the long-breathed verses often lengthen out still far-
ther at the end of the free-flowing strophes.

A fine example from the earlier tome is "Ciudad del paraíso"
("City of Paradise"), dedicated "To Málaga, my city," yet to which
Hyde's translation does signal injustice. "Angélica ciudad que, más
alta que el mar, presides sus espumas" becomes "town that stands
like an angel over the sea and rules its waves." Even granted that the
central panel of this verbal triptych, *más alta que el mar*, with its mar-
moreal assonance given final chiseling by the framing parallelism of
más and *mar*, cannot be reproduced in English, something like "ex-
alted above the sea" might come nearer the mark, and "angelic city"
is better than "town . . . like an angel." And, "rules the waves" hav-
ing been pre-empted by Britannia, I would opt for "rules over its
foam."

Consider Aleixandre's "Acaso de una reja florida una guitarra
triste / cantaba la súbita canción suspendida en el tiempo; / quieta la
noche, más quieto el amante, / bajo la luna eterna que instantánea
transcurre." "Suspended in time, a sad guitar seemed to sing / the
unexpected song of a flower-filled lattice. / The night was quiet and
the suitor even quieter / under the momentary moon that flows by
forever." Thus Hyde; a more Jekyllish translation might run: "Per-
haps from a flowery shelf a sad guitar / sang the sudden tune sus-
pended in time; / quiet the night and quieter the lover / under the
eternal moon rushing by in a trice." What is particularly inept about
Hyde's version is the inversion; the progression from flowery shelf
to suspension in time follows the order in which the senses appre-
hend the phenomena in question; moreover, the song belongs to the
lover, not to the lattice. Again, the movement from *momentary* to
forever is incorrect, and *flows* is too slow; this suggests duration,
whereas impermanence is intended: though the moon is eternal, for
the lover and for us it rushes by in an instant. And look now at the
final couplet: "Allí el cielo eras tú, ciudad que en él morabas. / Ciu-
dad que en él volabas con tus alas abiertas." Hyde translates: "You
were the sky and the sky was your home, / city that used to fly with
your wings spread wide." Not so. Málaga, on a cliff overlooking the
sea, becomes the sky for someone gazing at it from below; so we
must get something like "There you were the sky, city that dwelled
in it"—*there* is important, for it means that elsewhere, where the

poet now lives, no such guardian city in the sky exists. Again, it is not that the city "used to fly" through the heavens; it still does, only no longer for the absent and sadly older poet. Hence we need a continuous action: "City that flew in it [the sky] with your wings outspread."

The poems in *Historia del corazón* are mostly successful, the vestiges of surrealism discreetly heightening the intensely individual, sensuous perceptions. Especially notable are "The Old Man and the Sun," "Her Hand Given Over," and "We Feed on Shadow." I quote from the second: "Once more I touch your hand / . . . to touch / . . . the skin with its wings and beneath that / the stony bone that can't be bribed, the sad bone that never gets any / love . . ." (Hyde). This should read: ". . . feeling under the winged skin the hard, unsubornable / bone, the sad bone that is beyond the reach of / love . . ." (literally: "as far as which love never extends").

But in Aleixandre's last phase, things go wrong again. In poems like "If Someone Could Have Told Me" (from *Poemas de la consumación*, 1965–1966), surrealism returns with a ravening vengeance; moreover, a fuzzy mysticism and populism set in. There are still fine passages, as in poems like "Whom I Write for" (or "Who I Write for," as Hyde, who, like his associates, is often ungrammatical, would have it) and "To My Dog," containing such a lovely line as "Residido en tu luz, immóvil en tu seguridad, no podiste más que entenderme," which in the original has that pithy lyricism, that one talent of Aleixandre's which it is death to Hyde. This should become something like "Dwelling in your light, motionless in your assurance, you could do no more than hear me." Yet Hyde renders it as "You live in your light, your security does not change, the best / you could do for me was understand."

One of the few effective late poems, "Llueve" ("It's Raining"), is no less tidily sabotaged by Robert Bly's translation. Take the beginning: "En esta tarde llueve, y llueve pura / tu imagen. . . ." This becomes in Bly: "This evening it's raining, and my picture of you is raining." Lost are the compression and the word order with its near-chiasmus, so important because it acts as a linking device between perceptions; we need something like "Tonight it rains, as rains your pure image." But, on the whole, the late work is uninspired, and suffers from a facile anti-intellectualism, as in this dictum from "Sound of the War," the last poem in the book: "Whoever touches lives. Whoever knows has died." Aleixandre is worth reading, but in a more fastidious selection and in more responsible translations than proffered here.

As Nobel laureates go, however, Aleixandre is a rather good one. Somewhat less can be said for Hermann Hesse, especially when he waxes mystically prolix, and when the verbosity is in verse. In fact, Hesse's early collections of poetry, up to and including the volume *Crisis* (1928), display some attractive short lyrics of the kind Richard Strauss set to music in his *Four Last Songs*—though even there the fourth, by Eichendorff, far outstrips the three by Hesse. What we get in *Hours in the Garden and Other Poems*, translated by Rika Lesser, is two long poems published as plaquettes in 1936 and 1937, and four shorter ones from the late period, including one published posthumously in 1962, the year of Hesse's death. There is no critical apparatus except for a brief, anonymous note on the back cover; it states that these poems were written while Hesse was working "on his great novel *The Glass Bead Game* [and] reflect the book's themes of mysticism and the search for perfection. . . . These poems elucidate Hesse's physical and metaphysical search for what he described as 'a sublime alchemy, an approach to a spirit that is unified in itself beyond all images.'" I find *The Glass Bead Game* (a.k.a. *Magister Ludi*) unreadable, and I am highly suspicious of any search for a sublime alchemy, not to mention a spirit unified in itself beyond all images.

In point of fact, "Hours in the Garden," the title poem, is an account of the horticultural activities of the poet in his garden at Montagnola. It is in hexameters, reminiscent of some of the duller productions of Klopstock, Goethe (*Hermann und Dorothea*), and any number of undistinguished German nature poets. Actually, the mode goes back all the way to Hesiod, and has not improved with wear. Here, for example, is a brief passage about the restorative blessings of Hesse's garden: "Jetzt auch flücht ich hierher, den Nacken glüh'nd von der Sonne, / Müde im Rücken, die Augen verwelkt, und will bis zum Mittag / Hier bei spielerisch mühlosem Tun mich erholen und weilen." In English, we get: "Now I, too, take refuge here, my neck red-hot from the sun, / My back tired, my eyelids drooping, and until noon I want / To rest and relax in playful,

effortless occupation." This is typical of Lesser's meterless, pedes-
trian translation, which is the last thing the already footling original
needs. What Hesse says is "Even now, I . . ." meaning "even in my
advanced age," and not, "I, too," like the family cat (earlier de-
scribed as escaping into the garden), which is what Lesser takes it to
mean. "Eyelids drooping" flattens *die Augen verwelkt* (with wilting
eyes) into mundane prose. Utterly prosaic, too, is "rest and relax"
for *erholen und weilen* (restore myself and linger); *bei spielerisch
mühlosem Tun* requires "playful*ly* effortless," an adverb rather than
Lesser's adjectival *playful.*

The other long poem, "The Lame Boy," is a well-meaning but
bathetic tribute and apology to a childhood playmate who, because
he was working-class, was never brought home by young Hermann.
The remaining pieces are insignificant, except insofar as they reveal
Lesser's translatoritis in refusing obvious, God-given rhymes that
would be perfect English equivalents for the originals. Where Hesse
writes "Und schwemmte, schlämmte sanft die Wurzel ein," Lesser
offers "Slowly poured sun-warmed water over [the roots]." But,
surely, "flooded, mudded in the root" would do the trick better.
Again, in the last poem, about the broken bough (himself), Hesse
concludes: "Hart klingt und zäh sein Gesang / . . . Noch einen
Sommer, noch einen Winter lang." And Lesser? "Its song sounds
harsh and stubborn, / . . . One more summer, one more winter
long." It would have taken very little juggling to move that *song* to
the end of the verse, and reap the benefit of an effortlessly accurate
rhyme.

Our third Nobel laureate is Eugenio Montale, whose *The Storm
& Other Poems* appears now in a complete translation by Charles
Wright—complete, alas, only in its inclusiveness. By its inconclu-
siveness or inexactitude, however, this translation of *La bufera e altro*
forfeits any serious claim to completeness. Not much needs to be
said about Montale, whose reputation is secure though, I must con-
fess, he is not a poet to whom I warm easily. Neither his "essential-
ism" nor his "hermetism" sits well with me, and there are poems in
La bufera of which I can make very little sense. In the main, I prefer
Montale's two previous collections, *Ossi di seppia* and *Le occasioni*, al-
though *The Storm* does contain such justly famous poems as "The
Eel" and "Hitler Spring," as well as several wildly imaged but deli-

cately worded lyrics in which, between rampaging skies and uncaring seas, the poet must eke out an ambiguous relationship with nature and a mysterious, many-named beloved, both of whom seem to give with one hand only to take with the other.

The Ligurian littoral is obsessively present ("each of us has a country like this one, even if altogether different, which must always remain *his* landscape, unchanging"), as is the elusive woman with the clouds of hair and rainbow eyes, and, however muted, the viciousness of war. But much, much is lost in Wright's translation, which sometimes misunderstands and, at other times, overelaborates and waters down the original. Very seldom does it have anything like Montale's verbal music, granted that our language does not sing as spontaneously as the Italian. But must the English of this poet and professor of English from the University of California at Irvine be quite so slapdash? "You are him," we read; and "you, leapt down from some height, alter its color." There is a ghastly, "and, too," *reveille* as a verb, and "different than." We get the over-accusative "that satisfied whomever [sic] would face the narrow gate," and the non-objective "meeting Diotima, she [sic] who resembled you"; and there are many missing subjunctives, as in "as though it feeds." Wright is thrown by proper names: *Ariete* (Aries, the ram) is left untranslated; so, too, is *Pafnuzio*, in whom Wright evidently fails to recognize Paphnutius, the hero of Anatole France's *Thaïs*. Again, in English, it must be the "hills of Monferrat," not the "hills of Monferrini," which is the Italian adjective for Monferratian, as it were.

Nevertheless, *The Storm & Other Poems* won the PEN translation prize, and was considered for a National Book Award until too many mistakes surfaced, notably *truffatissimi agi* (ill-gotten gains, or comforts) rendered as "wily needles," based on a confusion between *agi* and *aghi*. But consider how Wright wrongs a poem like "The Shadow of the Magnolia," which begins: "L'ombra della magnolia giapponese / si sfoltisce o che i bocci paonazzi / sono caduti," literally: "The shadow of the Japanese magnolia is thinned out now that the purplish buds have fallen." But Wright gives us: "The shadow of the Japanese magnolia / drapes thinner, bonier fingers over the ground now / that its purple blooms are gone. . . ." This is sticking a cuckoo's egg into Montale's verse, and a cuckoo metaphor it is: draped fingers on the ground? When Montale writes *la via più dura,*

Wright carelessly turns the harder way (*via*) into a harder life (*vita*); *le fredde banchine del tuo fiume* (the cold wharves of your river) becomes "the hoarfrost of your river banks"; constellations that remain "indistinct" in Montale are "unfocused" in Wright; "the shiver of frost does not bend you" becomes "you are not jarred by the stutter and shiver of sleet," with the prolixity weakening the image. Similarly, "the file that cuts finely" turns into "the carver's file, once subtle and true," which is both inaccurate and verbose. "The empty crust of the singer" (presumably the bark of the tree formerly inhabited by songbirds) becomes "the hollow hull," introducing an irrelevant boat image. Montale: ". . . l'oltrocielo / che ti conduce e in cui mi getto, cefalo / saltato in secco al novilunio. // Addio." ("The beyond / that leads you and into which I hurl myself, mullet / that has jumped onto land at the new moon. // Good-bye.") Wright: ". . . the other side of the sky / that leads you on. There I swim, break water, / a fish in the high dry air under the new moon. // Addio." "The other side of the sky" is overliteral and cumbersome, "leads you on" has negative overtones, "I swim, break water" merely breaks wind, and "a fish in the high dry air" is plain nonsense. Moreover, leaving the *addio* untranslated is an affectation—as if, somehow, the Italian word contained profundities the English equivalent could not render.

But it is not only Montale's meanings and images that suffer; his very rhythm and melody are undermined. In the text, the syllabic count does not greatly vary from line to line: "non e più / il tempo dell'unisono vocale, / Clizia, il tempo del nume illimitato / che divora e reinsangua i suoi fedeli. / Spendersi era più facile, morire . . ." And Wright? "It is no longer, / Clizia, a season of singing in unison, a time / when the limitless god devours his faithful, then gives them back their blood. / Giving up was easier, dying. . . ." Note the disparity between the last two quoted verses (the second of which is two verses in Montale), and observe, incidentally, that *spendersi* is to consume or spend oneself, not "giving up." If this is not evidence enough, the reader is invited to examine what Wright does to "The Eel," particularly to its ending, where, for example, *immersi nel tuo fango* (submerged in your mud) becomes "up to our hairlines in your breathing mud." And such stuff wins translation prizes!

We come now to the brace of matinee idols—Russian ones, and

thus, more appropriately, street-corner or sports-stadium favorites:
Yevgeny Yevtushenko and Andrei Voznesensky, specialists, in Arthur
Miller's phrase about the latter, in carving out "a private speech for
public occasions, an intimacy which is yet open-armed about the
world." Neither of these poets is to be taken very seriously, although
Voznesensky started out better than he is in *Nostalgia for the Present*,
and although this new collection is still superior to Yevtushenko's
current *The Face Behind the Face*. What we have here is a kind of wit
writing, *vers de société* (but Marxist *société*): neat poems with *pointes*
simple enough for any alert collective-farm worker to get the point.
Or else it is indeed private speech for public occasions—the poet
pronouncing on political, social, artistic matters of general interest
in a way that even the worst commissar must recognize as not quite
the party line, but that will be tolerated by the party as a court
jester's outspokenness was by his feudal lord or king. True, jesters
sometimes got whipped, as did these poets when, on occasion, they
went too far. But, for the most part, they know where to stop, and
the state puts up with them as a reasonably harmless safety valve for
public discontent. I suppose they enjoy this privilege—for which
prose writers would be sent to the Gulag—because they are mostly
heard, not read; because the ear is assumed to be less retentive than
the eye (or printed paper), and because ugly facts couched in verse
may be written off as mere poetic licence.

Thus Yevtushenko (translated by Arthur Boyars and Simon
Franklin—I can't say how well, no Russian text being included) ends
"Mother":

> When we grow old,
>   then with delayed penance
> We come to our mothers,
>   to mounds of moist earth;
> Then, holding nothing back,
>   we pour out
>   to them
> Everything that once,
>   during their lifetimes, we could not say.

As can be seen, Yevtushenko has spotted the new Western trends in
spacing and line breaks, but he cannot be pronounced an apt copy-

cat: except for the absurd "we pour out / to them," this looks rather like an exercise in diagramming a sentence.

If the foregoing was the private Yevtushenko face, here now is the public one:

Oh, how repulsive,
When one defeated
By scum
Proceeds to suck up to it.

Don't puff yourself up
Into terrible turbulence,
Don't drop down
To kiss all the arses!

Rebelliousness expressed in such pious generalizations is no match for the specific evils of totalitarianism. Whatever may have been the case formerly, nowadays the face behind Yevtushenko's face is just another mask.

Voznesensky's *Nostalgia for the Present* is, like his previous collection, *Antiworlds*, translated by a consortium, extending all the way from Wilbur and Kunitz down to Ginsberg and Bly. Take, at random, "Lines to Robert Lowell," as rendered by Louis Simpson and Vera Dunham (who, with Max Hayward, was co-editor of the book). Though the poem begins in Russian "Peace / to your dust / foresighted President," the translators, for no good reason, start out "Bless / your grave, Mr. President. / You have been clairvoyant." Wordy and inaccurate; surely *mir* (peace), which runs through the poem as a refrain, is a reference to the peace movement's slogan, and should not be turned into a sanctimonious blessing. Then, again for no reason, the translators suddenly become chary, and fail to translate lines 7 and 9 altogether. A little later, "Peace to my heart / and to millions of sun strokes" becomes "Bless my heart / and millions of hearts that stagger / at a touch of the sun." Again, where Voznesensky says that "the profession of birthing is older than that of killing," Simpson and Dunham translate: "the art of creation / is older than the art of killing," which is a very different kettle of private speech.

But what about the poetry? At the end of the volume, there is a

historic narrative in verse episodes interspersed with prose docu-
ments—the story must read better in the prose account by George
Alexander Lensen, from which Voznesensky adapted it—followed
by a number of indifferent *calligrammes*. For the rest, it is slick, self-
assured verse a good century behind the times. Here is a typical
closing stanza, loosely but at least elegantly and rhymingly, trans-
lated by Richard Wilbur: "A deep stream of love. / A bright rapids
of sorrow. / A high wall of forgiveness. / And pain's clean, piercing
arrow." And here is a quatrain from "Family Graveyard. To the
Memory of Robert Lowell," honorably translated by William Jay
Smith and Fred Starr: "The family graves lie deep within the wood:
/ Your parents both are there, but where in the dark are you? / The
bookmarks in the book have been removed, / One cannot find the
page as one leafs through." What can I say? I hope that Yevtushenko
and Voznesensky are still favorites with the Russian crowds—they
are a lot better than their nearest American equivalent, Rod Mc-
Kuen. But if you want a superior Russian popular poet—a balladeer
who sets his verses to music and sings them to his own guitar ac-
companiment—I recommend Bulat Okudjava, preferable to both
Comrade Y. and Comrade V.

That brings us to Karol Wojtyla's *Easter Vigil & Other Poems*,
translated by Jerzy Peterkiewicz, with only one poem reproduced in
the Polish original. Wojtyla is, of course, better known as Pope John
Paul II, but these poems were written pseudonymously while he was
still rising from curate to bishop; they could be described as pre-
Vatican vaticinations. Though some are longer and more ambitious,
the short "Girl disappointed in love" is representative:

> With mercury we measure pain
> as we measure the heat of bodies and air
> but this is not how to discover our limits—
> you think you are the center of things.
> If you could only grasp that you are not:
> the center is He,
> and He, too, finds no love—
> why don't you see?
>
> The human heart—what is it for?
> Cosmic temperature. Heart. Mercury.

This, I submit, fails on two counts: as poetry and as compassion. Loss of love will not be illuminated, let alone consoled, by such simplicities (*sancta simplicitas*, indeed!); and as poetry, or even pietistic poetry, this is sorry stuff. At the utmost, the last hemistich could perhaps be sold to the Ford Motor Company for use as a commercial: "HEART. MERCURY." Call it popetry, and leave it at that.

Another Pole, Czeslaw Milosz, is a respected poet (winner of the Neustadt International Poetry Prize—whatever that is), author of a number of prose works among which *The Captive Mind* stands out as a worldwide success, and now a professor in the Slavic Department of the University of California at Berkeley. The poems in *Bells in Winter*, interspersed with prose, are of several kinds: philosophical, science-oriented, historical, surreal, phantasmagoric, satirical, Western American or Eastern European in their landscapes. Christianity and war hover in the background; not infrequently, the setting is academia, with its own little wars. At times, this is pleasant enough middle-of-the-road poetry, as in the opening of "Ars Poetica?":

> I have always aspired to a more spacious form
> that would be free from the claims of poetry or prose
> and would let us understand each other without exposing
> the author or reader to sublime agonies.
> In the very essence of poetry there is something indecent:
> a thing is brought forth which we didn't know we had in us,
> so we blink our eyes, as if a tiger had sprung out
> and stood in the light, lashing his tail.

This has the urbane tone of a civilized man speaking to his equals, but there is not much real poetry in it: sophisticated conversation must, to rise into poetry, become fiercely emblematic, unexpectedly archetypal. The diction, as translated by the author and Lillian Vallee, is not exciting either: "sublime agonies" or that tiger "lashing his tail." Yet sometimes Milosz is even more facile, as in the sequence of prose and verse aphorisms, "Notes," where we find such trivia as "*Consolation:* Calm down. Both your sins and your good deeds will be lost in oblivion."

At other times, the tone is more visionary: "We were flying over a range of snowpeaked mountains / And throwing dice for the soul of the condor. / —Should we grant reprieve to the condor? / —No, we won't grant reprieve to the condor. / It didn't eat from the tree of knowledge and so it must perish." This, like so much of Milosz, is religiously tinted vagueness, and comes from a sequence of six fairly long poems, "From the Rising of the Sun," which is a sort of *summa poetica*, a kind of Polish-Lithuanian *Waste Land* (Milosz was born in Lithuania) written in any number of forms, all of them rather uninteresting. It contains a goodly amount of autobiography, e.g., ". . . my shameful secret: / That, like the mermaid from Andersen's tale / I tried to walk correctly but a thin pain / Reminded me that I was foolish to try to imitate people"; some spiritual autobiography, as in this list of kindred literary spirits: "Chiaromonte / Miomandre / Petöfi / Mickiewicz"—an oddly unassimilated group, though the last two were leading romantic poets in their respective countries; and quite a bit of cosmic questioning: "Who can tell what purpose is served by destinies / And whether to have lived on earth means little / Or much." But, in the end, most of this is rather windy, amorphous, unmemorable, with a tendency to veer into opacity or banality.

There are also occasional linguistic lapses: "as if the city . . . was consumed by fire"; "so I ran further"; "some lazy earthly spirits" for *earth* spirits. There is modish spacing on the page; slashes and double slashes make gratuitous appearances:

> And lo our little sun // warms the frozen earth again
> Riding past green corn // palm in hand // the King enters
>   Jerusalem.

But nowhere do I find strong evidence that Milosz is, as the poet and cultural politician Joseph Brodsky claims for him on the jacket, "one of the greatest poets of our time, perhaps the greatest." By far the best piece in this collection is a short, wistful yet wry, lyric dating back to 1936, "Encounter":

> We were riding through frozen fields in a wagon at dawn.
> A red wing rose in the darkness.
>
> And suddenly a hare ran across the road
> One of us pointed to it with his hand.

That was long ago. Today neither of them is alive,
Not the hare, not the man who made the gesture.

O my love, where are they, where are they going
The flash of a hand, streak of movement, rustle of pebbles.
I ask not out of sorrow, but in wonder.

That, at least, is straightforward, unaffected, affecting.

Now let us leap back in time for some recent translations of classics. First, chronologically, we have *The Poems of Catullus*, translated by Frederic Raphael (novelist, film and television scenarist, and former Cambridge classical scholar) and Kenneth McLeish (translator of classical drama, author of children's books, and former Oxford classical scholar). This, as you might have guessed, is not a translation at all, but another of those numerous versions or updatings to which *miser* Catullus is particularly prone; the penalty for having been one of the most "modern" poets of antiquity is, it seems, to be perennially modernized into specious contemporaneity. The tone of these "translations" is aptly heralded in the Introduction, where the beginning of Catullus's affair with Clodia, alias Lesbia, elicits the comment, "What better way to mark one's arrival in smart society than by humping the hostess?"

In the very first poem, our Oxbridge translators give us a whopping grammatical error: ". . . you alone of Italy's sons has [sic] dared." But let us examine more closely the better known Poem II, "Passer, deliciae meae puellae." Here, typically, *acris solet incitare morsus*—Lesbia's teasing her pet sparrow into biting more sharply—becomes sexualized into "provoke the little pecker's peck." The phallicization continues: "For serious feelings, let them all go hang," with an obvious double entendre on the "hang." Like others before them, the translators fuse fragment IIa with this poem, and (referring to Atalanta's losing the footrace for stooping to pick up the golden apples) render *quod zonam soluit diu ligatam* (which loosed her too-long-tied girdle) as "And pushed her over, at last, into love's free zone." There is method in this madness: the English cognate of *zona*, zone (as in James Joyce's "Begin thou softly to unzone / Thy girlish bosom unto him") means "girdle" as well as "region," but from this to "love's free zone" is a misleading leap: where Lesbia was concerned, Catullus wanted her charms to be anything but the free zone that she, to his misery, considered them.

One more specimen, from one of the most famous of all, Poem V, "Vivamus, mea Lesbia, atque amemus." Even that opening ("Let us live, my Lesbia, and let us love") is falsified by "We can live, my Lesbia, and love." Why turn the urgency of *let* into the nonchalance of *can*? Presumably, just to be different. Again, the translators allow the sound of the Latin to govern their English: "asinine rumors" because of the original's *unius assis* (fractured Latin!); but where does the parenthetic remark in "The sun rises (they tell us); the sun sets" come from? A tribute to Hemingway? The beauty of the original lies largely in that plural "Suns may set and rise," a plural that makes the sun and the cosmos bigger, more impersonal, infinite. And the end of the poem is totally botched. First, the gratuitous and prosy "We *must* do it over and over— / It's obvious—surely you see?" Then the flatfooted "If even we lose track of the figures, / No one can tax us for loving at all," with a pun on *tax*. But compare the original: "Let us confound our reckoning, so we ourselves won't know it, / And that no ill-wisher can give us the evil eye / When he learns that there can be so many kisses." Surely, the presence of malicious people out to blight an unblemished passion is more dramatic than that vague "No one can," even with its jab at the tax collector. And, surely, the command, "Let us confound!" is more impassioned than that hypothetical "If even we . . ." Providently, the publisher has not provided the Latin text to shame these English versions.

We arrive, next, at a selection and translation, *Poems of Pierre de Ronsard*, by Nicholas Kilmer, a lecturer at the Swain School of Design and previous translator of Horace and Petrarch. He has also, as the jacket copy informs us, "romantically illustrated" his translations with his own line drawings. It is immediately apparent that Kilmer can draw lines better than he can translate them. If ever a poet needed rhymed translation, Ronsard is he; Humbert Wolfe, for example, charmingly transposed the *Sonnets for Helen* into rhymed English verse. But Kilmer's licence goes beyond rhymelessness: he will translate a perfect sonnet in end-stopped hexameters into thirteen lines of enjambed free verse! Thus "D'un sang froid, noir, et lent, je sens glacer mon coeur, / Quand quelcun parle à vous, ou quand quelcun vous touche: / Une ire autour du coeur me dresse

l'escarmouche, / Jaloux contre celuy qui reçoit tant d'honneur" be-
comes five lines:

> If someone speaks to you, or touches
> Your body, I feel my heart slowly
> Go cold, and cover with black blood
>
> Anger surrounds my brain with skirmishing.
> It is jealousy that anyone should be so honored.

Clearly, the stately, chilling progression of line 1—*froid, noir, lent,
glacer*—must be observed by a translator; equally clearly, Ronsard's
reverse movement from effect to cause is more dramatic than
Kilmer's customary order. "I feel my heart . . . cover . . . with blood"
is not English; but even were it, semantically and physiologically,
plausible, it still would not be frightening; a heart *freezing*, however,
is scary. Anger (*ire*), moreover, surrounds Ronsard's heart, not his
brain; and even the most literal rendering, "Jealous of him who re-
ceives so much honor," is livelier, more committed, than the passive
and almost impersonal "It is jealousy that anyone should be so hon-
ored."

Kilmer's ineptitude and perversity go further yet. In his Intro-
duction, the translator correctly states that Ronsard "tends to begin
with his visual argument and proceed to the abstract," only to add
that he, Kilmer, finds it "occasionally more telling to reverse this
order." And so, as he proudly announces, he takes from the sonnet
"Comme on voit sur la branche au mois de May la rose. . . ." Ron-
sard's "final line and [places] it at the beginning." The reason—if
you can call it that—is that Kilmer feels "obliged to bring about
[Ronsard's results] by whatever means seem adequately efficient
[wonderful phrase, that!], courteous, and technically sound." And he
continues: "My poems will be at times more vivid than Ronsard's;
more elliptical; more surprising"—a Stakhanovite endeavor quite
uncalled for; we would be quite happy with the good old unvivid
Ronsard.

In the sonnet in question, the poet proceeds from the spring rose
prematurely destroyed by showers or *excessive ardeur* (a fine, myste-
rious phrase that Kilmer vivifies into "hot winds") to a prematurely
dead friend, to whom he offers a basket of flowers, "Afin que vif, &

mort, ton corps ne soit que roses." That is a charming compliment, to which the poem builds up conventionally, but gracefully and touchingly. When Kilmer, however, begins with "Your body will be roses, living or dead," he not only gives away the show, he also commits an outrage against grammar, and thus against meaning: it is now the roses that are "living or dead," and a body of dead roses may be elliptical and surprising, but it also, quite literally, stinks.

Andrey Bely (1880–1934), the great Russian symbolist and mystic, was equally distinguished as a poet and as a novelist. In verse, his last major performance was *Pervoie svidanie, The First Encounter* (1921), now available in a translation by Gerald Janeček, with notes and comments by Nina Berberova, who knew the poet personally. The notes and comments are not without interest, but the translation, regrettably, is. What can we expect from translators (Berberova helped Janeček in various ways) who begin with the following head-note: "We gratefully acknowledge Professors Simon Karlinsky and Robert Hughes . . . for their invaluable and friendly help . . ."? You can acknowledge the help of Professors K. and H., but you cannot acknowledge them for their help. Forthwith, in the Introduction, Professor Janeček writes "no direct references . . . are explicit," which is redundant. We then hear about a four-point translation program in which there are first, second, third, and fourth priorities. Yet when something places third or fourth, how can it be a priority? Next, we learn that lines scanning ˇ ˇ – ˇ ˇ – are " 'paeonic' (as Bely would call them)"—would anyone call them anything else? Thereupon we get "overly important" for overimportant, and then "above-considered effects." After this, a perfunctory genuflection to the pseudoscience of semiology is hardly surprising. Moreover, a prose work of Bely's is thrice transliterated as *Glossalolya*. Since the Greek word, like its English and Russian equivalents, is "glosso-lalia," either (as I suspect) Janeček keeps getting the title wrong, or he fails to explain something that, unannotated, reflects badly on Bely. Professor Berberova's Preliminary Remarks, in turn, give us such solecisms as "two syllables and less," "amount of pyrrhics," and *"eena meena mina mo,"* which is not so much a solecism as a misspelling.

Turning now to the poem, it takes us no more than the first four lines to realize that the translation is hopeless. Bely's autobiographical-philosophical-mystical poem of 1319 lines depends for its formal beauty on its iambic tetrameter—rather strict, but with cogent and subtle variations—with an a-b-a-b (occasionally a-b-b-a) rhyme scheme. Incidentally, Bely's fellow symbolist Nikolai Gumilyov wrote back in 1909 that Bely had "no real understanding of iambic tetrameter," largely because in *Urn* he failed to follow Pushkin's example of switching to "the fourth paeon as a variant that added the greatest sonority to his poetry." One wonders how Gumilyov, who was executed in the year *The First Encounter* was published, would have rated its versification. In any case, even without knowing Russian, the reader will grasp that "Kirkoyo rudokopniyi gnom / Soglasnih hrusty rushit v tomi ... / Ya—stilisticheskyi priom, / Yazikovye idiomy!" cannot be conveyed by "With pick in hand a miner-gnome / Crumbles the consonant crackle into tomes ... / I'm—a device of style, / The idioms of our language," where the accidental near-rhyme (in an unrhymed translation!) falls in the wrong place, and where we blithely shift from tetrameter to pentameter to dimeter within four verses. This lamentable performance deserves no further consideration.

To wash the bad taste out of our mouths, let us hasten to an outstanding contemporary poet conscientiously translated in two separate versions: the Yugoslav Vasko Popa, whom we can read both in *Collected Poems 1943–1976*, translated by Anne Pennington (and rather grandiosely and fuzzily introduced by Ted Hughes), and in the much less inclusive *Homage to the Lame Wolf,* translated by Charles Simic. Even though, like the poet Charles Simic, I am Yugoslavian by birth, I had not until now come to grips with Popa, and I must confess that reading him makes me feel joyous—not as a Yugoslav, but as a poetry lover.

Vasko Popa is a Serb who lives in Belgrade, but was born (1922) in the Banat, the Danubian province in which Austro-Hungarian and Romanian influences—and, through them, general Western ones—can be experienced with particular intensity. This may have contributed to the cosmopolitan, universal nature of his poetry, consolidated by studies at the universities of Belgrade, Vienna, and Bucharest. But being born in the burgh of Grebenats, Popa is also in close touch with the fertile Pannonian soil that, despite foreign admixtures, is fundamentally Serbian. Hence, perhaps, the strong Serbian folk elements in this poetry.

Only the utterly nearsighted would number Popa among the

epigones of surrealism (such as Aleixandre and Milosz in some of their poetry, and Jean Follain and Robert Marteau, whom I am about to discuss, in all of theirs). Popa creates an animistic, anthropomorphic, mythic world out of an iridescent to-and-fro traffic between earth and cosmos, animate and inanimate, body and mind—even such personified abstractions as above and below, outside and inside, then and now. Within a very simple semantic structure—without rhyme, meter, often even stanzaic form—there are metaphors, personifications, symbols so daringly complex yet ingenuously playful as to create a strange simultaneity of the ordinary, mundane, transient with the irrational, transcendent, sempiternal. It would be a not entirely useless oversimplification to say that the witty and tragic, mysterious and childlike Popa is a cross between Blake and Jacques Prévert, between Murillo and Hieronymus Bosch. Many of Popa's poems form small cycles (which is Blakean, too) criss-crossed by further interrelationships.

Take the early poem, "On the Hat Stand" (thus Pennington; I'd say "On the Clothes Rack"):

The collars have bitten through
The necks of hanging emptinesses

Second thoughts hatch out [actually "Afterthoughts"]
In the warm hats

Fingers of twilight peep [actually "The twilight's fingers"]
From the widowed sleeves

Green terror sprouts
In the tame pleats

This is characteristic of that curious interpenetration of the human and non-human, concrete and abstract, humor and horror in Popa's work. The very next poem in the minicycle "Besieged Serenity" from the volume *Bark* (so Pennington—to me, *Rind* seems slightly preferable) is "In Forgetting":

From the distant darkness
The plain stuck out its tongue
The uncontrollable plain

Spilt events
Strewn faded words
Levelled faces

Here and there
A hand of smoke [or "An occasional hand . . ."]
Sighs without oars
Thoughts without wings
Homeless glances

Here and there
A flower of mist [or "An occasional flower . . ."]

Unsaddled shadows
More and more quietly paw [or "Ever more quietly dig in"]
The hot ash of laughter

Here, as so often, Popa manages to personify a mood, a feeling, an abstraction—in this case, oblivion doing its work of dissolution. The fascination lies not only in images as simple as they are strange ("sighs without oars," i.e., floating out aimlessly), but also in the eerie interplay of the embodied and disembodied (which is turning into which?), and in the beauty with which decomposition—mental but also, by implication, physical—is expressed and endured.

Or take, from the cycle "List" (or "Catalogue"), comprising homely fauna and flora sometimes reminiscent of Jules Renard's, the poem "Duck":

She waddles through the dust
In which no fish are smiling [actually "laughing," i.e., gaping]
Within her sides she carries [why not "flanks"?]
The restlessness of water [actually "waters"]

Clumsy
She waddles slowly
The thinking reed
Will catch her anyway

Never
Never will she be able

To walk
As she was able
To plough the mirrors

Details are enormously telling: the attempt to prosper on shore—transference of water to land—is halfway between metaphor and plain statement, a literal description of the duck (which, by the way, is "she" only because of the Serbian noun's feminine gender); the "thinking reed," which, though Pascalian, is perfectly apt from a duck's point of view; the final coming full circle—transference of land to water—in "plough the mirrors," where water is endowed with the reflecting, broadening virtues of the mirror.

Herewith a love poem from the beautifully entitled cycle "Far Within Us," in which war, separation, and reunion form three sub-themes; this being one of thirty untitled lyrics:

If it were not for your eyes [literally "If your eyes were not"]
There would be no sky
In our blind dwelling [or "apartment"]

If it were not for your laughter ["If your laughter were not"]
The walls would never
Vanish from our eyes [literally "the eyes"]

If it were not for your nightingales [as above]
The tender willows would never
Step over the threshold

If it were not for your arms
The sun would never
Spend the night in our sleep

The master images in Popa are the sun (life, joy, goodness) and nothingness; like Ormazd and Ahriman, they are locked in eternal combat. Hence the first verse of each tercet ends on *not*, which the beloved's sunny attributes, culminating in her full solarity, variously overcome by inducing the organic outer world to penetrate the man-made enclosure, by turning negation into a shining, natural assent.

I could go on quoting forever, but let me end with a poem rendered by both translators. Here, again, is Pennington with "A Conceited Mistake":

Once upon a time there was a mistake
So silly so small
That no one would ever have noticed it

It couldn't bear
To see itself to hear itself
It invented all manner of things

Just to prove
That it didn't really exist
It invented space

To put its proofs in
And time to keep its proofs
And the world to see its proofs
All it invented was not so silly
Nor so small
But was of course mistaken

Could it have been otherwise

Here now is Simic's "Proud Error": "Once upon a time there was an error / So ridiculous so minute / No one could have paid attention to it // It couldn't stand / To see or hear itself // It made up all sorts of nonsense / Just to prove / That it really didn't exist // It imagined a space / To fit all its proofs in / And time to guard its proofs / And the world to witness them // All that it imagined / Was not so ridiculous / Or so minute / But was of course in error // Was anything else possible." As for me, I would translate as follows: "Haughty Error": "Once upon a time there was an error / So ridiculous so small / That no one could have noticed it // It did not even want / To look at to hear itself // The things it invented / Just to prove / That in fact it didn't exist // It invented space / To place its proofs into it / And time to guard its proofs / And the world to behold its proofs // Everything it invented / Wasn't really so ridiculous / Or so small / But of course it was erroneous // Could it have been otherwise." From this, the reader may judge for himself where I agree with Pennington, where with Simic. On the whole, Simic tends to make things simple, which is right—but sometimes he oversimplifies. Pennington, generally, is more idiomatic—but she sometimes overelaborates or even misunderstands.

Thus "Pig," in Pennington's version, begins: "Only when she felt / The savage knife in her throat / Did the red veil / Explain the game . . ." whereas, properly, it should be "Only when she [really "it," the pig] felt / The furious knife in her throat / Did the red curtain / Explain the play to her . . ." Pennington overlooked the image of life as a tragedy on which blood descends like the final red theatrical curtain. Sometimes she misreads, as when, in "Before Play," she turns "with all one's weight" into "one's own weight," mistaking *svom* (all) for *svojom* (one's own). But, by and large, she does nobly by a sizable work in a remote language. And to think that I have no room to quote from those superb cycles, "Games," "One Bone to Another," and "Give Me Back My Rags" (actually "little rags")! Yet even from the foregoing examples, readers should be able to tell that the difference between a pope and a Popa is as between heaven and earth—between an imaginary heaven and an imaginatively realized earth.

II

César Vallejo: The Complete Posthumous Poetry. Tr. by Clayton Eshleman and José Rubia Barcia. Bi-lingual text.

Songs of Cifar and the Sweet Sea: Selections from "Songs of Cifar, 1967–1977," by Pablo Antonio Cuadra. Tr. and ed. by Grace Schulman and Ann McCarthy de Zavala. Bi-lingual text.

A World Rich in Anniversaries, by Jean Follain. Tr. by Mary Feeney and William Matthews.

Salamander: Selected Poems of Robert Marteau. Tr. by Anne Winters. Bi-lingual text.

Bertolt Brecht: Poems 1913–1956. Ed. by John Willett and Ralph L. Manheim.

The Oresteia of Aeschylus. Tr. by Robert Lowell.

Angelos Sikelianos: Selected Poems. Tr. by Edmund Keeley and Philip Sherrard. Bi-lingual text.

Ritsos in Parentheses. Tr. by Edmund Keeley. Bi-lingual text.

We come now to the winner of the last National Book Award in translation that, in all likelihood, will ever be given: César Vallejo's

The Complete Posthumous Poetry, translated by Clayton Eshleman and José Rubia Barcia, and published by the University of California Press (1978). Eshleman, the principal translator, writes in his Introduction that his goal was a rendering "in which the meaning of every bit of the original is preserved as literally as possible" while also yielding "an engaging poem in English . . . done with grace," which, he finds, is "nearly impossible." In his case, alas, entirely.

Clayton Eshleman devoted years of his life to translating Vallejo without much recognition and remuneration. One must admire his zeal; yet the most stubborn dedication without the needed sensitivity and talent is not worth much. The present version is the second Eshleman published and, in many instances, his nineteenth draft; still, it may be less a service than a disservice to Vallejo if it discourages other publishers and better translators from undertaking this huge task in the near future. The Introduction alone contains in its nineteen pages grammatical errors and clumsinesses such as "who he began to live with," "identifies with," "intrigued with," "a translation viewpoint," "retraced my direction [i.e., steps]," "neither Neruda or Vallejo," "to even further add," "culminates the relationship," "there are less of [deliberate misspellings]"—to name only the most obvious; and, apropos misspellings, we get "facsimilies" and "expatriots" (for expatriates).

By way of style, Eshleman provides such gems as Vallejo's having "forced the teeth of revolution into the gums of his personal life"; "It was as if a hand of wet sand came out of [Vallejo's] original and 'quicked' me in"; "I now realized that there was a whole wailing cathedral of desires, half-desires, mad-desires, anti-desires, all of which, in the Vallejo poem, seemed to be caught on the edge of no-desire. . . . What made him reach desiring desire? . . . I was in the presence of a mile-thick spirit."

The next problem is that Eshleman uses Vallejo to peddle his own poetry. The Introduction is full of such painful irrelevancies (and dangling constructions) as "In giving birth to myself, William Blake's poetry also became very important. I wanted to converse with Blake and knew I could not do this in the sense of Clayton talking with William. . . ." And more, much more, about Eshleman's poetry, complete with bio-bibliographical references, not to mention such lapses in logic as when we read about "dreams in which

Vallejo's corpse, fully dressed, with muddy shoes, was laid in bed be-
tween Barbara and myself," well before we learn that Barbara was
the wife Clayton had prior to his "present wife Caryl." About a bad
edition of Vallejo we are told that "in one case one poem [was] made
of two, and in another, two poems [were] made into one," which a
less than mile-thick mind would perceive as identical statements.

After several variations, the grand theme receives its finest for-
mulation: "We have tried very hard not to make [Vallejo] any more
clear in English than he is in Spanish. . . . We do not see ourselves
recreating a text in English; rather, we hope to make one in Spanish
visible to an English reader." Very well; in that case you print the
Spanish text along with a literal translation, preferably at the bottom
of the page in smaller print, as in *The Penguin Book of Spanish Verse*.
But Eshleman (I tend to exculpate Barcia, who seems to have func-
tioned mainly as an interpreter of meanings and refrained from ac-
tual Englishing) will have it both ways; he proudly prints his English
facing the originals and goes on to say: "Our goal has been to
achieve a translation that reads as great poetry in English while at
the same moment it is exactly what Vallejo is saying in Spanish."
Even with the modest disclaimer, "Obviously, this is not purely pos-
sible," this is hopelessly naive or arrogant—especially coming from
the coiner of such phrases as "purely possible."

The translator, like it or not, must have an interpretation of what
he is translating. If he translates something that, to him, is nonsense,
or a set of Chinese boxes with endless meanings within meanings—
something so unstable and shifting in value that he cannot get a bead
on it—his translation must lack the requisite passion, commitment,
shapeliness, and impact. And when poems are as obscure, elusive,
remote from reality as Vallejo's (to their detriment, I fear) often are,
some kind of meaning must be settled on, lest the reader of the
translation be utterly lost. How—to give a hypothetical example—is
he to interpret, in a totally unhelpful context, the word *bear*? As giv-
ing birth, carrying a burden, or a furry beast? Eshleman admits that
some choices had to be made; but, when they are not avoided in
some way, they tend to be extremely quirky. Frequently there is no
way of recreating multiplicity of meaning in another language: puns,
overtones, associations, connotations, allusions seldom translate; the
best thing is to convey as firmly as can be the chief meaning, ex-

plaining the others, if necessary, in a footnote. And one had better make use of whatever beauties, elegancies, riches the translator's language possesses, and hope that something emotionally, intellectually, aesthetically equivalent will emerge. As for "great poetry in English," except on the off chance that the translator himself is a very considerable poet and miraculously in tune with the original, one had better forget about it altogether.

Herewith a small selection from Eshleman's malpractices. I open the book at random at page 11, and find, among other things, "A half of drachm" for half a dram; "The family surrounds the night table [of a dying man] during a high dividend," where *por espacio* means "for the space of"—i.e., long enough to inherit—a high dividend; "I do not know what this woman is to the sick man, who kisses him and cannot heal him" for "I do not know what this woman who kisses him is to this sick man"; and, just overleaf (p. 12), the illiterate spelling "ecstacy." I flip over to page 33, where I find Vallejo's *hun* (for *un*) rendered as "aa": "Time has aa centipedal fear of clocks." Vallejo's frequent capricious misspellings and neologisms present a serious problem for the translator. Except perhaps in a footnote, it is best to ignore them, as David Smith has done in his translation of Vallejo's *Trilce*. In any case, "aa" is impossible; it is the kind of eye- and earsore that *hun*, with its mute *h*, would not be in Spanish.

Take now the moving poem "Altura y pelos" ("Height and Hair"), whose three stanzas all end with a lament in the form of incremental repetition: first, "¡Yo que tan sólo he nacido!"; then, "¡Yo que solamente he nacido!"; and finally, "¡Ay! yo que sólo he nacido solamente!" Eshleman translates: "I who was born so alone"—correct; "I who solely was born!"—barbarous; and "Aie! I who alone was solely born"—unconscionable and unspeakable, what with that "Aie! I . . ." only needing one more *ay* to become "The Donkey Serenade." Clearly, we need something like "I who was born so alone!"; "I who was only born!"; and "I, alas, who was only born—so alone!" But at least we are spared the utter abomination of "I who so alone've been born!" with which Eshleman came up in an earlier volume of Vallejo translations, *Poemas Humanos* (1968).

Consider a few additional, scattered howlers. "Masterfully" for "magisterially"; "French Comedy" for "the Comédie Française";

"smiling at my lips" for "with a smile on my lips"; repeated instances of "aches me" for "hurts me"; the jargon of "intuit" and "incredible amount"; walking "leaned on our misfortune" for "leaning" etc.; frequent occurrences of "who" for "whom"; nonsense words, e.g., "impunibly" and "earthlyly," where Vallejo uses good Spanish words; "I suffer, like I say" (a very frequent error); misspellings such as "knowledgeable," "stupified," "annoint" (more than once); un-English constructions, e.g., "prying on me," "as it is said" (for "as they say"), "refrain yourself" (for "restrain yourself"), "meaning-possibility"; total illiteracy as in "the corpse might lay down" or "without father nor mother"; an impossible ablative absolute: "at the end of the battle, and the combatant dead"; the absurd fondness for omitting the article, as in "where scarlet index, and where bronze cot" or "war gives tomb"; crazy apostrophes, e.g., "t'hell with'm"; and all those ghastly attempts to reproduce Vallejo's weird spellings with "whasp," "skabbard," "navell," "magesty," etc., etc. And then the tin ear, as in "sick sickle," "wind paper . . . flesh pen" (for "paper of wind . . . pen of flesh"), "wood hearts" (for "wooden hearts"), and so on and on.

Eshleman is also careless enough, for all his alleged scruples, to turn "the world looks Spanish until death" into "Spanish unto death," "judging from the comb" into the nonsensical "off the comb," "my unconscious" into the literal but un-English "profound I," "falls to the bottom" into "falls thoroughly." A poem entitled "epistle to the transients" in the text, becomes "epistle to those passing through" in the notes.

I wish I could quote entire devastated poems, instead of merely this third strophe from "The hungry man's wheel," which concerns stones:

> At least the one they could have found lying across and alone in
>   an insult,
> that one give it to me now!
> At least the twisted and crowned, on which echoes
> only once the walk of moral rectitude,
> or, at least, that other one, that flung in dignified curve
> will drop by itself,
> acting as a true core,
> that one give it to me now!

Even without referring to the original, one can tell that this is not English, and, therefore, worthless. Or take these four verses:

> I drink your blood in regard to Christ the hard,
> I eat your bone in regard to Christ the soft,
> because I love you, two to two, Alfonso,
> and I could almost say so, eternally.

This grates as excruciatingly on the ear as on the mind, what with "in regard to," "Christ the soft" (*dulce*), "two to two," and that supererogatory *so*.

But let me conclude with a couple of horrible examples from "Los mendigos pelean por España" ("The beggars fight for Spain"), where *encarnízanse en llorar* becomes "they [the beggars] mercilessly cry" rather than "incarnate themselves in weeping," and *arrastrando sus títulos de fuerza* becomes "dragging their titles of strength" rather than "seizing their titles by force." And then we get the unforgettable line, "that combat in which no longer is anyone defeated." If at least the judges of the National Book Awards had made clear that this was the best translation into pidgin English!

From Vallejo, "a poet whose poetry had a rough surface, as rugged to the touch as a wild animal's skin" (Neruda), we proceed to another, smoother and smaller, Latin American poet, the Nicaraguan Pablo Antonio Cuadra (born 1912), whose *Songs of Cifar and the Sweet Sea* (*Selections from "Songs of Cifar, 1967–1977"*) have been translated by Grace Schulman and Ann McCarthy de Zavala. There is something unpretentious about these little poems that makes them appealing even though I find them, for the most part, insignificant. Loosely related yet nonsequential, resembling folk poetry yet with a more sophisticated frame of reference, they concern imaginary but realistic figures from around Lake Nicaragua. The Lake, or The Great Lake, as the people call it, is a body of sweet water, 92 by 34 miles, containing many small islands as well as sharks and shad. To Cuadra and the folk who live by it, it is big and precious enough to be "the sweet sea." But, even with sharks in it, it is a bit small for a sea, and the verse it has inspired is a bit too small for poetry.

These songs are mostly about Cifar—sailor, fisherman, adventurer, harp player, and lover—and the women he carries on with, as well as about the natural, and occasionally supernatural, phenomena of the region. Although Miss Schulman tries to make a case for the mythic and ecumenical resonance of this poetry, I find it merely graceful and provincial. Take the opening poem, "The Birth of Cifar":

> There is an island in the shadows
> slender
> as the hand of an Indian god.
> It offers red fruit
> to the birds
> and, to the shipwrecked,
> the sweet shade of trees.
> There Cifar, the sailor,
> was born.
> His mother's time came
> as she rowed alone to Zapatera.
> She steered the boat to a pool
> while sharks and shad
> circled,
> drawn by the blood.

This is a faithful, unassuming rendition (though, unlike Eshleman, the translators don't boast about it), taking liberties only with the line breaks. It is simple and tasteful stuff, but probably too simple, with not enough happening between the lines. Consider, in its entirety, "The Call": "Cifar / quiet your song. / Cifar / do not cover / your ears with music: / That limitless / Blue / calls you." The two central verses containing the one image are effective, but the rest is trivial. Another poem ends with "and the wind / sounds / like a moan," which, like the call of the limitless Blue, is banal. Still another—part of a subcycle in which an insufferable guru, the Master of Tarca, pontificates darkly—concludes with: "That which is known / is the unknown!" This is feeble stuff, not even Nicaraguan lake poetry—more like puddle prose.

And yet there are moments when Cuadra comes alive, especially (needless to say) in the Spanish, where the floating assonances help:

Se oyen lejanos	The cocks
los gallos.	are heard in the distance.
El viento	The wind

sopla en la brasa del lucero.	blows on the hot coal of the
Parece	morning star.
que ya amanece.	Already it seems to be dawn.

Too bad that in English, along with the assonance, the terseness goes: the six words of the fourth verse lose by becoming nine. But the translations, throughout the book, are clean and accurate except for a few mistakes, some of which are noted in the generally appreciative (too appreciative) notice by Edmund L. King in *The Hudson Review* (Spring, 1980), which likens these loosely strung poems to a Spanish *romancero*. The main errors listed by King are "river carpenter" (actually "boatwright") for *carpintero de ribera*, and "The Cockroach" for Cifar's nickname, *El Cachero*. Far from lacking any literal meaning, as the translators assert, this is, King points out, a Central-Americanism meaning something like "The Hustler." King might have added that a *periplus* is not a "voyager," as Miss Schulman seems to think, but a cautious sea voyage that hugs the shore. Cuadra's poetry, to its disadvantage, is definitely a periplus; so too, to its advantage, is the translation.

Jean Follain (1903–1971) has always struck me as an overrated poet, even though the vociferous overrating was practiced by a tiny enough band. Follain was a lawyer and a judge, and was at one time associated with a group that included Max Jacob, Pierre Reverdy, and Léon-Paul Fargue, to all of whom he was appreciably inferior. *A World Rich in Anniversaries* is a selection and translation of prose poems from *Tout Instant* (1957) and *Appareil de la terre* (1964) by Mary Feeney and William Matthews.

These pieces are either bizarre, seminonsensical anecdotes or quaint catalogues of objects in a whimsical landscape or eccentric interior. The technique is cubist or surreal, and distinctly epigonous. (Since the publication of the first part of this review, I received a card from Charles Simic declaring, "You are wrong about Surrealism. Read early Eluard." Early Eluard is fine; it is the later, tired surrealism, with its sycophants and rehashers, that I find useless.) Consider the following, reprinted in its entirety:

> A crossroads, said to be treacherous. But quiet. A man was seen there whittling green wood for a boy in an impeccably pleated black smock. It makes him look like he's in mourning, even in girl's clothing, in a landscape whose every leaf seems in place for

eternity. The stew they eat in each of the outlying farms smells the same as ever. On a treetrunk is a tattered auction notice officially posted during a regime to be followed by one only slightly bloodier.

A typical Follain procedure, this: begin as a grotesque anecdote and end as a shaggy-dog story. The components of this prose poem, not very stimulating in themselves, do not interact in a suggestive enough way. Yet the translators are also to blame. "Sarreau... faisant deuil et même travesti" could be more succinctly rendered as "having an air of mourning, indeed drag." "De toute éternité" is not "for eternity" but something like "since time immemorial." The "fermes de l'alentour" are neighboring, not "outlying," farms. I don't mind that "tattered" auction notice, though yellowing or crumbling would be nearer the mark; "like he's in mourning" is sad English. And *que suivit* is "that was followed by" rather than "to be followed." In translating prose poetry, one truly need not take such liberties.

The Feeney & Matthews liberties are, in fact, mostly sloppinesses. Elsewhere our translators render "Voices [*des voix*] no longer scare her" as "Certain voices" etc., which is a different matter. By what colorblindness does a tawny (*fauve*) autumn become "sepia"? There is worse. In one poem, a crone of ninety, whose three daughters all died aged seventy or more, keeps saying, "C'est malheureux, je n'ai pas pu en élever une." ("What bad luck! I couldn't raise one of them.") But we get: "It's a shame, I couldn't write one of them." Write? Pure nonsense, and the death of the joke. Well, in some cases at least a poet gets the translators he deserves.

Perhaps the fault lies in my unbelieving nature, but I found *Salamander: Selected Poems of Robert Marteau*, translated by Anne Winters, not just bad but actually repellent. Repellent in its literal sense: so opaque as to resist penetration and so causing withdrawal. Marteau is a Frenchman who has moved to Canada—a bad sign; in 1963, when he was thirty-eight, his answer to a question about the great event of his life was "Seeing Claudel's *Le Soulier de satin*"—a worse sign. But the really bad news is that Marteau's poetry is a perfect example of belated surrealism gone berserk, and that it relies on alchemy for its philosophy and imaginative framework. In her Introduction, Miss Winters, who has worked very closely with Marteau, quotes him as saying that the aim of his poetry is, like that of alchemy, "to conquer, or rather reanimate, matter, which has fallen asleep; to awaken its inner waves so that it may again become that living, vibratory, celestial matter, the very light emanated from the Principle . . ." As might be guessed, this dread pursuit gets mixed up with Christianity, Greek myths, bullfighting, various pagan cults, and anything the poet, a veritable Marteau *sans maître*, wishes to drag into his mystic mishmash. What good is it to reanimate dormant matter if, in the process, you put the reader to sleep?

Alchemy has, in one way or another, affected many poets since the romantics, and Rimbaud appropriated as much of it as could be exploited for poetic purposes—perhaps more. It can still prove of marginal value to a poet such as Popa, who uses it playfully; to make it one's central, humorless concern seems to me obscurantist, antiquarian, and self-defeating. I can see why, after all that Georgian *rus in urbe*—or, rather, *urbs in rure*—Eliot and Pound opted for their *trobar clus*; but in an age when poetry is in great danger of cutting itself off completely from a vast majority of readers, doggedly arcane cultism seems to me an ill-advised procedure. And when it sets out to become absorbed by a mystique as exploded as astrology or alchemy, it is being downright perverse. The Great Work is about as useful to Marteau as the Golden Dawn was to Yeats: not very, but Yeats at least had the sense to move on.

Here is how alchemy works in the poem "Charente, Again," as described by Miss Winters: "The country is the poet's own *terre noire* [the *materia prima* whose first alchemical phase is dissolution and putrefaction]. . . . The sequence of images follows the major stages of the overall alchemical injunction *Solve et coagula*. . . . In the first lines the landscape is obscurely decomposing: 'Strewn on bundles of rotting brushwood.' In the third and fourth stanzas, the fermented mass is distilled . . . until the alchemical whiteness appears ('On the ermine's track / A bundle of whetted arrows / Trails from alcohol's frosty gloves'). Distillation is followed by . . . sublimation ('All thought / Disappears in the presence of prayer'). . . . We sense that refinement in the imagination may not be less subtle than in the retort [and no less alembicated!]. . . . At the close the poet has restored Charente . . . to its most crystalline, irreducible form: 'Black seed, homeland and powder blown in my eyes, / These make my furnace, where the Fall and windfallen / Images turn into truth.' The language of the alchemical treatises, as well as the actual procedures, is reflected in Marteau's poetry—particularly in the bewildering fusions of allegory and laboratory procedures."

Do not think for a moment that this "bewildering" is intended as anything but a term of praise by Miss Winters, whose translations, though sometimes attempting to be explanatory, are often plentifully bewildering themselves. Thus the last three lines translated above read in French: "Graine noire, poudre et pays dans mes yeux, / D'eux, je fais mon four et je change en vérité / Ce qui n'est que chute, images tombées." Surely, the first line alludes to the locution *la poudre aux yeux* (eyewash), so that "dust in my eyes" would do better than "powder blown in my eyes"; and if we are going to abide by the alchemical imagery, the next two lines could use more literalness, e.g., "Of them I make my furnace and change into truth / what is only a fall, only fallen [or tumbled] images." Winters's capitalized *Fall* is overallegorical, her *windfallen* overspecific, and her impersonal construction, losing the active *je fais*, puts an end to the *Grand'Oeuvre*.

Look now at a few verses from "Tauraux de Bayonne" ("Bulls in Bayonne") and at their translation. This long poem begins: "Nous voici dans la cuve et sur les planches liés; / Un soleil d'arachide et de crin reste entre les toitures; / Ocre soir que les pigeons becquètent! . . ." Winters translates: "Here we are in the wine-vat and bound on the boards; / The sun like a nut-colored mane between the rooftops; / And pigeons peck at the ochre evening . . ." Yet the text, full of Martelian inversions and invocations (Marteau is obsessed with these archaic and shallow devices), reads: "Here we are in the vat and to the boards fastened; / A sun of earth-nut and horse-hair remains among the rooftops; / Ochre evening that the pigeons peck at!"

A little further into the poem, we read: "Nuit, que des chevaux conduisent en tournant, / Vous descendez comme le vis au centre d'un pressoir / Et sans doute du sang se mêle au moût de la vendange. / Comme des oiseleurs à cheval sur la frontière épient le passage des migrations, / Je vous vois en costume de lumière à la pliure des deux mondes. / Tout un peuple vous croit grimés quand seuls vous êtes nus . . ." And Winters:

Night driven by turning horses
Wound down like the central screw of a press
And blood no doubt sharpens the must of the vintage.
As on the frontier fowlers on horseback spy the passing
    migrations,
I see you costumed in light where the two worlds fold under.
A whole people sees you in greasepaint when you are the only
    nudes . . .

Again Winters omits the apostrophe to Night. We should get something like: "Night, whom turning horses draw, / You descend like the screw at the center of a wine press / And doubtless blood mingles with the must of the vintage. / As fowlers on horseback on the frontier spy on the passing migrations, / I see you in a garment of light where two worlds fold under. / A whole nation thinks you're made up to look old when you alone are naked. . . ." To be noted also is that *spy* is an intransitive verb: "spy on" is needed; that with "where the two worlds fold under" Winters found a clever way around *pliure* (the noun *fold* in English would be ambiguous—it might suggest a pen); that "a whole people" is not idiomatic English; and that *grimer* is to make old with make-up—for any other making up, *maquiller* is indicated. But the verse is opaque beyond a translator's ministrations: after the singular *you* in the address to Night, a plural *you* (indicated by the *s* in *grimés*) suddenly takes over without any logical antecedent; three lines below, a *he* appears out of nowhere to add to the confusion.

Winters herself is no less mysterious than Marteau: when he writes, "Un vent s'élève qui plaque en haut les fumées des crématoires," she translates, "A wind rises to fan out the crematory smoke on high." But *plaquer* does not mean "to fan out"; it means "to plaster down, lay on, or stand someone up." The translator seems to be (perhaps unconsciously) ashamed of Marteau's windier excesses, and tries to tone them down with her translations. Thus when Marteau inverts away as in "d'aucun secours nous sont les feux," she straightens this "of no help to us are the beacons" into "no beacon can help us." What, I wonder, is the alchemical significance of inversion?

Nevertheless, Miss Winters's procedure, especially when contrasted with, let's say, Clayton Eshleman's, is of paramount interest. Whereas Eshleman believes in reproducing every convolution, complication, eccentricity, and wart of the text, Miss Winters evidently chooses to simplify, if not, indeed, to interpret. It is as if Eshleman's Vallejo arrived in English on a tourist visa with no intention of settling down; Miss Winters's Marteau, however, comes in as an immigrant striving to become naturalized in English. This is an important distinction, and I regret to state it in terms of so poor a poet as Marteau and so dismal a translator as Eshleman. Yet both concepts have their good and bad sides, although if a choice has to be made, I tend to favor the Winters one; but, more than the system, what matters is the practitioner. No methodology can affect the translation anywhere near so much as the genius of the translator. In fact, the translator of genius has no method: what he provides may be identical or equivalent—either way, it feels so right that one hardly stops to question it.

We come, with a sense of relief, to Bertolt Brecht, who is much better known as a playwright than as a poet (at least outside Germany), even though his poetry is the equal of his dramaturgy and in some ways perhaps superior to it. In his verse chronicle in *The Nation* of July 17, 1958, Randall Jarrell alighted with enthusiasm on the slender volume of Brecht translations by H. R. Hays, some of which originally appeared in *Poetry*. Wrote Jarrell: "Through most of [Brecht's] *Selected Poems* one is touching real people and the real world—and in our times, generally, one gets to touch only a real poet." In Brecht's poetry, which is extraordinarily unintroverted and unselfconscious, the poet is a superior reporter whose canny, almost prosaic, didacticism nevertheless slips across into poetry. There is terseness and irony, matter-of-fact understatement, powerful use of anticlimax, and an unblinking, almost lidless, lucidity of outlook. And then, out of nowhere, a sudden touch of heart-wrenching lyricism. Then on again, as if nothing had happened.

The ability to deal all but impersonally with personal experience, making the poet virtually into an absent presence, is related to the *Neue Sachlichkeit* (New Objectivity) movement and derives in part from Frank Wedekind and the cabaret poets. Much of it has a kind of tender harshness, a restrained violence that is—well—Brechtian; yet a world-weary irony can occasionally be heard as well. Consider "The Mask of Evil," tidily translated by Hays:

On my wall hangs a Japanese carving
The mask of an evil demon, decorated with gold lacquer.
Sympathetically I observe
The swollen veins of the forehead, indicating
What a strain it is to be evil.

John Willett and Ralph Manheim, the co-editors of *Bertolt Brecht: Poems 1913–1956*, have undertaken the difficult and noble task of assembling translations from various hands that would render Brecht's poetry as rhymed verse where that is called for, and, for the rest, into free forms that would duplicate the exact nature of the freedoms taken. They picked some five hundred of the approximately thousand poems that have so far been made available (East German political and moral censorship still withholds some), arranged them as nearly as possible chronologically, and have supplied, with the help of Erich Fried, a good critical apparatus. There is a concise and cogent Introduction, a not ungenerous selection from Brecht's various writings about poetry in general and his own in particular, and a set of generous explanatory and bibliographical notes. Unfortunately, the editors so wanted the translations to be poems in their own right that, except for titles, nary a line of the German text is included anywhere in any form. (There are, however, page references to the two principal German editions.) Another drawback: it takes some fairly complex maneuvering to trace a given poem's translator among the thirty-five contributors—or perhaps thirty-four, because although Manheim's name is twice listed as a translator, no specific translations is credited to him. He may, of course, have participated in the translations by committee, of which there are a few.

As might be expected, the work is uneven, especially in the rhymed translations, which, to be sure, present enormous problems. Willett himself took on many of these rhymed translations, and handled them, on the whole, creditably. Take the last stanza of the famous "Remembering Marie A.":

As for the kiss, I'd long ago forgot it
But for the cloud that floated in the sky
I know that still, and shall forever know it

It was quite white and moved in very high.
It may be that the plum trees still are blooming
That woman's seventh child may now be there
And yet that cloud had only bloomed for minutes
When I looked up, it vanished on the air.

That has a nice movement and sound, though on closer examination one can find flaws. Thus the fourth line, "Sie war sehr weiss und kam von oben her," could be better rendered as "It was so white and came down from on high." Then, Willett has ignored that, despite the pentametric context, the sixth line is in hexameter—hypertrophic, no doubt, to suggest Brecht's comic disgust with such overproduction (seven children!). In the next line, Willett almost kills the point: "Doch jene Wolke blühte nur Minuten" should be translated "That cloud, however, bloomed only for minutes." "And yet" implies a relation between the girl's being a woman now with seven children and the cloud's transience; whereas the relation is first between the poet and the woman (forgotten despite her enduring and reproducing), then between the poet and the cloud (remembered in spite of its transitoriness).

Sidney H. Bremer, on the other hand, has no luck with the difficult "On the Infanticide Marie Farrar." Here is the original: "Marie Farrar, geboren im April / Unmündig, merkmallos, rachitisch, Waise / Bislang angeblich unbescholten, will / Ein Kind ermordet haben in der Weise: / Sie sagt, sie habe schon im zweiten Monat / Bei einer Frau in einem Kellerhaus / Versucht es abzutreiben mit zwei Spritzen / Angeblich schmerzhaft, doch ging's nicht heraus. / *Doch ihr, ich bitte euch, wollt nicht in Zorn verfallen / Denn alle Kreatur braucht Hilf von allen.*" Bremer offers: "Marie Farrar: month of birth, April / An orphaned minor; rickets; birthmarks, none; previously / Of good character, admits that she did kill / Her child as follows here in summary. / She visited a woman in a basement / During her second month, so she reported / And there was given two injections / Which, though they hurt, did not abort it. / But you I beg, make not your anger manifest / For all that lives needs help from all the rest." First, the meter: Brecht's verse is, until the refrain, regularly decasyllabic, with alternating masculine and feminine rhymes; Bremer's verse can at times hardly be scanned. The first line is some kind of tetrameter, vaguely trochaic; the second, rhythmless prose. Then come four iambic pentameter lines, then two lines in tetrameter. The refrain follows Brecht's metrical schema, but, in the German, the longer line calls attention also to a change in tone from that of a police report to that of a humane voice, which the English flubs. As for the rhyme, it may be too much to ask for the masculine-feminine alternation in English; surely, however, *April—did kill, previously—summary* are not to be countenanced. "But you I beg, make not your anger manifest" is, moreover, scarcely English.

"Will ein Kind ermordet haben" is *"Claims* to have murdered a child," which is very different from *admits:* it makes the girl's confession voluntary and expiatory, while maintaining the narrator's detached tone. "So she reported" is doubly wrong: it should be in the present tense, to conform with the ongoing narration (but then it wouldn't rhyme!), and it should be at the head of Marie's declarations, to make the impersonality or skepticism of the narration (presumably taken from an official document) extend to all that follows rather than pop up in the middle. In German, the injections to induce abortion are "allegedly painful": the police report (or whatever it is) does not take Marie's suffering on faith; Bremer's "though they hurt," which accepts it as a fact, loses the irony. In the refrain, where the voice of the poet takes over, we are not being asked merely to repress ("make not . . . manifest") our anger; rather, we are enjoined, out of pity and charity, not to be moved to anger at all.

Sometimes the editors' injunction to stick as close as possible to the original's word order and line breaks wreaks havoc with the translation, as in Stephen Spender's version of "Concerning the Label Emigrant," where we read: "Restlessly we wait thus, as near as we can to the frontier / Awaiting the day of return, every smallest alteration / Observing beyond the boundary . . ." This corresponds closely enough to "Unruhig sitzen wir so, möglichst nahe den Grenzen / Wartend des Tags der Rückkehr, jede kleinste Veränderung / Jenseits der Grenze beobachtend . . ." Yet the German "restlessly we *sit"* is better than *wait:* it avoids the near-duplication with *awaiting* and it conjures up a quasi-paradox: people sitting but restless, with the *sitting* further suggesting enforced idleness, unemployment. The real problem, though, is that "every smallest alteration observing beyond the boundary" simply isn't English.

At other times a respected translator such as Michael Hamburger blows a poem, as in the case of "Radwechsel": "Ich sitze am Strassenhang. / Der Fahrer wechselt das rad. / Ich bin nicht gern, wo ich herkomme. / Ich bin nicht gern, wo ich hinfahre. / Warum sehe ich den Radwechsel / Mit Ungeduld?" In "Changing the Wheel," Hamburger gives us: "I sit by the roadside. / The driver changes the wheel. / I do not like the place I have come from. / I do not like the place I am going to. / Why with impatience do I / Watch him changing the wheel?" First, in English, one changes tires, not wheels. Second, the German does not mention *place*; it says, "I don't feel good where I'm coming from, / I don't feel good where I'm going." The reference can be to times, dispensations, systems—as well as places. There are political implications here (the date, 1953, is that of the East German Rising), which *places* minimizes or misses. And the last two lines—which, incidentally, disregard the editors' directive—are disastrous. They could easily have been rendered literally: "Why do I watch the changing of tires / With impatience?" Without following the German word order, Hamburger makes hash of the English all the same. Moreover, he loses the devastating terseness of the last line by introducing a misleading *him:* Brecht is not watching the driver—he is watching the change, any change, with the impatience that characterized his restless nature. The new tire will bring about change, even if only from the frying pan into the fire; but anything is better than standing still.

My position now becomes awkward: I have to deal with translations from the Greek, even though—Classical, modern demotic, or modern literary—it is all Greek to me. Let me begin with Robert Lowell's acting version of the *Oresteia.* I have written elsewhere on how I feel about Lowell's *Imitations* (bad, very bad), but here the situation is different, different even from Lowell's rendering of the *Prometheus Bound.* There is serious doubt in my mind whether there is just and sufficient cause for such an acting version. Greek tragedies, with the possible exception of some by Euripides, seem to me unactable in the present theater, even if one proceeds "to trim, cut and be direct enough to satisfy . . . at a first hearing the simple ears of a theater audience." Those simple ears will not be taken in that easily by something insuperably alien to them; but Lowell writes also about satisfying his own mind with this adaptation, which may be easier. I myself would prefer an attempt to transpose into English, as accurately as possible, the full text, especially the powerful Aeschylean imagery (after all, Aeschylus was the greatest poet, not playwright, among Greek dramatists) and try to satisfy the discriminating eyes and ears of poetry lovers.

Erich Segal has shown in the London *Times Literary Supplement* (January 25, 1980) how Lowell, while basing himself on Richmond Lattimore's version—itself not always accurate and sometimes ponderous and prosaic—proceeded to throw out many of the *Oresteia's* finest and most elaborately germane images. This is, presumably, part of making the work accessible to plebeian sensibilities, a poor idea, although certain strategies, such as assigning choric speeches or songs to individual voices and adding explanatory stage directions, are generally helpful. But Segal also praises Lowell for some of his additions to the text, and additions, no matter how deft, are always illegitimate.

The great problem with Lowell was—I can find no other word for it—a stubborn quirkiness. Why, else, say "meathouse," when English has the perfectly good "slaughterhouse"? I am not happy either about showily modern usage: why speak of "the menacing vibration of the voices" when "tremor," "trill," or something metaphorical would serve better? The same holds for the Chorus's question to Cassandra, "Did you sleep with Apollo?" where the expression is crudely contemporary. (Peter Arnott translates: "And did you lie with him and take his seed?") Here is a typical telescoped passage of the Chorus from *The Libation Bearers*—or, as Lowell more popularly retitles it, the *Orestes*. It occurs just before Orestes brings out the corpses of Clytemnestra and Aegisthus, and is about three times longer in the Greek: "Time makes all things right perhaps. / Orestes has washed the blood from his house. / He has cast out its age-old furies. / The dice have fallen right." This is not very cadenced, festive, or majestic, but it does move fast—if that is a virtue in this context. Note, however, that "right perhaps" is Lowell's interpolation and a feeble one; the Greek simply says that time brings all things to pass. The repetition of "right" is likewise less

than apt: "washed the blood" does not necessarily convey the origi-
nal's notion of ritual purification.

Now take Orestes' self-justifying speech, the part that Lattimore
translates as: "What does she seem to be? / Some water snake, some
viper / Whose touch is rot even to him who felt no fang / strike. . . ."
Lowell has: "An asp? a watersnake? / Even before it was touched,
this brutal / coil of scales rotted our hands." That "even before it
was touched" is nonsense; it is precisely touching the skin that
causes rot, whether or not the deadly fang strikes. And when the
Chorus says of Orestes that "his suffering is just about to bloom"
(Robert Fagles) or "pain flowers for him" (Lattimore), Lowell, for
no good reason, flattens out the line into "His torture increases."
With like prosaism, Lowell invents a curious bit of stage business
about Orestes' stumbling and becoming partially entangled in
Agamemnon's robe, and then writes:

> Not yet, not yet, I am entangled
> in my kingship. I grieve for what I have done.
> I have triumphed, my triumph is stained.
> No pride, no pride!

Bear in mind that this is the passage Lattimore renders as: "Now I
can praise him, now I can stand by to mourn / and speak before this
web that killed my father; yet / I grieve for the thing done, the
death, and all our race. / I have won; but my victory is soiled, and
has no pride." Observe, first, the rather schematic parallelism in
Lowell between "Not yet, not yet" and "No pride, no pride!" And
what does that "not yet" mean? Presumably that it is too soon, as
Lowell says earlier, "to trample on the web that killed him." But the
Aeschylean sentiment is quite different, almost the opposite: now
that he has been avenged is the time to praise and mourn Agamem-
non—no question of gloating, as Lowell's version suggests. Most
displeasing, here as elsewhere, is all that parataxis—those simple,
simplistic sentences like beads on an abacus being unceremoniously
ticked off. Even the reiteration in "I have triumphed, my triumph is
stained" adds to the sense of undue haste (hardly have I triumphed
but that my triumph is over), rather like those accelerated life cycles
of insects in a nature documentary. And on "No pride, no pride!"
you can practically see Orestes shaking his head like a carping ped-
agogue.

And how does Lowell end his *Orestes?* With this verse about the Furies: "You don't see them, but I do." This is a double crime. Not only has Lowell cut the beautiful concluding utterance of the Chorus, but he has also provided an ending that could not be surpassed for anticlimactic flatfootedness. This *Oresteia* may have graces, and you may see them. But I don't.

We come now to two modern Greek poets. First, Angelos Sikelianos (1884–1951), whose *Selected Poems* were translated (and, in some instances, retranslated) by Edmund Keeley and Philip Sherrard. Sikelianos was a mixture of neo-romanticism and symbolism from the West (mostly French) with intense, home-grown nationalism, which in his case was more cultural and mystical than political—he and his American first wife tried, with much effort and expense, to revive the Delphic Games. A friend of the first Greek modernist, Kostis Palamas, and, off and on, of Nikos Kazantzakis, Sikelianos was also influenced by his brother-in-law, Raymond Duncan, Isadora's brother. He was active in reviving Greek tragedy both at home and abroad, and himself wrote a number of tragedies. He also fought in the Balkan War and endured hardship during the German occupation in World War II. Most extraordinary was his death: paralyzed by a stroke, and perhaps dejected when the Greek Academy failed to make him a member, he died from drinking Lysol, which his maid had mistakenly given him instead of Nujol.

Sikelianos's vision, as the translators expound in their Introduction, combines elements of Orphism, Pythagoreanism, the mysteries of Eleusis (which the poet studied extensively), and the cult of Delphi as a religious-cultural-athletic center. His world view combined that of the Pre-Socratics with Christianity, Dionysus rubbing shoulders with Jesus. The poet is a seer mediating between the visible and invisible worlds, between the mortal and the divine. If this sounds both somewhat vague and a trifle commonplace, so, I fear, is much of the poetry—although, of course, I cannot appreciate "the resonances and surprises that Sikelianos's quite magnificent use of demotic brings to the Greek reader." Perhaps Sikelianos has indeed "produced some of the most striking lyrical poetry written in the twentieth century," as Constantine Trypanis has argued, but on the evidence of these translations I cannot see it. In fact, the poetry strikes me as so old-fashioned even for its time that I am surprised that it was written in *Demotiki,* the spoken language, rather than in the archaizing, stilted *Katharevousa*. This is particularly true of the early poems, e.g., the sonnets here unfortunately translated into rhymeless verse, and a poem such as "Aphrodite Rising," which ends: "Nymphs of the breeze, hurry; Cymothoe, Glauce, come grip me / under my arms. / I did not think I'd find myself so suddenly caught up / in the sun's embrace." In the Greek, the short lines rhyme; but neither rhyme nor magnificent use of demotic can mitigate such triviality.

Or consider the ending of "The First Rain":

> I could not, as I breathed,
> choose among the scents,
> but culled them all, and drank them
> as one drinks joy and sorrow
> suddenly sent by fate;
> I drank them all,
> and when I touched your waist,
> my blood became a nightingale,
> became like the running waters.

The sound, even I can tell, is better in the Greek, but there is something hopelessly commonplace about drinking joy or sorrow suddenly sent by fate—even if it is mixed with rain water (wouldn't Perrier be better?); and though the blood becoming a nightingale gives off a baroque trill, it is undercut by that mundane comparison (on a rainy day, remember!) to the running waters. The images tend to be somewhat predictable in this poetry: the poet's horse turns into Pegasus, the lead goat in a herd is metamorphosed into the god Pan, a dying man's bed is "the mystical trireme of Dionysus," and so on in almost formulaic cross-references between ancient and modern Greece. Take this image from "The Village Wedding": "His body drinks the sun, / drinks as a hot beach of fine sand / the ever-renewing foam." (Note, incidentally, the lapse in the English here: either "like a hot beach" or "as a hot beach does" is required.) I am disturbed by the contrary nature of the things compared, though this is doubtless intentional; still, I cannot equate a body's drinking the sun, and thus parching, with a sandy beach being flooded by foam.

Look now at the conclusion of the longest poem in the late manner, "Daedalus":

> . . . father, at those times
> when life's bitterness weighs with its full burden
> on our hearts, and our strength can be roused no more by youth
> but only by the Will that stands watchful
> even over the grave, because to It the sea
> which hugs the drowned remorselessly is itself shallow,
> and shallow too the earth where the dead sleep;
>
> in the dawn hours, as still we struggle on,
> while the living and the dead both lie in the same
> dreamless or dream-laden slumber, do not stop
> ascending in front of us, but climb always
> with slow even wings the heavens of our Thought,
> eternal Daedalus, Dawnstar of the Beyond.

This strikes me as a decent minor poetry (shouldn't the twentieth-century poet let the sleeping dead lie?), very competently translated. Everything works here: cadence, imagery, sentiment, and thought harmonize skillfully, but without great originality or depth. Yet there are no awkwardnesses, as in this image from the long, earlier poem, "A Village Wedding," where the bridegroom is exhorted by the poet: "Let him now reap the deepest field / of creative fragrance." Not only does the abstract "creative" (even if taken in the humbler sense of "procreative") clash with the very specific "fragrance," but also the reduction of sexual fulfillment to a mere olfactory experience, however pleasant, strikes me as, if I may put it so, anticlimactic. Nor does the translators', presumably unintentional, jingle—*reap deepest*—prove helpful.

In the main, though, the translators have done a respectably less than brilliant job, and I am a trifle disturbed by their steady bypassing of subjunctives (e.g., "as though a whole world is coming apart," etc.) and consistent misspelling of "anointed" as "annointed" (pp. 59 and 144). They are careless at times: in "Dionysus Encradled," for instance, an "infant" would be more suitable than a "baby"; "in vain I strain" (twice in the same poem) jars with its uncalled-for rhyme.

Occasionally they even lapse into translatorese, as in "Because I Deeply Praised," where we find "here life starts, here ends" and "for secret is earth's live creative pulse." Still, they have done well enough to convince me that Sikelianos is a repetitious poet with a few, constantly reiterated, conceits. There is the notion of the past contained in the present: "I'd taken this same road centuries before" ("The Sacred Way"), "And the rhythm of our horses now / . . . still lives / under obscure hoofprints of ancient horses / left in the same holy ground" ("Attic"); and there is the related concept of two worlds in one: "the living and the dead both lie in the same / dreamless or dream-laden slumber" ("Daedalus"). "Everything, visible and invisible, we and the heroes and the gods, too, / move forward inside the same eternal sphere!" ("Attic"). All these samenesses have a way of becoming all the same to the reader, whether the rhetoric waxes too rhapsodic or the rhapsode turns into a mere rhetorician.

Edmund Keeley, flying solo this time, has also given us *Ritsos in Parentheses*, and in Yannis Ritsos we have, I believe, a major poet, with whom it is as fitting to conclude the second half of my chronicle as it was to end the first with Vasko Popa. Yannis Ritsos (born 1909) is the poet who unjustly lost the Nobel Prize to his considerably less interesting compatriot Odysseus Elytis—mainly, I suppose, because Ritsos is a Communist and Elytis is not. Ritsos has suffered, at various times, imprisonment, banishment, a ban on publication, and the public burning of his books. This has not prevented him from publishing (by 1978) 77 volumes of poetry (ranging from very long to very short poems), two volumes of plays, ten of translations, and one book of essays. He has also had his share of domestic and foreign honors, and is surely the only poet who, with perfect justice, was granted in the same year (1977) the Lenin Prize and election to the Académie Mallarmé. And, indeed, people and symbols mingle with perfect ease in his poetry, an ease that encompasses, as it must, misunderstandings, suffering, even horror, but that remains an un-attitudinizing, natural relationship arrived at through absolute mastery of artifice. Take, for example, "In the Ruins of an Ancient Temple":

The museum guard was smoking in front of the sheepfold.
The sheep were grazing among the marble ruins.
Farther down the woman were washing in the river.

You could hear the beat of the hammer in the blacksmith's shop.
The shepherd whistled. The sheep ran to him
as though the marble ruins were running. The water's thick
    nape
shone with coolness behind the oleanders. A woman
spread her washed clothing on the shrubs and the statues—
she spread her husband's underpants on Hera's shoulders.

Foreign, peaceful, silent intimacy—years on years. Down on the
    shore
the fishermen passed by with broad baskets full of fish
on their heads, as though they were carrying long and narrow
    flashes of light:
gold, rose, and violet—the same as that procession bearing
the long, richly embroidered veil of the goddess that we cut up
    the other day
to arrange as curtains and tablecloths in our emptied houses.

To me this says infinitely more about the relationship of ancient and
modern Greece than Sikelianos's horse turning into Pegasus. "Foreign, peaceful, silent intimacy—years of years." The numinous becoming the useful, the veil of the mystery finding practical
application in saving the houses from their poverty. But this is a two-way street: at the same time, the sheep become works of statuary art,
and the fish in the basket, a holy radiance. There is peasant good
humor here: if the goddess loses her veil, never mind—she gains a
pair of underpants for a shawl. The mythic Then and the anxious
Now are not, as in Sikelianos, the same, but a pair of teasingly complementary friends: the old gods need humanizing; the new, impoverished tables and window frames need a touch of the divine.

There are strange, ambivalent relationships between pairs of
human beings as well: wistful, ironic, mysterious. Consider this brief
poem, "Completeness Almost": "You know, death doesn't exist, he
said to her. / I know, yes, now that I'm dead, she answered. / Your
two shirts are ironed, in the drawer, / the only thing I'm missing is
a small rose." Somehow the dead woman still takes care of the living man, ironing his shirts by proxy. And she no longer feels his
deadly indifference—if only he would bring her a tiny, symbolic
tribute of remembrance. Or is this a living woman who, having accepted her man's uninterestedness as death in life, finds the strength

to carry on in performing as best she can the humdrum tasks of living? If only, on occasion, the man would extend an emblematic gesture across the real abyss! Perhaps neither of these interpretations is correct, but surely present in the poem are wistfulness, irony, mystery.

The poems of *Ritsos in Parentheses* were culled from three sources: a volume titled *Parentheses, 1946–47*; a second collection, *Parentheses, 1950–61*, still unpublished in Greek; and *The Distant* (1977), containing verse written in 1975. In the succinct, incisive Introduction, Keeley identifies the themes of Ritsos' poetry—the progression from greater to lesser sharing, from stouter to slenderer hope: "The poet's thirty-year journey from *Parentheses, 1946–47* to *The Distant* has been one of bitter catharsis, a progress from his focus on so-called simple things and more or less abortive gestures to a focus on bare—not to say barren—essentials and primitive rituals performed by those whose deity appears to be an infinitely distant, absolutely white, unapproachable and silent ambiguity."

What I find remarkable about Ritsos' poetry is its ability to make extraordinary constructs out of the most unforcedly ordinary ingredients—surreality out of reality. And seem not even to make it, just find it. Footling details are taken out of context and seen either strictly for themselves or in some dizzyingly vast framework. Sensory experiences are detoured through some other than the obvious sense, yet without any showy, programmatic synaesthesia. Colors are expressionistically heightened or nudged in a direction they might have only hoped or feared to take. The actions of dreamers, eccentrics, or creatures impaled on despair are viewed with the alert amorality of a child. For instance: "Poor Saturday night music coming from the neighborhood dancing school, / poor music, frozen, with wooden shoes— / every time the unpainted door opens the music rushes out into the street . . ." This music is, clearly, seen rather than heard. "She fell asleep smelling a star . . ." This woman has brought the unattainable closer by changing senses to reach it, the intimacy of smell succeeding where the factuality of the regard fails. Of another woman: "Her back / is a bitterly sad hill loaded with many dead— / the family's dead, her dead, your own death"— many remotenesses concentrated into a single proximity. ". . . And the three handsome young men, linked shoulder to shoulder (the one in the middle a statue), / strolling reluctantly in the sunlit insouciance of death." Is the youth in the middle only frozen into a statue or is this a picture of total destruction in which the beauty of flesh and marble, art and life, perish together? Man and world interpenetrate with a wry kinship: ". . . the mountains / grew larger and sharper like the teeth of the one who hungered."

Yet sometimes the images leave reality virtually unchanged and still manage to get at something inscrutable or ineffable: ". . . the old jester in front of the dark mirror / washes off his painted tears so that he can weep"; or "The four windows hang rhyming quatrains / of sky and sea in the rooms." And sometimes there is no imagery at all, only an insistently resonant situation or incident, as in the three-line poem "Spring": "They sat down in the field facing each other, / took their shoes off, and bare like that, their shoes / touched in the tall grass. And they stayed." Are these two creatures lovers turning into friends or friends changing into lovers? Or are they either or both communing with something bigger? Or look at "Brief Dialogue":

> The sky turned desolate behind the houses.
> Why are you crying? he asked, buckling his belt.
> The world is beautiful, she answered,
> so beautiful, with such an awful headache; and the bed
> is a silent, fierce animal getting ready to leave.

Is the headache really the world's or is it, metonymically, the woman's? Is the sadness of this parting projected onto the world or does the world rush to identify itself with the woman about to be abandoned? Or are the lovers parting only routinely and temporarily, yet with the woman perceiving even so that something nears its end: the passionate love-beast of the bed disappearing into a piece of perfunctory furniture? As Ritsos puts it in "The Meaning of Simplicity," with which the book opens;

> I hide behind simple things so you'll find me;
> if you don't find me, you'll find the things,
> you'll touch what my hand has touched,
> our hand-prints will merge.
>
> The August moon glitters in the kitchen
> like a tin-plated pot (it gets that way because of what I'm saying
>   to you),

> it lights up the empty house and the house's kneeling silence—
> always the silence remains kneeling.

> Every word is a doorway
> to a meeting, one often cancelled,
> and that's when a word is true: when it insists on the meeting.

This tricky simplicity is perceptively analyzed in the Introduction, and, on the whole, Keeley's translations read convincingly. Only now and then is there a false note—ungrammatical, unidiomatic, or simply flat. It is disconcerting to read "which of the two persuades you the most," or to encounter the awkward tenses and redundancy of "I've left the key in the same place you knew about." So, too, "It didn't matter if you'd be late" is curiously unidiomatic for an American translator, and "if the dead don't have any territory, we too don't have territory to stand on" is incorrect usage for "we don't have territory to stand on either" or "neither have we any territory to stand on." Consider this lovely verse: "And she is so beautiful as the denial of her most beautiful self," where the "so" has to be "as." "Moon's light" in one poem is as grammatically and sonorously disturbing as "tree's trunk" in another. English demands either "moonlight" or "light of the moon," in which it is seconded by the aesthetic ear; "tree trunk" is not all that euphonious in itself, but the extra sibilant makes it truly ugly.

These are, however, footling objections to what is basically a readable rendering of a greatly needed poetic voice in what looks like a judicious selection from an enormous oeuvre. Let me illustrate Ritsos' range by quoting a political poem, but, again, with the political made both highly personal and transcendent.

> The deep voice was heard in the deeper night.
> Then the tanks went by. Then day broke.
> Then the voice was heard again, shorter, farther in.
> The wall was white. The bread red. The ladder
> rested almost vertical against the antique lamppost. The old
>   woman
> collected the black stones one by one in a paper bag.

> TOWARD SATURDAY

This is, by simpler means, as ominous and hallucinatory as a painting by De Chirico. And it gains its power chiefly from that old woman and her black stones. What are these black stones, and why gather them? And why in something as flimsy as a paper bag? There is poverty here and the irrational devastation of war, but also something crazier yet and more unsettling, as in that near-vertical ladder. It is as if the tanks had thundered madness onto this scene.

Ritsos, on the evidence of these poems, is also a great bard of loneliness, but of loneliness ennobled and overcome. Poem after poem, image upon image, suffuses aloneness with a gallows humor that begins to mitigate its ravages and makes the person in the poem a Pyrrhic winner. There are many superb poems about both the solitary and the sadder, shared loneliness, notably "Self-sufficiency?" and "Miniature." But the essence is conveyed about as well by the shorter "Inertia":

> He sat alone in the darkness of the room smoking.
> Nothing was visible. Only the glow of his cigarette
> moved slowly now and then, carefully,
> as though he were feeding a sick girl
> with a silver spoon, or as though he were treating
> some star's wound with a small lancet.

Note that although loneliness is given a dignity here, it is a comic dignity based on hyperbole and make-believe. Yet even this helps. Yannis Ritsos is a true poet.

I suppose that after reviewing twenty volumes of poetry in translation, one is expected to make some brief closing remarks about the art of translation itself, if only to fix in the reader's mind the criteria from which the criticism proceeded. The second issue of the now defunct periodical *Delos* (1968) featured answers to a questionnaire on translation. I still agree with most of what I said there, which included the following: "A good translation is, to borrow words from Rilke about the unicorn, an animal of which there isn't any. But, like the unicorn, it exists sufficiently; more than, for example, the Tasmanian tiger, which, though it does exist, does so considerably less for most people than the unicorn. I mean that a near-success in translating a major work is worth more than complete success in writing a minor one." And I went on to "make a desperate stab" at defining a good translation: "one that to a sensitive and informed reader—perhaps even an expert—reads, first, like *an* original and, second, like *the* original." In the mean time, I gather, the Tasmanian tiger (or wolf) may have become extinct; the unicorn, too, has rather faded from memory. Translation, however, as the foregoing shows, continues. And it is, at least occasionally, successful.

1980–1981

Victimized Verlaine

IS THERE ANYTHING harder to define than poetry? Beyond matters of prosody, imagery, cadence, and such—the mysterious essence and quiddity of poetry? What, for instance, makes the odd verse quintessentially poetic, engraved on the mind, conjuring up voluptuous feelings when we repeat it to ourselves as a mantra? The quality that, in J. A. Cuddon's apt phrase, "at once transcends and supports the meaning"? Take, for example, Thomas Nashe's "Brightness falls from the air; / Queens have died young and fair," where the second verse is more charged with feeling, yet the first lingers more hauntingly in the memory. (I realize that some think *air* a textual corruption for *hair*, but let us not split hairs.) The entire verse is an image, with the progression of vowels from brighter to darker mirroring the meaning; but it is that unusual *falls* rather than, say, *fades* that shocks the line into poetry.

Or take Auden's "Lay your sleeping head, my love, / Human on my faithless arm," where, again, the second verse is more charged and provocative, but the first is more "poetic." Partly so because, instead of the expected *sleepy*, we get the almost paradoxical *sleeping*; and partly because of those liquid *l*'s at the beginning, middle, and end of the line—the medial *l*, as it were, slightly masked by the *s* that precedes it—as if hooded by a lowered eyelid. It is in such near-intangibles that poetry resides; they are what, in Frost's famous dictum, poetry is—that which is lost in translation.

This elusive quintessence is also what makes the simplest poetry hard to translate: Heine's, for instance, or Verlaine's. And that is what makes *One Hundred and One Poems by Paul Verlaine*, translated by Norman R. Shapiro, so regrettably useless. Useless, that is, as verse translation, which is what Shapiro thinks he is doing. I turned immediately to "Chanson d'automne," that very famous lyric from Verlaine's first collection, *Poèmes saturniens* (1866). Shapiro properly gives the French and English on facing pages; the present format unfortunately prevents this.

> Les sanglots longs
> Des violons
>   De l'automne
> Blessent mon coeur
> D'une langueur
>   Monotone.

> The autumn's throbbing
> Strings moan, sobbing,
>   Drone their dole;
> Long-drawn and low,
> Each tremolo
>   Sears my soul.

Immediately apparent is that Shapiro cannot render the regular interlacing of masculine and feminine rhyme, which contributes much to the poem's music. The schema is aabccb, with a and c masculine, and b feminine. Shapiro's *throbbing* and *sobbing* are top-heavy and, incidentally, the only feminine rhymes offered in the entire eighteen-line poem, and those in the wrong place.

But consider the extreme simplicity of the French, which translates literally: "The long sobs / Of the violins / Of autumn / Wound my heart / With a languor / Monotonous." How spare this diction is as opposed to Shapiro's verbosity and prolixity which even lose the crucial *violins: strings* could refer to any number of nebulous instruments. Shapiro's vocabulary is both recherché and obsolescent: *tremolo* and *dole*; Verlaine's is a distillation of everyday language. Its instantaneous music is in the repeated closed *o* sounds that then shift slightly to the open *o*'s of *monotone*, like a distant echo to which the mute *e* adds its dying fall. In Verlaine, the lines flow; in Shapiro, we get the jarring staccato of a seeming quasi-molossus, "Strings, moan, sobbing," that loses Verlaine's *langueur*, yet another key word Shapiro forfeits. "Long-drawn and low" would be acceptable, were it not for the *rime riche*, anathema in English, of *low* and *tremolo*. "Drone their dole" sounds nice, but is both verbose and archaizing.

> Tout suffocant
> Et blême, quand
> > Sonne l'heure,
> Je me souviens
> Des jours anciens
> > Et je pleure;

> When tolls the hour
> I think of our
> > Days gone by;
> Pallid as death
> I gasp for breath
> > And I cry.

Literally: "All suffocating / And pale, when / The hour strikes, / I remember / The old days / And weep." But who here is this "we" implicit in "our days"? The point is the poet's isolation, the I that is not part of any we. *Pallid* is a poeticism, and "as death" a cliché; "gasp for breath" might pass but for that hackneyed rhyme *death/breath*. And even that seemingly harmless *I* in "And I cry" feels pleonastic after "I gasp." "And cry" would be natural here, even if it muddies the scansion.

> Et je m'en vais
> Au vent mauvais
> > Qui m'emporte
> Deçà, delà
> Pareil à la
> > Feuille morte.

> And like a dead
> Leaf, buffeted,
> > Tempest-tossed,
> I ride the air—

Now here, now there—
    Aimless, lost . . .

Literally: "And I go away / In the ill wind / That carries me off /
Hither and yon / Like unto the / Dead leaf." Note the stark denud-
edness of the original, which contains nothing so fancy as *buffeted*,
or so literary as *tempest-tossed*. "I ride the air" makes it all sound like
a joyride; even "Now here, now there" suggests something more of
a nervous dilettantism than grim compulsion. Worst is that "Aim-
less, lost . . ." with that added, attitudinizing ellipsis: it is both
pleonastic and didactic. And having the dead leaf appear at the top
of the stanza, rather than at the end, robs it of the climactic termi-
nal position that brings the poem back to the initial *automne*, which
is to say full circle.

    It can be argued, of course, that the dead leaf is a commonplace,
as dead as foliage in the fall. But Verlaine's quadrisyllabic lines,
which know when to run on and when to be end-stopped, triumph
with their carefully wrought musicality. Observe how *morte*
sonorously returns us to the earlier *monotone*, and how the very or-
dinary "Deçà, delà" taps into the poet's purpose; though the locu-
tion designates diverse locations, *deçà* and *delà* sound so alike, almost
identical: a change of place that may bring only sterile sameness.
And the dead leaf at the bottom of the poem conveys the ground, fi-
nality, finitude. Not aimlessness and loss, which has the pathos of
the *poète maudit*, but just the plain, dead end.

    Consider, next, the famous "Clair de lune" that opens Verlaine's
second collection, *Fêtes galantes* (1869), and has been set to music by
more than one composer. It suffices to look at the first line and at
the last of its three quatrains. The poem begins: "Votre âme est un
paysage choisi" (Your soul is a chosen landscape), with *choisi* achiev-
ing multiple and suggestive meanings. Thus *choice*, something supe-
rior and exquisite; *elect*, something instilled with divine grace;
selected, picked out from various possibilities and willed into being—
excogitated. So we have possibilities of superiority (refinement),
transcendence (religious privilege, as of a chosen people), and art-
fulness (elucubration), opening up within a simple modifier. And
what does Shapiro give us? "Your soul is like a landscape fantasy,"
which lacks even the concreteness of plain *paysage*, and suggests a

vague daydream or a grandiose landscape architect's scheme to transform his back garden into Versailles.

Now for the conclusion:

Au calme clair de lune triste et beau
Qui fait rêver les oiseaux dans les arbres
Et sangloter d'extase les jets d'eau,
Les grands jets d'eau sveltes parmi les marbres.

The calm, pale moonlight, whose sad beauty beaming
Sets the birds softly dreaming in the trees
And makes the marbled fountains, gushing, streaming—
Slender jet-fountains—sob their ecstasies.

Examine how thoroughly Shapiro misses the boat. That the moonlight is pale is self-evident and unnecessary; but what is that "sad beauty, beaming" meant to do? If it is sad, how can it beam? *Beaming*, in English, signifies contentment, perhaps even smugness. It is there only for the rhyme, and subverts the simple dignity of *triste et beau*, which also sets up a discreet, self-effacing inner rhyme with *oiseaux*. (Nothing so obvious as *beaming/dreaming*.) And whereas Verlaine's birds are merely dreaming—probably denoting their silence or tiny chirps—Shapiro's are "softly dreaming," which makes one wonder what hard or loud dreaming would be like. Next, we do not want "marbled fountains" this early: for full impact, marble (not *marbled*, which suggests paper) should be withheld until the final panorama. And again, that "gushing, streaming" won't do for the simple *jets d'eau*, which avoids frenetic tautology.

But the great loss is the bungling of the closing picture, whose effect works through plainness and a striking contrast. It is, literally, "And cause to sob with ecstasy the water jets, / The great jets of water, slender amid the marbles." Shapiro's "sob their ecstasies" is less direct and sexual than "sob with ecstasy," and, in any case, belongs in the penultimate verse right next to the spouts of water. That placement more strongly suggests the ecstasy of ejaculation, and justifies the last line's rapt incremental repetition: "Les grands jets d'eau," contrasted in their svelteness with the weight—in both sense and sound—of the final *marbres*. The plural conveys not so much a single marble basin as ample statuary (nymphs, fauns) surrounding the jet of water and making that high spurt even more orgasmic. And remember: this entire *paysage* is a trope for the beloved's soul, with Verlaine's metaphor more vivid than Shapiro's simile. "Your soul is *like*," etc. And what sort of gobbledygook is "jet-fountains"?

"Colloque sentimental," a favorite of mine from the same collection, begins "Dans le vieux parc solitaire et glacé, / Deux formes ont tout à l'heure passé." Ernest Dowson has translated this as "Into the lonely park all frozen fast, / Awhile ago there were two forms who passed." Not perfect, but much better than Shapiro's "In the drear park, beneath a chill, bleak sky, / Two shapes, two silhouettes come passing by." Note again the tautology: "chill, bleak" and, ludicrously, "two shapes, two silhouettes." And again, the obsolete *drear*, and the, to my ear, clunky molossus "chill, bleak sky." And why substitute the present tense for the sadder, more distancing past? The entire poem is translated as disastrously as its opening couplet.

Now for a later poem, the celebrated "Il pleure dans mon coeur," from the Mendelssohnianly titled *Romances sans paroles* (1874) which begins

> Il pleure dans mon coeur
> Comme il pleut sur la ville;
> Quelle est cette langueur
> Qui pénètre mon coeur?
>
> Like city's rain, my heart
> Rains teardrops too. What now,
> This languorous ache, this smart
> That pierces, wounds my heart?

Granted, *pleure-pleut* cannot be adequately Englished; even so, "city's rain" is as tin-eared and ungrammatical as it gets. Why not, at the worst, "city rain"? And whatfor that "What now," without even the excuse of a needed rhyme? And could anything be wordier and clumsier than "This languorous ache, this smart / That pierces, wounds . . ."? Why not just *penetrates*, as in the text, or *suffuses*?

Still later, from *Sagesse* (1881), a stanza of the windowside poem "Le Ciel est, par-dessus le toit," which runs:

> Mon Dieu, mon Dieu, la vie est là,
>   Simple et tranquille.

Cette paisible rumeur là
 Vient de la ville.

My God, my God, out there . . . That's where
 Real life is found.
A simple town . . . And everywhere,
 Its gentle sound.

Could anything be more pedestrian and bathetic than "out there . . .
That's where"? No less absurd is "A simple town," where the town
is not simple, only its distant rumor feels *peaceful*, and thus inviting.

Finally, the seminal "Art poétique" from *Jadis et naguère* (1884),
with its famous opening "De la musique avant toute chose" whose
penultimate stanza reads,

De la musique encore et toujours:
Que ton vers soit la chose envolée
Qu'on sent qui fuit d'une âme en allée
Vers d'autres cieux à d'autres amours.

Music first and foremost, and forever!
Let your verse be what goes scaring, sighing,
Set free, fleeing from the soul gone flying
Off to other skies and loves, wherever.

Literally: "Music yet again and forever! / Let your verse be the
winged thing / To be felt issuing from a soul in transit / Toward
other skies, to other loves." Redundance here has wrought its mas-
terpiece. I also relish the aeronautical trope "the soul gone flying,"
and that wonderfully offhand *wherever*.

Norman Shapiro's verse translations are a powerful argument
for prose translation—unless the translator is a man of Richard
Wilbur's stature.

1999

Index

A NOTE ON THE AUTHOR

John Simon writes drama criticism for *New York* magazine and music criticism for the *New Leader*. He has written film criticism for a variety of magazines, including *New York*, *Esquire*, and twenty-one years for the *National Review*. He has also been a columnist on language for *Esquire*, and drama critic for the *Hudson Review* and for *Commonweal*. Mr. Simon has received the George Polk Memorial Award in Criticism and the George Jean Nathan Award in Dramatic Criticism, as well as the American Academy of Arts and Letters Award. Author of a dozen books of criticism—on film, literature, and theatre—he lives in New York City.